T0144548

CANCER PREDICTION FOR INDUSTRIAL IOT 4.0: A MACHINE LEARNING PERSPECTIVE

Chapman & Hall/CRC Internet of Things: Data-Centric Intelligent Computing, Informatics, and Communication

Series Editors:

Souvik Pal
Global Institute of Management and Technology, India

Dac-Nhuong Le
Haiphong University, Vietnam

The role of adaptation, machine learning, computational intelligence, and data analytics in the field of Internet of Things (IoT) systems is becoming increasingly essential and intertwined. The capability of an intelligent system is growing depending upon various self-decision-making algorithms in IoT devices. IoT-based smart systems generate a large amount of data that cannot be processed by traditional data processing algorithms and applications. Hence, this book series involves different computational methods incorporated within the system with the help of analytics reasoning, learning methods, artificial intelligence, and sense-making in big data, which is most concerned in IoT-enabled environment.

This series will attract researchers and practitioners who are working in information technology and computer science in the field of intelligent computing paradigm, big data, machine learning, sensor data, IoT, and data sciences. The main aim of the series is to make available a range of books on all aspects of learning, analytics, and advanced intelligent systems and related technologies. This series will cover the theory, research, development, and applications of learning, computational analytics, data processing, and machine learning algorithms, as embedded in the fields of engineering, computer science, and information technology.

Security of Internet of Things Nodes: Challenges, Attacks, and Countermeasures
Chinmay Chakraborty, Sree Ranjani Rajendran, and Muhammad Habib Ur Rehman

Cancer Prediction for Industrial IoT 4.0: A Machine Learning Perspective
Meenu Gupta, Rachna Jain, Arun Solanki, and Fadi Al-Turjman

For more information on this series, please visit: https://www.routledge.com/Chapman–HallCRC-Internet-of-Things/book-series/IOT

Cancer Prediction for Industrial IoT 4.0: A Machine Learning Perspective

Edited by
Meenu Gupta, Rachna Jain, Arun Solanki, and
Fadi Al-Turjman

CRC Press
Taylor & Francis Group
Boca Raton London New York

CRC Press is an imprint of the
Taylor & Francis Group, an **informa** business

A CHAPMAN & HALL BOOK

First edition published 2022
by CRC Press
6000 Broken Sound Parkway NW, Suite 300, Boca Raton, FL 33487-2742

and by CRC Press
2 Park Square, Milton Park, Abingdon, Oxon, OX14 4RN

Library of Congress Cataloging-in-Publication Data
Names: Gupta, Meenu, editor. | Jain, Rachna D., editor. | Solanki, Arun,   1985- editor. | Al-Turjman, Fadi, editor.
Title: Cancer prediction for industrial Iot 4.0 : a machine learning   perspective / edited by Dr. Meenu Gupta, Associate Professor, Chandigarh University, Punjab, Dr. Rachna Jain, Assistant Professor, Bharati Vidyapeeth's College of Engineering, New Delhi, Dr. Arun Solanki, Gautam Buddha University, Noida, Dr. Fadi Al-Turjman, Near East University, Nicosia.
Description: First edition. | Boca Raton : C&Hl/CRC Press, 2022. | Series: Chapman & Hall/CRC internet of things: data-centric intelligent computing, informatics, and communication | Includes bibliographical references and index. | Summary: "This book presents the developments in machine learning with data mining, and their influence in Industrial IoT 4.0 for cancer prediction. It explores a comprehensive analysis of the gradual evolution of Industrial IoT 4.0 and machine learning technologies for establishing a new-generation and improving the productivity of healthcare industries. Covers the fundamentals, history, reality and challenges in Industrial IoT 4.0 D iscusses the concepts and analysis of Industrial IoT 4.0 Highlights machine learning-based deep learning and data mining concepts for automated Industrial 4.0 in the prediction of cancer Includes applications of industrial IoT 4.0 in the prediction of cancer with different real-world examples Focuses on strategies and tools for prediction of cancer in Industrial IoT 4.0 P resents case studies/success stories T alks about the future prospectus of Industrial IoT 4.0 This book is aimed primarily at graduates and researchers working in machine learning and data mining. Researchers and healthcare specialists studying cancer will also find this book useful"-- Provided by publisher.
Identifiers: LCCN 2021032674 (print) | LCCN 2021032675 (ebook) | ISBN 9781032028781 (hardback) | ISBN 9781032028798 (paperback) | ISBN 9781003185604 (ebook)
Subjects: LCSH: Cancer--Research--Technological innovations. | Machine learning.
Classification: LCC RC267 .C3648 2022 (print) | LCC RC267 (ebook) | DDC 616.99/400285--dc23
LC record available at https://lccn.loc.gov/2021032674
LC ebook record available at https://lccn.loc.gov/2021032675

ISBN: 978-1-032-02878-1 (hbk)
ISBN: 978-1-032-02879-8 (pbk)
ISBN: 978-1-003-18560-4 (ebk)

DOI: 10.1201/9781003185604

Typeset in Minion
by MPS Limited, Dehradun

Contents

Preface

Cancer treatments can cause changes to the human appearance, such as hair loss or loss of a body part. Whether these changes are temporary or permanent, they can change how people feel about themselves and make them feel self-conscious and less confident. **Machine learning** is a branch of artificial intelligence that uses numerous techniques to complete tasks, improving itself after every iteration. Pathologists are accurate at diagnosing **cancer** but have an accuracy rate of only 60% when **predicting cancer development**. Machine learning classifiers are very popular for detecting breast cancer. Several research studies have been conducted in this area.

Machine learning is one of the fastest developing research areas in computer science and includes the logical amount of data to form precise decisions. Traditional distributed machine learning algorithms deem a trusted central server, data reliability, and sharing and emphasize the critical security issue in machine learning models to enhance the accuracy of the results. Furthermore, machine learning techniques have the remarkable ability of data analysis. Novel and advanced data models are growing by using data mining techniques. The use of machine learning and data mining technology can provide significantly precise results.

This book presents recent advances in machine learning and its influence on cancer prediction. It explores a comprehensive analysis of the gradual evolution of cancer prediction and treatment with machine learning technologies for establishing the new generation of a secure, trusted environment and improving the productivity of the healthcare industry. The book discusses how machine learning can be used in the prediction of cancer.

Each chapter presents machine learning use in lung cancer, breast cancer, and other types of cancer with the introduction of the field. The idea behind this book is to simplify the journey of aspiring engineers/doctors across the world. This book contains 11 chapters. We hope that readers make the most of this volume and enjoy reading it. Suggestions and feedback are always welcome.

Meenu Gupta, Rachna Jain, Arun Solanki, and Fadi Al-Turjman

Editors

Dr. Meenu Gupta earned her PhD in computer science and engineering with an emphasis on traffic accident severity problems from the Ansal University, Gurugram, India (2020). She earned an M.Tech in computer science and engineering from the M.D. University, Rohtak, India (2010), and she graduated in information technology at the K.U.K University, Kurukshetra, India (2006). She is currently an Associate Professor in Chandigarh University. She has 13 years of teaching experience. Dr. Gupta's areas of research are machine learning, intelligent systems, and data mining, with specific interests in artificial intelligence, image processing and analysis, smart cities, data analysis, and human/brain–machine interaction. She has four authored books on engineering STREAM. She also submitted one edited book to CRC Press on healthcare. She worked as a reviewer for many journals including *Big Data, CMC, Scientific Report, TSP*, etc. She is a life member of ISTE and IAENG. Dr. Gupta has authored or co-authored more than 50 papers in refereed international journals (SCI/SCIE/WoS/Scopus/etc.), conferences, and more than 20 book chapters. She also chaired the IEEE International Conference and convened many workshops/FDPs.

Dr. Rachna Jain is an Assistant Professor (Computer Science Department) in Bharati Vidyapeeth's College of Engineering (GGSIPU), where she has been since 2007. She earned her PhD in computer science from Banasthali Vidyapith in 2017. She earned her ME degree in 2011 from Delhi College of Engineering (Delhi University) with specialization in computer technology and applications. She earned her B.Tech (Computer Science) in 2006 from N.C. College of Engineering, Kurukshetra University. Dr. Jain's current research interests are cloud computing, fuzzy logic, network and information security, swarm intelligence, big data and IoT, deep learning, and machine learning. She has contributed more than 10 book chapters to various books. She has also served as Session Chair in various international conferences. Dr. Jain is CO-PI of the DST Project titled "Design an Autonomous Intelligent Drone for City Surveillance." She has a total of 14+ years of academic/research experience with more than 50 publications in various national and international conferences and international journals (Scopus/ISI/SCI) of high repute.

Dr. Arun Solanki is an Assistant Professor in the Department of Computer Science and Engineering, Gautam Buddha University, Greater Noida, India, where he has been working since 2009. He has worked as Time Table Coordinator, Member Examination, Admissions, Sports Council, Digital Information Cell, and other university teams from time to time. He earned an M.Tech. degree in computer engineering from YMCA University, Faridabad, Haryana, India. He earned his PhD in computer science and engineering from Gautam Buddha University in 2014. He has supervised more than 60 M.Tech. dissertations under his guidance.

His research interests span expert system, machine learning, and search engines. He has published many research articles in SCI/ Scopus indexed international journals/ conferences such as IEEE, Elsevier, Springer, etc. He has participated in many international conferences. He has been a technical and advisory committee member of many conferences. He has organized several FDP, conferences, workshops, and seminars. He has chaired many sessions at international conferences. Dr. Solanki is working as Associate Editor in *International Journal of Web-Based Learning and Teaching Technologies (IJWLTT)*, IGI publisher. He has been working as Guest Editor for special issues in *Recent Patents on Computer Science*, Bentham Science Publishers. Dr. Solanki is the editor of many books with reputed publishers including IGI Global, CRC Press, and AAP. He is working as a reviewer for Springer, IGI Global, Elsevier, and other reputed journal publishers.

Prof. Dr. Fadi Al-Turjman earned his PhD in computer science from Queen's University, Canada, in 2011. He is the Associate Dean for Research and the Founding Director of the International Research Center for AI and IoT at Near East University, Nicosia, Cyprus. Prof. Al-Turjman is the head of the Artificial Intelligence Engineering Department, and a leading authority in the areas of smart/intelligent IoT systems, wireless, and mobile networks' architectures, protocols, deployments, and performance evaluation in Artificial Intelligence of Things (AIoT). His publication history spans more than 350 SCI/E publications, in addition to numerous key note and plenary talks at flagship venues. He has authored and edited more than 40 books about cognition, security, and wireless sensor networks' deployments in smart IoT environments, which have been published by well-reputed publishers such as Taylor & Francis, Elsevier, IET, and Springer. He has received several recognitions and best paper awards at top international conferences. He also received the prestigious Best Research Paper Award from *Elsevier Computer Communications Journal* for the period 2015–2018, in addition to the Top Researcher Award for 2018 at Antalya Bilim University, Turkey. Prof. Al-Turjman has led a number of international symposia and workshops in flagship communication society conferences. Currently, he serves as book series editor and the lead guest/associate editor for several top tier journals, including the *IEEE Communications Surveys and Tutorials* (IF 23.9) and the *Elsevier Sustainable Cities and Society* (IF 5.7), in addition to organizing international conferences and symposia on the most up-to-date research topics in AI and IoT.

Contributors

Ritu Aggarwal
Maharishi Markandeshwar University
  Mullana
Ambala, Haryana, India

Ruchir Ahluwalia
Bharati Vidyapeeth's College of Engineering

Shakeel Ahmed
King Faisal University
Saudi Arabia

Ajat Shatru Arora
Sant Longowal Institute of Engineering
  and Technology
Deemed-to-be-University
Longowal Sangrur, Punjab, India

Rishika Garg
Bharati Vidyapeeth's College of Engineering
Delhi, India

Mehdi Gheisari
Islamic Azad University
Iran

Bhawna Gupta
Panipat College of Engineering
Panipat, India

Rachna Jain
Bharati Vidyapeeth's College of Engineering
New Delhi

Rishit Jain
Bharati Vidyapeeth's College of Engineering

Gurmanik Kaur
Sant Baba Bhag Singh University
Khiala, Jalandhar, Punjab, India

Zaved Ahmed Khan
Department of Biotechnology Engineering
University
Institute of Engineering
Chandigarh University
Gharuan, Mohali (Punjab)

Ashish Kumar
Bharati Vidyapeeth's College of Engineering
New Delhi

Surekha Manhas
University Institute of Biotechnology
Chandigarh University
Gharuan, Mohali, Punjab

Preeti Nagrath
Bharati Vidyapeeth's College of Engineering
Delhi, India

Harsh Patel
Institute of Technology
Nirma University
Ahmedabad

Dr. Chander Prabha
Chandigarh University
Mohali, Punjab, India

Revant Singh Rai
Bharati Vidyapeeth's College of Engineering
New Delhi

Meet Shah
Institute of Technology
Nirma University
Ahmedabad

Geetika Sharma
Chandigarh University
Mohali, Punjab, India

Soham Taneja
Bharati Vidyapeeth's College of Engineering
Delhi, India

Prateek Thakral
Jaypee University of Information Technology
Waknaghat, Solan, India

Jai Prakash Verma
Institute of Technology
Nirma University
Ahmedabad

CHAPTER 1

Investigation of IoMT-Based Cancer Detection and Prediction

Meet Shah, Harsh Patel, Jai Prakash Verma, and Rachna Jain

CONTENTS

1.1 INTRODUCTION

According to the World Health Organization, the top two causes of cancer death in 2020 were lung cancer and colon and rectum cancer [1]. A quick, safe, and accurate early-stage cancer diagnosis can save millions of lives through proper diagnosis and treatment. There are many screening procedures for cancer diagnosis that work under different conditions and for different types of cancer. Medical practitioners analyze these results for patient diagnosis and treatment, but a misinterpretation of the data or human error can lead to misdiagnosis. To combat these issues, machine learning and deep learning (ML/DL) techniques, combined with the Internet of Medical Things (IoMT), have been a boon for cancer prediction, diagnosis, treatment, and patient care. The majority of this research has been carried out on breast, lung, and prostate cancer [2]. DL architectures generally suffer from tuning a huge number of parameters and require huge data to train. The goal of this chapter is to propose an IoMT-driven DL framework for detection and classification of the top two deadliest cancers – lung cancer and colon cancer – using transfer learning. A publicly available dataset, i.e., LC25000 [3], is used for this research. Upon feature extraction from pre-trained convolutional neural network (CNN) models like VGGNet [4], ResNet50 [5], and DenseNet121 [6], features were fed into a dense and flattened layer for cancer and its sub-type classification depending on the type of cancer. We evaluated the proposed approach by analyzing accuracy, precision, recall, and F1 score. The results showed that CNN pre-trained model ResNet-50 achieved the highest classification rate of 98.53% and 99.93% for the lung cancer and colon cancer datasets, respectively.

1.2 CANCER DIAGNOSIS AND RESEARCH

Cancer is a genetic disease caused by the unregulated growth of normal cells into tumor cells that happens in a multistage process. According to the World Health Organization, almost 19.3 million cancer cases were reported in 2020, and an estimated 28.4 million cases are projected to occur in 2040 [7]. Cancer is more likely to be treated successfully if diagnosed at an early stage. Moreover, early detection and diagnosis also decrease mental and physical pain suffered by patients. For example, 9 out of 10 patients diagnosed with lung cancer at its earliest stage survive for at least 1 year, which is reduced to just 2 out of 10 patients when lung cancer is diagnosed at the most advanced stage [8]. To detect lung cancer, there are many non-invasive imaging techniques such as computed tomography (CT) scan, chest magnetic resonance imaging (MRI) scan, and positron emission tomography (PET) scan. To detect colon cancer, there is CT scan, colonography, and PET scan. Although these imaging methods can show the tumor size, shape, and position, they are sometimes followed by a biopsy to further determine whether the tumor is cancerous and the grade of cancer. Types of biopsy include endoscopic biopsy, where the doctor inserts a thin, flexible tube called an endoscope via the patient's mouth or rectum to look for the tumor and also to collect a small tissue sample; needle biopsy, where the doctor uses a special needle to collect tissue samples from a suspicious area; or surgical biopsy, where the doctor makes an incision in the skin to access and collect tissue samples from a suspicious area. These biopsies provide a histological assessment of the microscopic structure of the tissue, and pathologists make the final diagnosis based on a visual inspection of histological samples under a microscope [9]. The process of microscopic examination of tissue to diagnose a disease is called histopathology [10].

1.2.1 Computational Analysis for Cancer Research

The rise in various forms of cancers and other illnesses has made pathologists key supporters in the medical industry, and doctors rely on them for accurate and efficient diagnosis. But the histopathological analysis is time-consuming, requires experience, and is prone to human error when done by pathologists [11]. Therefore, we propose computer-aided diagnosis (CAD) that can automatically and accurately classify benign and malignant tissues to relieve the pathologists' workload and provide a second opinion to the doctors. CAD and detection of cancer can be done with the help of state-of-art ML/DL techniques combined with the IoMT to provide the highest possible accuracy.

1.2.2 Role of the IoMT in Cancer Detection and Prediction

In the last decade, the Internet of Things (IoT) has seen great applications in healthcare and has come to be known as the Internet of Medical Things (IoMT) [12]. The IoMT, sometimes described as the Healthcare IoT, refers to the network of medical equipment such as sensors and imaging machines and their use to enhance patient health in future directions. IoMT devices include smart wearable devices, implants, smart pills, and smart drones that are equipped with sensors and other computing resources [13]. IoMT devices can be used to provide virtual care for patients with long-term illness; to provide medication monitoring; for location tracking of patients in order to create an analytical feedback loop between IoMT devices; and for research groups, doctors, pharmaceutical companies, and patients themselves. Generally, IoMT devices have a limited amount of memory, computational power, and communication capability [14]. Therefore, data from IoMT devices are collected and analyzed in the cloud for further processing [15]. These data can be CT scan images, MRI scan images, patients' vitals, etc. The goal of IoMT technology is to save time and effort of doctors and thus reduce the burden on health systems [12]. Due to many IoMT devices generating a large amount of data, we require ML/DL algorithms for efficient analysis.

1.2.3 Role of ML/DL Techniques in Cancer Detection and Prediction

ML is a subset of artificial intelligence (AI) and consists of algorithms that learn automatically through experience. DL is a part of ML based on an artificial neural network (ANN) that mimics the function of the human brain. Both ML and DL techniques play an important role in cancer detection and prediction [16–20]. These ML/DL techniques usually work by segmenting or detecting abnormalities and classifying the segmented area or tumor into benign or malignant. On the other hand, these techniques might also be trying to predict the risk of cancer to a patient based on his/her diagnostic history rather than detecting if he/she has cancer or not. DL methods can automatically learn features from large amounts of raw images and perform cancer detection and classification. The use of ML/DL techniques for cancer detection allows us to move from a reactive approach to a more proactive, personalized approach for cancer detection and prediction.

1.3 LITERATURE REVIEW

In cancer detection and prediction, ML/DL techniques are widely used on medical imaging data obtained from CT scans, MRI, PET, mammography, etc. As shown in Table 1.1, ML/DL cancer detection models usually work by tumor detection, segmentation, feature extraction, and classification. To detect cancer from medical images, feature extraction is a key step to identify tumor regions and tumors of various shapes and sizes. Luckily, ML/DL techniques can learn hierarchical feature representation directly from raw image data so researchers don't have to focus on feature engineering. ML/DL techniques have seen huge success in the field of cancer research in recent years due to massive parallel architectures and graphic processing units (GPUs). IoMT can offer real-time monitoring of patients in their everyday lives, such as tracking patient medication orders and using predictive diagnosis when combined with ML/DL techniques. Table 1.1 shows a summary of research done in the area of cancer prediction, detection, and classification using IoMT.

1.4 PROPOSED METHODOLOGY

The flowchart of the proposed IoMT architecture is shown in Figure 1.1. In the beginning, the patient is examined using IoMT devices, and the captured data are sent to the cloud. This data can be medical imaging data such as CT scans, MRIs, PET scans, etc., or histopathological sample images. Once in the cloud, data are pre-processed, and feature extraction is done on input images using pre-trained CNN architectures such as VGG16 [4], ResNet-50 [5], DenseNet-121 [6], etc. The pre-processing includes the removal of the noise present in the images. This helps in better feature capturing from the images. Data augmentation is also a part of pre-processing, where the images are flipped, rotated, cropped, and sheared to increase the dataset sample size because DL methods require a large dataset to train on. These extracted features are classified using ANN, but it can be any ML algorithm such as SVM, Random Forest, etc. Finally, the results are sent to the doctor or pathologist to act as a second opinion.

1.5 TRANSFER LEARNING

Training of CNNs from scratch requires a large amount of data and a great deal of computation time. These challenges lead to transfer learning, an advanced ML concept.

TABLE 1.1
A Summary of Different Research Work Done in the Area of Cancer

Reference	Type of Cancer	Summary
[21]	All types of cancer	The authors designed a densely connected encoder-decoder structure and also proposed an adaptive segmentation algorithm for shallow and deep features from CT scan images.
[22]	All types of cancer	The authors presented a new training scheme called ETS-DNN for DL networks in an edge computing enabled IoMT system.
[23]	Lung cancer, Brain cancer	The authors proposed an optimal feature selection using the opposition-based crow search (OCS) algorithm for effective medical image classification in IoMT.
[24]	Spinal cancer	The authors used the hierarchical hidden Markov random model field (HHMRF) to predict vertebral tumors from MRI images.
[25]	Blood cancer	The authors developed an IoMT-based framework for quick and safe detection of leukemia, a type of blood cancer using DL models DenseNet-121 and Resnet-334.
[26]	Brain cancer	The authors used a partial tree (PART), an association rule learner, with advanced features set to detect brain tumors in various stages from medical images in an IoMT-based approach.
[27]	Skin cancer	The authors proposed a new model, Optimal Segmentation and Restricted Boltzmann Machines (OS-RBM), for skin lesion detection and classification.
[28]	Blood cancer	Three pre-trained CNN architectures, Alexnet, Caffenet, and Vgg-f, were used for feature extraction, and support-vector machine (SVM) was used for leukemia classification.
[29]	Cervical cancer	A radiomics and VGG19 fusion model was used to extract high-level features from multiparametric MRI and classified using SVM to predict lymph-vascular space invasion.
[23]	Lung cancer	The authors proposed an optimal feature selection DL model with OCS.
[30]	Lung cancer	The authors successfully predicted future risk of lung cancer from low-dose CT scan images with the help of an integrated DL method, i.e., a combination of a long short-term memory network and CNN.
[31]	Colon cancer	The authors proposed a CAD system where colon cancer is detected from wireless capsule endoscopy (WCE) images using color histogram and SVM.
[32]	Colon cancer	The authors used a DL approach for colon cancer detection that can train using limited data or cancer data from a different organ using Cycle-GANs.

Transfer learning focuses on storing the knowledge gained while solving one problem and applying it to a different but related problem. The model selection depends on the target problem, and we might choose to re-train some of the layers of the model. Training the model on various datasets helps to generalize the data knowledge of the model, which helps to attain better training accuracy.

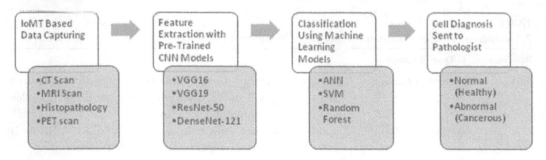

FIGURE 1.1   Proposed IoMT architecture.

1.5.1   Pre-Trained Models

After performing data augmentation when required, CNNs come into the picture. CNNs can automatically learn from raw data. A typical CNN begins with convolutional and pooling layers and ends with a fully connected layer. New models can be trained by assembling different numbers of convolutional, pooling, and dense layers. In the presented work, we use various pre-trained networks VGGNet [4], ResNet50 [5], and DenseNet121 [6]. In this section, we explain various pre-trained CNNs used in our work to identify different types of cancer based on their subtypes.

1.5.2   VGG16 and VGG19

The VGG16 and VGG19 [4] networks are simple in the sense that they use only 3 × 3 convolutional layers stacked on top of each other in increasing depth. Reducing volume size is handled by 2 × 2 max pooling. The "16" and "19" in their names stand for the number of weight layers, as shown in Figure 1.2. Due to a large number of weights, the training is very slow and needs a large disk space. The VGG16 performs as well as VGG19 despite having fewer layers, as we will see in the Results and Comparative Analysis section. The VGG network consists of 13 convolutional layers, pooling, rectification, and three fully connected layers in the infrastructure. The model design and execution are similar to the Alexnet [33] model but are able to perform better due to the enhanced complexity provided in the VGG networks.

The major difference between the VGG16 and the VGG19 is the total number of layers present in the neural network, which provide an edge over each other according to the use case the models are being deployed for. The convolutional layers in the VGG networks are followed by a max-pooling layer, which helps in the normalization of the results obtained from the convolutional layers. The VGG16 and VGG19 are two of the five total neural networks present in the VGG network series but are the best performing ones due to the uniform kernel size present throughout the infrastructure. The normalization of the outputs from the layers is done using the SoftMax activation function, whereas the convolutional layers contain ReLu and leaky ReLu as the activation functions in the layers. The major outstanding feature of the VGG networks is the small filter strategy, which helps in enhanced results on the dataset given.

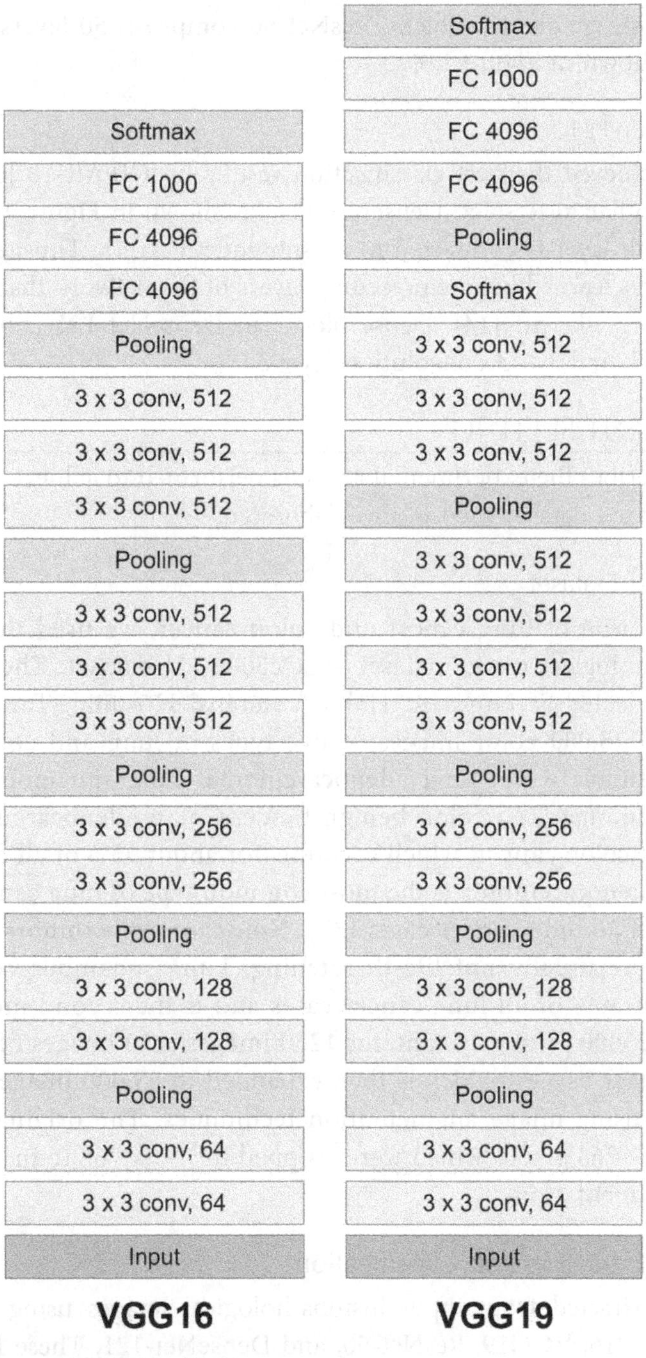

	Softmax
	FC 1000
Softmax	FC 4096
FC 1000	FC 4096
FC 4096	Pooling
FC 4096	Softmax
Pooling	3 x 3 conv, 512
3 x 3 conv, 512	3 x 3 conv, 512
3 x 3 conv, 512	3 x 3 conv, 512
3 x 3 conv, 512	Pooling
Pooling	3 x 3 conv, 512
3 x 3 conv, 512	3 x 3 conv, 512
3 x 3 conv, 512	3 x 3 conv, 512
3 x 3 conv, 512	3 x 3 conv, 512
Pooling	Pooling
3 x 3 conv, 256	3 x 3 conv, 256
3 x 3 conv, 256	3 x 3 conv, 256
Pooling	Pooling
3 x 3 conv, 128	3 x 3 conv, 128
3 x 3 conv, 128	3 x 3 conv, 128
Pooling	Pooling
3 x 3 conv, 64	3 x 3 conv, 64
3 x 3 conv, 64	3 x 3 conv, 64
Input	Input
VGG16	**VGG19**

FIGURE 1.2   VGG16 and VGG19 architecture.

1.5.3   ResNet-50

ResNet-50 [5] solves the accuracy degradation problem. When network depth increases, accuracy gets saturated and then degrades rapidly. Residual blocks in ResNet-50 use skip connections, which allow a type of shortcut path for the gradient to follow through and solve the vanishing gradient problem. ResNet-50 comprises 50 layers, and the network architecture is shown in Figure 1.3.

1.5.4 DenseNet-121

DenseNet [6] achieved the best classification results on CIFAR-10 [34] and ImageNet datasets [35]. Similar to ResNet, DenseNet-121 (as shown in Figure 1.4) consists of 121 layers, where each layer is connected to all subsequent layers. Thus, each layer receives important features learned by any preceding layers of the network that makes training of the network more efficient [14]. Dense blocks in DenseNet-121 consist of batch normalization, ReLU, and 3×3 convolution layers.

1.6 EXPERIMENT SETTING

This section describes the experimental analysis performed to achieve defined objectives. A description of the dataset used is also elaborated.

1.6.1 Source of Dataset

For the classification of lung cancer and colon cancer, we used the lung and colon cancer histopathological image dataset – LC25000 [3] dataset. The LC25000 dataset images were collected at James A. Haley Veterans' Hospital, Tampa, Florida. This dataset contains 25,000 color images of five types of lung and colon tissues, which include lung benign tissue, lung adenocarcinoma, lung squamous cell carcinoma, colon adenocarcinoma, and colon benign tissue. Colon adenocarcinoma is the most common type of colon cancer, which accounts for about 95% of all colon cancer cases [36], and lung adenocarcinoma is the most common type of lung cancer, which counts for about 40% of all lung cancer cases [37]. Non-cancerous tumors are called benign tumors, which are usually not life-threatening. Lung squamous cell carcinoma accounts for about 30% of all lung cancer cases and is the second most common lung cancer [37]. LC25000 primarily contains 1250 images (250 images of each type × 5) of pathological cancer tissues, which is then expanded to 25,000 images (5000 images of each type × 5) using image augmentation techniques. The original images were of resolution 1024×768 pixels, which were cropped to 768×768 to make them square to apply image augmentation.

1.6.2 Feature Extraction and Classification

Features were extracted from input histopathological images using pre-trained CNN architectures VGG16, VGG19, ResNet-50, and DenseNet-121. These features were then utilized by ANN to classify the image into sub-types of cancer depending on the type of cancer. The dataset used for this work [3] divides lung histopathological images into three classes – lung benign tissue, lung adenocarcinoma, and lung squamous cell carcinoma – and divides colon histopathological images into two classes: colon adenocarcinoma and colon benign tissue.

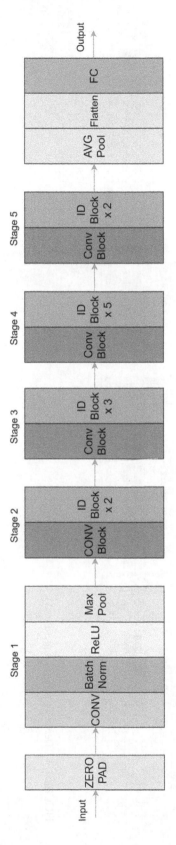

FIGURE 1.3 ResNet-50 architecture.

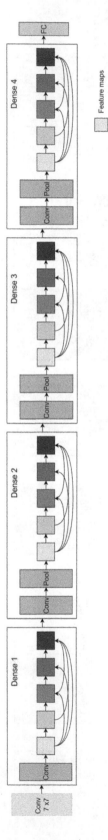

FIGURE 1.4 DenseNet-121 architecture.

1.6.3 Pre-Processing and Training

Input images were resized to 128 × 128 pixels from their original 768 × 768 size to fit all the images into memory at once. Downsizing the images poses the risk of deforming patterns and features inside the image, but it's necessary to reduce the space and time complexity of training. All the layers of pre-trained CNN models are kept as is, with the weights from their training on the "Imagenet" [35] dataset except the fully connected layer. We replaced the fully connected layers in each pre-trained CNN model with an ANN of size 128 × 64 × 32 × 16 × 8 × 2 for the colon cancer classification task and size 128 × 64 × 32 × 16 × 8 × 2 for the lung cancer classification task, i.e., 128 neurons in the first layer, 64 neurons in the second layer, and so on. The proposed IOMT architecture is trained on four different pre-trained CNN models, and then results were fed into ANN for classification with the help of transfer learning. For the experimentation, data were divided into 75%–10%–15% training–validation–testing split without shuffling. Comparison between different pre-trained CNN models with the combination of ANN classifier is shown in Tables 1.2 and 1.3.

1.6.4 Model Evaluation Metrics

To evaluate the different pre-trained models, we use class-wise precision (eq 1.1), recall (eq 1.2), F1 score (eq 1.3), and overall accuracy (eq 1.4), as shown in Tables 1.2 and 1.3.

$$\text{Precision} = \frac{TP}{TP + FP} \tag{1.1}$$

Here, TP = True Positive, i.e., the number of instances where the model correctly classified positive class as the positive class. FP = False Positive, i.e., the number of instances where the model incorrectly classified negative class as the positive class.

$$\text{Recall} = \frac{TP}{TP + FN} \tag{1.2}$$

Here, FN = False Negative, i.e., the number of instances where the model incorrectly classified positive class as the negative class.

$$\text{F1} - \text{score} = \frac{2 * \text{Precision} * \text{Recall}}{\text{Precision} + \text{Recall}} \tag{1.3}$$

The F1 score is essentially a harmonic mean of precision and recall. We use the F1 score as a way of combining both precision and recall.

$$\text{Accuracy} = \frac{TP + TN}{TP + TN + FP + FN} \tag{1.4}$$

TABLE 1.2
Performance of Pre-Trained Models on Lung Cancer Classification

Pre-Trained Architecture	Class	Precision (%)	Recall (%)	F1 Score (%)	Overall Accuracy (%)
VGG16	Benign	100	91.77	95.71	96.93
	Adenocarcinoma	100	100	100	
	Sq. Cell Carcinoma	92.56	98.96	95.65	
VGG19	Benign	96.45	95.69	96.07	97.33
	Adenocarcinoma	100	99.73	99.86	
	Sq. Cell Carcinoma	95.59	96.63	96.11	
ResNet-50	Benign	99.21	96.54	97.86	98.53
	Adenocarcinoma	98.7	100	99.34	
	Sq. Cell Carcinoma	97.64	99.15	98.39	
DenseNet-121	Benign	91.64	92.73	92.18	94.71
	Adenocarcinoma	98.68	100	99.33	
	Sq. Cell Carcinoma	93.78	91.39	92.57	

TABLE 1.3
Performance of Pre-Trained Models on Colon Cancer Classification

Pre-Trained Architecture	Class	Precision (%)	Recall (%)	F1 Score (%)	Overall Accuracy (%)
VGG16	Benign	100	98.85	99.42	99.4
	Adenocarcinoma	98.77	100	99.38	
VGG19	Benign	99.36	100	99.68	99.67
	Adenocarcinoma	100	99.3	99.65	
ResNet-50	Benign	99.86	100	99.93	99.93
	Adenocarcinoma	100	99.87	99.93	
DenseNet-121	Benign	99.44	94.78	97.05	97.13
	Adenocarcinoma	95.05	99.47	97.21	

Here, TN = True Negative, i.e., the number of instances where the model correctly classified negative class as the negative class.

1.7 RESULTS AND COMPARATIVE ANALYSIS

Table 1.2 shows the comparison between different pre-trained CNN models used for feature extraction using ANN for classification of lung cancer. Table 1.3 shows the same but for the colon cancer classification. As mentioned in Section 6.3, we evaluate these models by measuring their class-wise precision (%), recall (%), F1 score (%), and overall accuracy (%). We see a common trend in both the tables that as the number of layers increases in the network architecture from 16 layers in VGG16 to 121 layers in DenseNet-121, we notice a decrease in all the evaluation metrics mentioned above. Up until ResNet-50, network performance improves and starts degrading as soon as the network layers are increased. This is since we have picked a smaller size for our input images (128 × 128), and as the layers increase, there is more downsizing of the input images. If we pick a smaller input size for our images, then there is going to be a significant loss in image features and deformity in patterns as we go down the network. That is why we see a decrease in network performance as we move down the table and have more layers in the network. It is clear from Tables 1.2 and 1.3 that ResNet-50 is the best model for lung cancer classification and also colon cancer classification. ResNet-50 achieves an overall accuracy of 98.53% for the lung cancer classification task and an overall accuracy of 99.93% for the colon cancer classification task. On the other hand, VGG19 is in second place with an overall accuracy of 97.33% on the lung cancer classification task and also achieves second place on the colon cancer classification task with an overall accuracy of 99.67%.

1.8 SUMMARY

In this chapter, we proposed an IoMT architecture for lung cancer and colon cancer sub-type classification. We extracted features from histopathological images using pre-trained CNN models and fed those features to ANN for classification. We compared different pre-trained CNN architectures and found that the ResNet-50 model's performance supersedes all other models –for both lung and colon cancer classification. After a diagnosis is generated by the network, the pathologist confirms the results. This proposed IoMT architecture aids doctors in an accurate diagnosis and helps save lives. This kind of proposed approach can help take the load off medical infrastructure (pathology labs, radiology labs, etc.), especially during pandemics such as COVID-19. For future work, it can be extended by training on a different dataset to include the classification of more types of cancer. Moreover, this IoMT architecture can be adapted to other diseases as well depending on the disease and the testing method.

REFERENCES

[1] Cancer. (2021b, March 3). The World Health Organization. https://www.who.int/news-room/fact-sheets/detail/cancer

[2] Ray, Susmita. "A Survey on Application of Machine Learning Algorithms in Cancer Prediction and Prognosis." Data Management, Analytics and Innovation. Springer, Singapore, 2021. 349–361.

[3] Borkowski, A.A., M.M. Bui, L.B. Thomas, C.P. Wilson, L.A. DeLand, and S.M. Mastorides. "Lung and Colon Cancer Histopathological Image Dataset (LC25000)." arXiv 2019, arXiv:1912.12142. [Google Scholar]

[4] Simonyan, Karen, and Andrew Zisserman. "Very Deep Convolutional Networks for Large-Scale Image Recognition." arXiv preprint arXiv:1409.1556 (2014).

[5] He, Kaiming, et al. "Deep Residual Learning for Image Recognition." Proceedings of the IEEE conference on computer vision and pattern recognition. 2016.

[6] Huang, Gao, et al. "Densely Connected Convolutional Networks." Proceedings of the IEEE conference on computer vision and pattern recognition. 2017.

[7] Sung, Hyuna, et al. "Global cancer statistics 2020: GLOBOCAN estimates of incidence and mortality worldwide for 36 cancers in 185 countries." CA: A Cancer Journal for Clinicians 71.3 (2021): 209–249.

[8] Cancer Research UK. (2021, January 22). Why is early diagnosis important? https://www.cancerresearchuk.org/about-cancer/cancer-symptoms/why-is-early-diagnosis-important

[9] Babaie, Morteza, and Hamid R. Tizhoosh. "Deep features for tissue-fold detection in histopathology images." European Congress on Digital Pathology. Springer, Cham, 2019.

[10] Wikipedia contributors. (2021, April 14). Histopathology. Wikipedia. https://en.wikipedia.org/wiki/Histopathology

[11] Yari, Yasin, Hieu Nguyen, and Thuy V. Nguyen. "Accuracy improvement in binary and multi-class classification of breast histopathology images." 2020 IEEE Eighth International Conference on Communications and Electronics (ICCE). IEEE, 2021.

[12] Din, Ikram Ud, et al. "A decade of Internet of Things: Analysis in the light of healthcare applications." Ieee Access 7 (2019): 89967–89979.

[13] Basatneh, Rami, Bijan Najafi, and David G. Armstrong. "Health sensors, smart home devices, and the internet of medical things: An opportunity for dramatic improvement in care for the lower extremity complications of diabetes." Journal of diabetes science and technology 12.3 (2018): 577–586.

[14] Khan, Sana Ullah, et al. "An e-Health care services framework for the detection and classification of breast cancer in breast cytology images as an IoMT application." Future Generation Computer Systems 98 (2019): 286–296.

[15] Janjua, Kanwal, et al. "Proactive forensics in iot: Privacy-aware log-preservation architecture in fog-enabled-cloud using holochain and containerization technologies." Electronics 9.7 (2020): 1172.

[16] Saba, Tanzila. "Recent advancement in cancer detection using machine learning: Systematic survey of decades, comparisons and challenges." Journal of Infection and Public Health 13.9 (2020): 1274–1289.

[17] Vaka, Anji Reddy, Badal Soni, and Sudheer Reddy. "Breast cancer detection by leveraging Machine Learning." ICT Express 6.4 (2020): 320–324.

[18] Mojrian, Sanaz, et al. "Hybrid machine learning model of extreme learning machine radial basis function for breast cancer detection and diagnosis; a multilayer fuzzy expert system." 2020 RIVF International Conference on Computing and Communication Technologies (RIVF). IEEE, 2020.

[19] Kadampur, Mohammad Ali, and Sulaiman Al Riyaee. "Skin cancer detection: Applying a deep learning based model driven architecture in the cloud for classifying dermal cell images." Informatics in Medicine Unlocked 18 (2020): 100282.

[20] Zheng, Jing, et al. "Deep learning assisted efficient AdaBoost algorithm for breast cancer detection and early diagnosis." IEEE Access 8 (2020): 96946–96954.

[21] Wang, Eric Ke, et al. "A deep learning based medical image segmentation technique in Internet-of-Medical-Things domain." Future Generation Computer Systems 108 (2020): 135–144.

[22] Pustokhina, Irina Valeryevna, et al. "An effective training scheme for deep neural network in edge computing enabled Internet of medical things (IoMT) systems." IEEE Access 8 (2020): 107112–107123.

[23] Raj, R. Joshua Samuel, et al. "Optimal feature selection-based medical image classification using deep learning model in internet of medical things." IEEE Access 8 (2020): 58006–58017.

[24] Alsiddiky, Abdulmonem, et al. "Magnetic resonance imaging evaluation of vertebral tumour prediction using hierarchical hidden Markov random field model on Internet of Medical Things (IoMT) platform." Measurement 159 (2020): 107772.

[25] Bibi, Nighat, et al. "IoMT-based Automated Detection and Classification of Leukemia Using Deep Learning." Journal of healthcare engineering 2020 (2020).

[26] Khan, Shah Rukh, et al. "IoMT-based computational approach for detecting brain tumour." Future Generation Computer Systems 109 (2020): 360–367.

[27] Anandaraj, A. Peter Soosai, et al. "Internet of Medical Things (IoMT) Enabled Skin Lesion Detection and Classification Using Optimal Segmentation and Restricted Boltzmann Machines." Cognitive Internet of Medical Things for Smart Healthcare. Springer, Cham, 2021. 195–209.

[28] Vogado, Luis HS, et al. "Leukemia diagnosis in blood slides using transfer learning in CNNs and SVM for classification." Engineering Applications of Artificial Intelligence 72 (2018): 415–422.

[29] Hua, Wenqing, et al. "Lymph-vascular space invasion prediction in cervical cancer: Exploring radiomics and deep learning multilevel features of tumor and peritumor tissue on multiparametric MRI." Biomedical Signal Processing and Control 58 (2020): 101869.

[30] Wang, Wei, et al. "An Integrated Deep Learning Algorithm for Detecting Lung Nodules with Low-dose CT and Its Application in 6G-enabled Internet of Medical Things." IEEE Internet of Things Journal (2020).

[31] Sundaram, P. Shanmuga, and N. Santhiyakumari. "An enhancement of computer aided approach for colon cancer detection in WCE images using ROI based color histogram and svm2." Journal of medical systems 43.2 (2019): 29.

[32] Tsirikoglou, Apostolia, et al. "A study of deep learning colon cancer detection in limited data access scenarios." arXiv preprint arXiv:2005.10326 (2020).

[33] Iandola, Forrest N., et al. "SqueezeNet: AlexNet-level accuracy with 50x fewer parameters and< 0.5 MB model size." arXiv preprint arXiv:1602.07360 (2016).

[34] CIFAR-10 and CIFAR-100 datasets. (n.d.). The CIFAR-10 dataset: The CIFAR-10 and CIFAR-100 are labeled subsets of the 80 million tiny images dataset. Retrieved June 2, 2021, from https://www.cs.toronto.edu/%7Ekriz/cifar.html

[35] Deng, Jia, et al. "Imagenet: A large-scale hierarchical image database." 2009 IEEE conference on computer vision and pattern recognition. Ieee, 2009.

[36] Types of Colorectal Cancer: Common, Rare and More. (n.d.). Cancer Treatment Centers of America. Retrieved June 2, 2021, from https://www.cancercenter.com/cancer-types/colorectal-cancer/types

[37] Types of Lung Cancer: Common, Rare and More Varieties. (n.d.). Cancer Treatment Centers of America. Retrieved June 2, 2021, from https://www.cancercenter.com/cancer-types/lung-cancer/types

CHAPTER 2

Histopathological Cancer Detection Using CNN

Soham Taneja, Rishika Garg, Preeti Nagrath, and Bhawna Gupta

CONTENTS

2.1 INTRODUCTION

The term "cancer" is used to refer to any disease that emerges from the irrepressible proliferation of cells in the body, leading to disruption of the functioning of other, normal cells. Cancer has consistently been a leading cause of death throughout the world [1]. What makes this disease one of the most notorious is its ability to exist in nearly any part of the body, especially in vital organs. In fact, among men, carcinoma tumors (cancerous tissues) were most likely to be found in the lungs, prostate, urinary bladder, colon, and rectum, with

DOI: 10.1201/9781003185604-2

prostate cancer being the most fatal. Among women, carcinoma tumors were most likely to be found in the lungs, breast, uterus, thyroid, and colon and rectum, with breast cancer being the most fatal [2]. Several hypotheses have been made to ascertain and understand the origin(s) of cancer, the most prominent one being the mutation theory proposed by Karl-Heinrich Bauer. However, all of these theories have been contradicted with data [3], making research in the detection and diagnosis of cancer even more important.

Histopathology is the inspection of specimens of tissue (obtained via pathology) at a microscopic level to identify and locate any traces of cancerous growth. The process of histopathology primarily consists of obtaining a fresh specimen, preserving it, and carrying out biochemical procedures to optimize its usability. The process ends with carefully observing the specimen under a microscope and scrutinizing its histological behavior [4].

As evident even from the condensed description of the process, it is a prolonged process involving the utmost precision, and it is strenuous. Moreover, a potential threat of sample misdiagnosis exists in the form of microscopic visual artefacts, which are incongruities found during visual representation. In histopathology, these can occur as structural details not pertaining to the specimen that occur due to errors during its processing.

Such errors [5], while quite rare, stand the chance of being nearly eradicated. In addition, the entire procedure can receive a boost in speed and possibly better accuracy as well. This potential is seen by introducing artificial intelligence (AI) to the field of histopathology.

In our research, we strive to find a novel method of performing histopathology by building a deep learning (DL) model that can detect metastatic cancerous growth in tissue specimen scans. The model is an ensemble of various convolutional neural network (CNN) techniques such as Inception Net, XceptionNet, ResNet, and DenseNet, which are all different types of DL-based image classification models.

The contributions made by our research are as follows:

- Introduction of a CNN-based system for the detection of metastatic cancer in histopathological scans of different types of tissue

- Creation of an ensemble model to combine the results obtained by individual models to reduce ambiguity and increase reliability

- Usage of a large dataset to train and validate the model to increase credibility

- Extending the potential of the proposed system to detect any kind of cancer in the body

The remainder of the chapter is organized as follows: Section 2.2 discusses the different kinds of cancer that are frequently detected in histopathological scans, which our AI solution is especially aimed towards. Section 2.3 shows the literature surveys we reviewed during the course of the research to identify the common problems faced when tackling similar issues. Section 2.4 discusses the details of the dataset used by us to train and test the proposed system. Section 2.5 talks about the methodology adopted to build the proposed system and Section 2.6 discusses the results obtained and what they mean. Finally, Section 2.7 contains concluding remarks about the study and future scope.

2.2 MAJOR TYPES OF CANCER DETECTED THROUGH HISTOPATHOLOGY

In this section, we describe the main kinds of cancer, whose detection depends on histopathology or histology.

1. Breast Cancer – This is the world's most prevalent cancer and a leading cause of death among women. Its symptoms are largely physical and can vary from patient to patient. What makes it worse is its likeliness to recur and the fact that it cannot be completely cured. This makes early detection all the more imperative. We explored a number of studies carried out on this issue [6–17] and tried to incorporate useful findings in our proposed solution.

2. Lung Cancer – Another very common type of cancer that can be detected using histopathology, lung cancer also has a high rate of mortality. If detected soon enough, a patient can survive, as this cancer often spreads to other organs if not treated early. We also took note of work done to alleviate this cancer [17–19] and tried to base our methods on our observations.

3. Prostate Cancer – This is also one of the commonly occurring types of cancer. This cancer almost always occurs in men and has implicit symptoms. It often takes time to grow, so early detection can mean early elimination, and since it is fully curable as well, we expect our proposed method to contribute towards the early detection of this cancer as well.

4. Colorectal Cancers – This term refers to cancers of the colon and the rectum, also called bowel cancer. It is the development of cancer from the colon or rectum (parts of the large intestine) and usually requires surgery for treatment. This cancer is curable as well, although it can recur after surgery, often resulting in fatalities. However, early detection can reduce the need for surgery, thereby helping the patient heal fully. Hence, we expect our solution to be capable of working in favor of this goal.

5. Hepatic (Liver) Cancer – This cancer begins in the cells of the liver. Its symptoms also tend to be physical, and it usually requires complex procedures as treatment. Like lung cancer, this cancer also spreads to other organs fast due to the proximity, decreasing the chances of survival. Therefore, like all other cancers, early detection is key. We went through some of the research work done with respect to this cancer [20] and expect our method to fare well.

2.3 LITERATURE REVIEW

A study carried out by Matko Šarić, Mladen Russo, Maja Stella, and Marjan Sikora compared the performances of VGG and Resnet on image patch level to aid diagnosticians in the diagnosis of lung cancer. However, this research could only prove that CNN in histopathology has potential due to the improvable accuracy achieved by the model developed despite being trained on a small dataset [18].

Liangqun Lu and Bernie J. Daigle, Jr. used three pre-trained CNN models; VGG16, Inception V3, and ResNet50 to identify characteristics from histopathological scans of cancerous tissues from the liver. While the accuracies obtained by the models are high, this research's only shortcomings were its restriction to liver cancer and the small size of the dataset used [20].

In the study conducted by Sara Hosseinzadeh Kassani et al., an ensemble DL-based approach (using VGG19, MobileNet, and DenseNet) for the classification of breast histology scans was proposed. The model was validated on four different datasets, achieving significant accuracies. The only shortcoming of this research was its restriction to breast cancer [6].

Mahesh Gour, Sweta Jain, and T. Sunil Kumar designed a residual learning-based 152-layered CNN named ResHist for the classification of histopathological images for breast cancer detection. They also made use of data augmentation. Though the system achieved a high degree of accuracy, the study was only carried out for breast cancer, and the dataset involved was very large [7].

Bijaya Kumar Hatuwal and Himal Chand Thapa used a CNN model to classify the types of lung cancer found in the dataset images. Their model showed good accuracy, but the study focused on basic CNN (ConvNet) and didn't delve deeper into its many algorithms [19].

The research by Ebrahim Mohammed Senan et al. proposed a CNN-based method using AlexNet for classifying breast cancer as "benign" or "malignant." Although the accuracies achieved by the system were high, the research fell short on simultaneously exploring more methods and extending the study to the classification of different types of tumors [8].

The study carried out by Şaban Öztürk and Bayram Akdemir examined the performance of a CNN model in classifying histopathological images based on their extent of pre-processing. However, this study picked up three different pre-processing techniques and ran the model on them, along with the original dataset, and found that "normal" (moderate) pre-processing resulted in the best accuracy. However, this research was restricted only to the AlexNet structure of CNN, thereby making the results somewhat unreliable for use with other models [21].

A study conducted by Meghana Dinesh Kumar et al. compared local binary patterns (LBP), deep features, and the bag-of-visual words (BoVW) scheme for classifying histopathological scans. They found the accuracy to be the highest with BoVW and lowest with LBP. However, this research conceded that deep solutions were capable of showing better scores if given a bigger dataset to train on, which was not the case in this scenario [22].

Noorul Wahab, Asifullah Khan, and Yeon Soo Lee, in their research, proposed a two-phase model to attenuate class biasness during the classification of mitotic and non-mitotic nuclei in histopathological scans of breast cancer using a deep CNN system. However, this study showed ambiguity in the results owing to the weakness of the dataset used [9].

The same set of researchers also carried out a study where they made use of transfer learning by using a pre-trained CNN for segmentation, followed by another hybrid-CNN (with weights transfer and custom layers) to classify mitoses in histopathological images pertaining to breast cancer. The system achieved an average accuracy but utilized a very small dataset [10].

The research conducted by Angel Cruz-Roa et al. introduced a new method for detecting breast cancer, called High-throughput Adaptive Sampling for whole-slide Histopathology Image analysis (HASHI), comprising a novel approach of flexible sampling centered on probability gradient and quasi-Monte Carlo sampling and a robust CNN-based representation-learning classification model. The limitations of this study were the inability of the system to differentiate between BCa and DCIS, and the use of FCN, which cannot be run on large images [11].

In the study carried out by Swathy C.K. and Resmi K. Ranjan, a method of detecting breast cancer in digital thermography and histopathology images using the image processing techniques in artificial neural networks (ANNs) was presented. Though their system achieved high accuracies, the dataset used during the course of the research was very small [12].

In the research carried out by Tahir Mahmood et al., a multi-stage mitotic cell detection method centered on faster R-CNN and deep CNNs was proposed to improve the second-opinion system in medicine in terms of speed and cost. However, this study fell short in its examination of DL by using relatively small datasets, even though DL is best trained with large datasets [23].

In their research, Zhigang Song et al. developed a system using deep CNN trained on a large dataset to help improve diagnostic accuracy in cases of gastric cancer. One shortcoming of this study was that it only focused on gastric cancer, which is one of the rarer-occurring cancers and is hard to diagnose, even by professionals. The second was the high computational cost of building and running the AI system they developed [24].

Yun Liu et al., in their study, explored a DL-based method called LYmph Node Assistant, or LYNA, for detecting Stage-IV breast cancer in sentinel lymph node specimens. The shortcomings of this study included the inability of LYNA to make position-dependent inferences and the lack of direct evaluation of the system's accuracy [13].

In the research conducted by Sumaiya Dabeer, Maha Mohammed Khan, and Saiful Islam, a DL-based architecture encompassing ML and image classification was presented for helping detect breast cancer. However, this study utilized data pre-processing methods that significantly altered the data and thus the accuracy [14].

A study by Abdullah-Al Nahid, Mohamad Ali Mehrabi, and Yinan Kong proposed using a group of DNN techniques based on various details obtained from the dataset (having biomedical breast cancer images) to perform image classification (as benign and malignant). However, the dataset used during this research was too weak to be used with a DNN model, introducing the possibility of an over-fitted model [15].

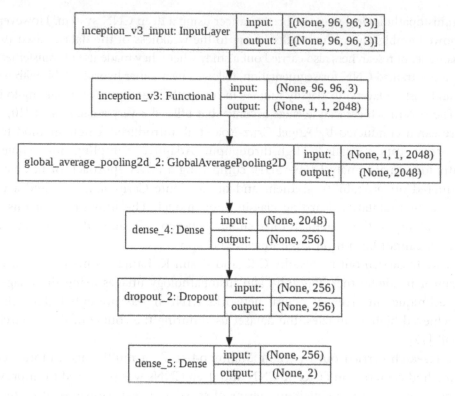

FIGURE 2.1   Inception V3 model architecture.

In their study, Naresh Khuriwal and Nidhi Mishra explored 12 different features to try to diagnose breast cancer and compare DL methods with ML methods. However, this research only focused on breast cancer, and the dataset used did not contain actual tissue scans [16].

The study by Hoa Hoang Ngoc Pham et al. presented a two-step DL algorithm to deal with the false-positive prediction of lung cancer, without cutting out on accurate detection. They used a DL algorithm to eliminate frequently misclassified non-cancerous regions, followed by the use of a DL-based classification model to spot cancerous cells. They used this method to increase the sensitivity of, and reduce the errors made by, their model. The research explored something that does not receive much attention, but in the process had limitations like the low specificity of the system, a small validation set, and its exclusion of true-negatives from the study [17].

2.4   DATASET

Our research made use of the dataset titled "Histopathologic Cancer Detection" obtained from Kaggle. We chose the refined version of this dataset on Kaggle over the original PCam one, as the latter contained duplicate images.

The dataset contains 2,20,023 small pathology images to classify, each allotted a unique image id. Each picture is also associated with an image label, wherein a positive label suggests that the 32 × 32px region at the center of a patch has a cancerous tissue occupying at least 1 pixel. This follows that the presence of even a single cancerous tissue in the

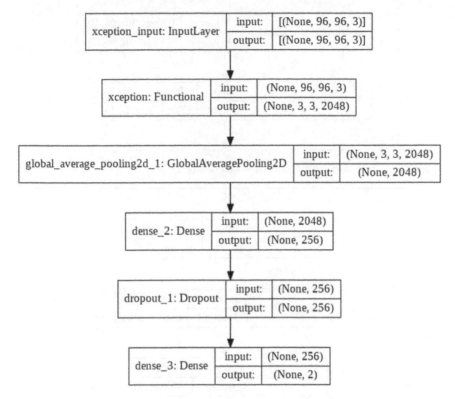

FIGURE 2.2 XceptionNet model architecture.

exterior of the patch does not affect the label, as this exterior only is provided so that fully convolutional models that do not use zero-padding can display consistent behavior when tested on whole-slide images.

The data were already partitioned into a train folder providing the ground truth for the images, and a test folder to predict the image labels for the files contained in it.

2.5 METHODOLOGY

2.5.1 Data Pre-Processing

The dataset contained three-dimensional images of varying sizes, which were then scaled down to fit the 96 × 96 × 3 dimensions.

The third axis contained three channels representing the RGB nature of the images. Following this, the data frame consisting of the list of labels for positive and negative images was loaded. Next, the data generator was initialized with directory paths as input. The data generator loaded images from those paths and sent them to the individual models in a batch size of 64 in each step. The images in the data generator were all rescaled within a range of 0–1 by dividing individual pixel values by 255.

2.5.2 Components of the Ensemble

Inception V3 – This type of CNN model, introduced by Google, originally used 22 layers in its architecture. We used its third version, or V3, a two-fold improved modification of

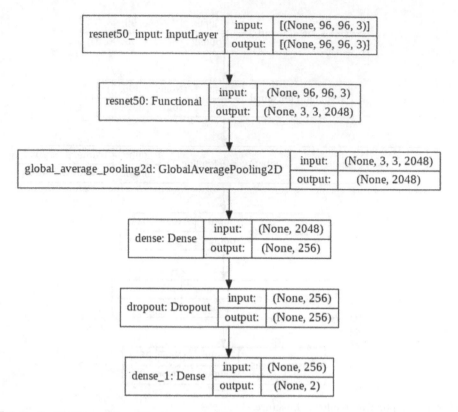

FIGURE 2.3 ResNet50 model architecture.

the first architecture. It uses label smoothing [25], has an RMSProp Optimizer, factorized 7 × 7 convolutions, and used BatchNorm in its auxiliary classifiers (Figure 2.1).

XceptionNet – This type of CNN model, made by François Chollet [26] (the creator of the Keras library), uses 71 layers in its architecture. It is an extension of Inception Net and has depth-wise separable convolutions. Its weight serialization is the smallest among all the other architectures (Figure 2.2).

ResNet50 – This type of CNN model, created by Kaiming He, Xiangyu Zhang, Shaoqing Ren, and Jian Sun [27], was inspired by the VGG19 model. It uses 34 layers in its architecture. We used its variant, ResNet 50, which was developed by IBM and uses 48 convolution layers in its architecture. It also has MaxPool and Average Pool layers, one of each. It uses 3.8 × 10^9 floating points operations (Figure 2.3).

DenseNet121 – This type of CNN model, proposed by Gao Huang, Zhuang Liu, Laurens Van Der Maaten, and Kilian Q. Weinberger [28], uses multi-layer "dense blocks" in its architecture. We used its variant, DenseNet121, which, as the name suggests, has 121 layers dedicated to different functions (Figure 2.4).

Each component was finalized with:

2D Global Average Pooling [29]
1 Dense Layer

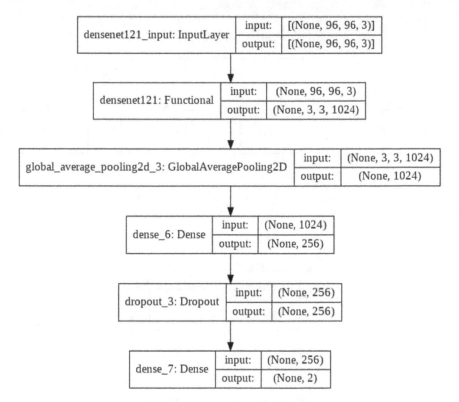

FIGURE 2.4   DenseNet121 model architecture.

1 Inference Layer
Compiler: Adamax Optimizer [30], Loss Function – Binary Cross-Entropy [31]
Metrics: F1 Score and Accuracy [32]

2.5.3   Ensemble Model

The results generated by the individual models were assembled, and the collective modes were calculated for all images of the dataset. Using these modes, the ensemble model was trained to generate its own set of results in terms of the confusion matrix, accuracy and loss curves, and a precision-recall table (Figure 2.5).

2.6   RESULTS AND DISCUSSION

2.6.1   Ensemble Components

Inception V3 – Figures 2.6 and 2.7 show the accuracy and loss curves for the training and validation sets when run through the Inception V3 model for 15 epochs. As can be seen, the model starts overfitting after six epochs, and the training loss decreases, whereas the validation loss does not improve. Figure 2.8 shows the confusion matrix obtained on validating the model. Some minor misclassifications can be seen in it.

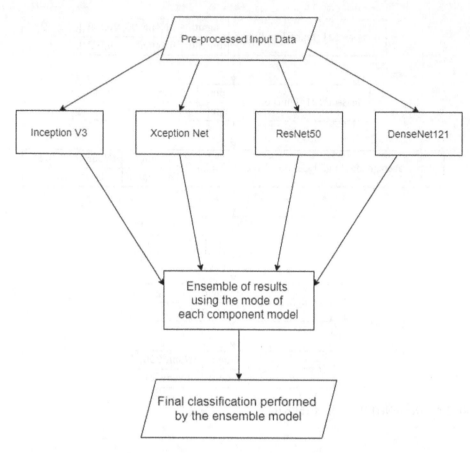

FIGURE 2.5   Working algorithm of ensemble model.

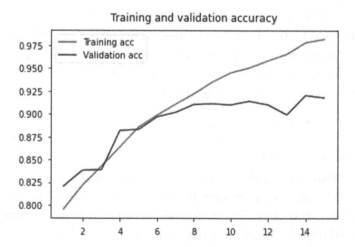

FIGURE 2.6   Accuracy and loss curves for inception V3 model training and validation.

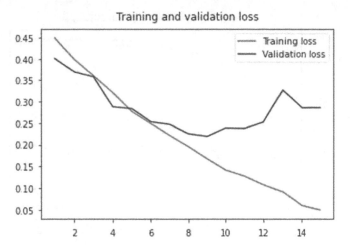

FIGURE 2.7   Accuracy and loss curves for inception V3 model training and validation.

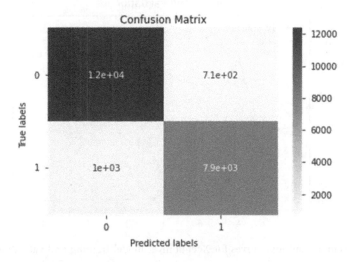

FIGURE 2.8   Confusion matrix obtained for inception V3.

	precision	recall	f1-score	support
0	0.92	0.95	0.93	13091
1	0.92	0.88	0.90	8912
accuracy			0.92	22003
macro avg	0.92	0.91	0.92	22003
weighted avg	0.92	0.92	0.92	22003

FIGURE 2.9   Precision, recall, and F1 scores obtained for inception V3.

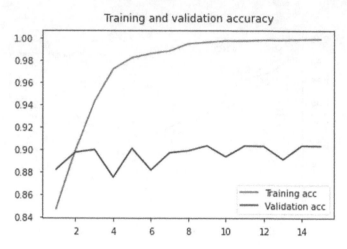

FIGURE 2.10   Accuracy and loss curves for XceptionNet model training and validation.

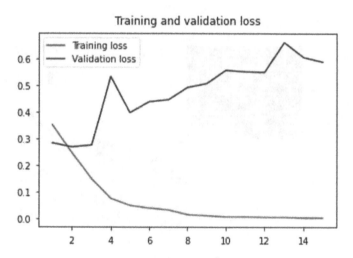

FIGURE 2.11   Accuracy and loss curves for XceptionNet model training and validation.

Finally, Figure 2.9 describes the model's performance (precision, recall, and F1 scores) on the validation set.

XceptionNet – Figures 2.10 and 2.11 show the accuracy and loss curves for the training and validation sets when run through the XceptionNet model for 15 epochs. As can be seen, the model starts overfitting after just three epochs, and the training loss falls, whereas the validation loss rises. Figure 2.12 shows the confusion matrix obtained on validating the model. Misclassifications can be seen. Lastly, Figure 2.13 describes the model's performance (precision, recall, and F1 scores) on the validation set. Clearly, this model is not as good as the previous one.

ResNet50 – Figures 2.14 and 2.15 show the accuracy and loss curves for the training and validation sets when run through the ResNet50 model for 15 epochs. As can be seen, the

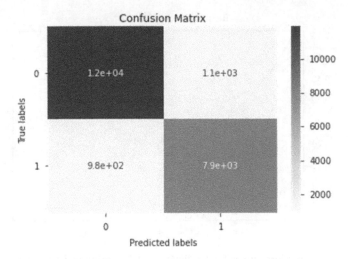

FIGURE 2.12   Confusion matrix obtained for XceptionNet.

	precision	recall	f1-score	support
0	0.92	0.91	0.92	13091
1	0.87	0.89	0.88	8912
accuracy			0.90	22003
macro avg	0.90	0.90	0.90	22003
weighted avg	0.90	0.90	0.90	22003

FIGURE 2.13   Precision, recall, and F1 scores obtained for XceptionNet.

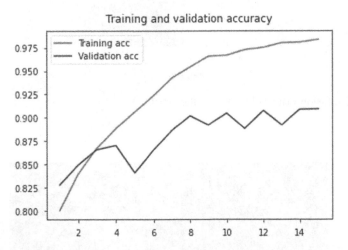

FIGURE 2.14   Accuracy and loss curves for ResNet50 model training and validation.

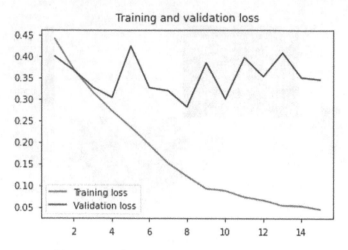

FIGURE 2.15   Accuracy and loss curves for ResNet50 model training and validation.

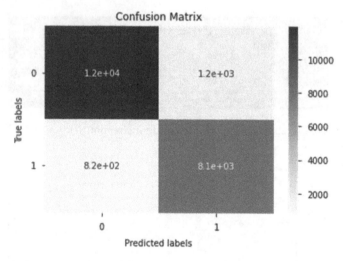

FIGURE 2.16   Confusion matrix obtained for ResNet50.

	precision	recall	f1-score	support
0	0.94	0.91	0.92	13091
1	0.87	0.91	0.89	8912
accuracy			0.91	22003
macro avg	0.90	0.91	0.91	22003
weighted avg	0.91	0.91	0.91	22003

FIGURE 2.17   Precision, recall, and F1 scores obtained for ResNet50.

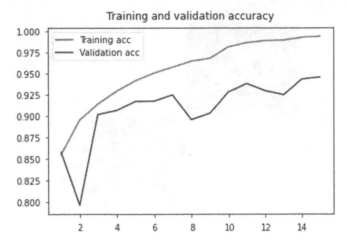

FIGURE 2.18   Accuracy and loss curves for DenseNet121 model training and validation.

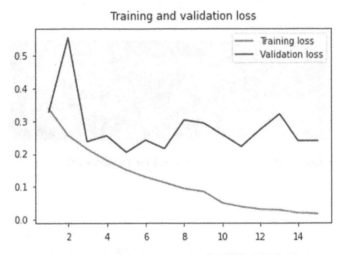

FIGURE 2.19   Accuracy and loss curves for DenseNet121 model training and validation.

model starts overfitting after four epochs, and the training loss decreases, whereas the validation loss changes unpredictably. Figure 2.16 shows the confusion matrix obtained on validating the model. Misclassifications can be seen in it. Finally, Figure 2.17 describes the model's performance (precision, recall, and F1 scores) on the validation set. This model is only slightly better than the previous one.

DenseNet121 – Figures 2.18 and 2.19 show the accuracy and loss curves for the training and validation sets when run through the DenseNet121 model for 15 epochs. As can be seen, the model starts overfitting only slightly after seven epochs, and the training loss decreases, whereas the validation loss does not change significantly. Figure 2.20 shows the confusion matrix obtained on validating the model. Some minor misclassifications can be seen. Lastly, Figure 2.21 describes the model's performance (precision, recall, and F1 scores) on the validation set. Clearly, this is the best-performing model out of the four individual models.

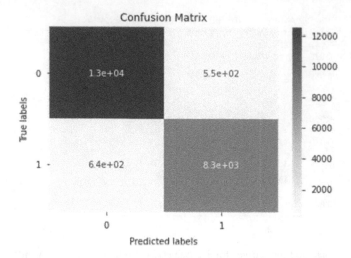

FIGURE 2.20   Confusion matrix obtained for DenseNet121.

	precision	recall	f1-score	support
0	0.95	0.96	0.95	13091
1	0.94	0.93	0.93	8912
accuracy			0.95	22003
macro avg	0.94	0.94	0.94	22003
weighted avg	0.95	0.95	0.95	22003

FIGURE 2.21   Precision, recall, and F1 scores obtained for DenseNet121.

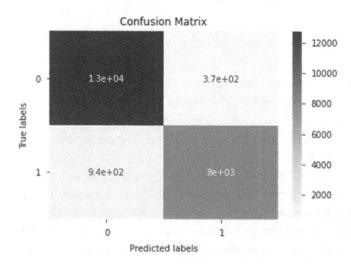

FIGURE 2.22   Confusion matrix obtained for the ensemble.

	precision	recall	f1-score	support
0	0.93	0.97	0.95	13091
1	0.96	0.89	0.92	8912
accuracy			0.94	22003
macro avg	0.94	0.93	0.94	22003
weighted avg	0.94	0.94	0.94	22003

FIGURE 2.23   Precision, recall, and F1 scores obtained for the ensemble.

TABLE 2.1
Comparison

Model	Accuracy	Macro Average	Weighted Average
Inception V3	92%	92%	92%
XceptionNet	90%	90%	90%
ResNet50	91%	91%	91%
DenseNet121	95%	94%	95%
Ensemble	94%	94%	94%

Ensemble Model – Figure 2.22 shows the confusion matrix obtained on validating the ensemble model for 15 epochs. Some minor misclassifications can be seen in it. Finally, Figure 2.23 describes the model's performance (precision, recall, and F1 scores) on the validation set.

Below is a table encapsulating the performances shown by the individual models against the ensemble Table 2.1.

Overall, it can be inferred that out of the individual models, DenseNet121 gave the most solid performance, even giving better results than the ensemble model itself. However, the ensemble model is still preferable as its results stem from the cross-evaluation of four different models, making it far more reliable, especially if other datasets will also be tested.

2.7 CONCLUSION

In our study, we looked at histopathology, the problems that come with it, and how the introduction of AI to this field can help solve these problems to a significant extent. We chose the robust CNN-based approach and, to get the best results, designed an ensemble model of four of the best CNN techniques: Inception Net, XceptionNet, ResNet, and DenseNet. We found that our ensemble model achieved a bulk accuracy of 94%, with the individual accuracies of the Inception V3, XceptionNet, ResNet50, and DenseNet121 being 92, 90, 91, and 95, respectively, showing that out of the four, DenseNet121 gave the highest score but is still not as reliable as the ensemble. Though future scope remains in the form of testing the system for actual application in medicine, the proposed system remains steady and has the potential to be incorporated in the field.

REFERENCES

[1] Nagai, Hiroki, and Young Hak Kim, "Cancer prevention from the perspective of global cancer burden patterns," *Journal of Thoracic Disease*, Vol. 9, No. 3, pp. 448–451, 2017.

[2] Koulm, Bhupendra, "Herbs for cancer treatment," *(Ch. 2 – Types of Cancer)*, pp. 53–146, 2019.

[3] Hanselmann, Rainer G. and Cornelius Welter, "Origin of cancer: An information, energy, and matter disease," *Frontiers in Cell and Developmental Biology*, Vol. 4, November 2016.

[4] Heaton, S.M., A.C. Weintrob, K. Downing et al. "Histopathological techniques for the diagnosis of combat-related invasive fungal wound infections," *BMC Clinical Pathology*, Vol. 16, p. 11, 2016.

[5] Karki, Shovana, "Errors: Detection and minimization in histopathology laboratories," *Journal of Pathology of Nepal*, September 2015.

[6] Kassani, Sara Hosseinzadeh, Peyman Hosseinzadeh Kassani, Michal J. Wesolowski, Kevin A. Schneider, and Ralph Deters, "Classification of histopathological biopsy images using ensemble of deep learning networks," CASCON '19: Proceedings of the 29th Annual International Conference on Computer Science and Software Engineering, November 2019, pp. 92–99.

[7] Gour, Mahesh, Sweta Jain, and T. Sunil Kumar, "Residual learning based CNN for breast cancer histopathological image classification," *International Journal of Imaging Systems and Technology*, August 2020.

[8] Senan, Ebrahim Mohammed, Fawaz Waselallah Alsaade, Mohammed Ibrahim Ahmed Al-Mashhadani, Theyazn H.H. Aldhyani, and Mosleh Hmoud Al-Adhaileh, "Classification of histopathological images for early detection of breast cancer using deep learning," *Journal of Applied Science and Engineering*, Vol. 24, No. 3, pp. 323–329, 2021.

[9] Wahab, Noorul, Asifullah Khan, and Yeon Soo Lee, "Two-phase deep convolutional neural network for reducing class skewness in histopathological images based breast cancer detection," *Computers in Biology and Medicine*, April 2017.

[10] Wahab, Noorul, Asifullah Khan, and Yeon Soo Lee, "Transfer learning based deep CNN for segmentation and detection of mitoses in breast cancer histopathological images," *Microscopy (Oxford, England)*, June 2019.

[11] Cruz-Roa, Angel, Hannah Gilmore, Ajay Basavanhally, Michael Feldman, Shridar Ganesan, Natalie Shih, John Tomaszewski, Anant Madabhushi, and Fabio Gonza´lez, "High-throughput adaptive sampling for whole-slide histopathology image analysis (HASHI) via convolutional neural networks: Application to invasive breast cancer detection," *PLoS One*, May 2018.

[12] Swathy, C.K. and Resmi K. Ranjan, "Breast cancer detection using histopathology and thermography images," *International Journal of Innovative Research in Science, Engineering and Technology*, April 2017.

[13] Liu, Yun, Timo Kohlberger, Mohammad Norouzi, George E. Dahl, Jenny L. Smith, Arash Mohtashamian, Niels Olson, Lily H. Peng, Jason D. Hipp, and Martin C. Stumpe, "Artificial intelligence-based breast cancer nodal metastasis detection: Insights into the black box for pathologists," *Archives of Pathology & Laboratory Medicine*, October 2018, pp. 859–868.

[14] Dabeer, Sumaiya, Maha Mohammed Khan, and Saiful Islam, "Cancer diagnosis in histopathological image: CNN based approach," *Informatics in Medicine Unlocked*, Vol. 16, August 2019.

[15] Nahid, Abdullah-Al, Mohamad Ali Mehrabi, and Yinan Kong, "Histopathological breast cancer image classification by deep neural network techniques guided by local clustering," *BioMed Research International*, Vol. 2018, March 2018.

[16] Khuriwal, Naresh and Nidhi Mishra, "Breast cancer detection from histopathological images using deep learning," 3rd International Conference and Workshops on Recent Advances and Innovations in Engineering, November 2018.

[17] Pham, Hoa Hoang Ngoc, Mitsuru Futakuchi, Andrey Bychkov, Tomoi Furukawa, Kishio Kuroda, and Junya Fukuoka, "Detection of lung cancer lymph node metastases from whole-slide histopathologic images using a two-step deep learning approach," *The American Journal of Pathology*, Vol. 189, December 2019.

[18] Šarić, M., M. Russo, M. Stella, and M. Sikora, "CNN-based method for lung cancer detection in whole slide histopathology images," 2019 4th International Conference on Smart and Sustainable Technologies (SpliTech), Split, Croatia, 2019, pp. 1–4.

[19] Hatuwal, Bijaya Kumar and Himal Chand Thapa, "Lung cancer detection using convolutional neural network on histopathological images," *International Journal of Computer Trends and Technology*, October 2020, pp. 21–24.

[20] Lu, Liangqun and Bernie J. Daigle Jr., "Prognostic analysis of histopathological images using pre-trained convolutional neural networks: Application to hepatocellular carcinoma," *PeerJ*, Vol. 8, e8668, 12 March 2020.

[21] Öztürk, Şaban and Bayram Akdemir, "Effects of histopathological image pre-processing on convolutional neural networks," *Procedia Computer Science*, June 2018.

[22] Kumar, Meghana Dinesh, Morteza Babaie, Shujin Zhu, Shivam Kalra, and H.R. Tizhoosh, "A comparative study of CNN, BoVW and LBP for classification of histopathological images," *IEEE Symposium Series on Computational Intelligence (SSCI)*, November 2017.

[23] Mahmood, Tahir, Muhammad Arsalan, Muhammad Owais, Min Beom Lee, and Kang Ryoung Park, "Artificial intelligence-based mitosis detection in breast cancer histopathology images using faster R-CNN and deep CNNs," *Journal of Clinical Medicine*, March 2020.

[24] Song, Zhigang, Shuangmei Zou, Weixun Zhou, Yong Huang, Liwei Shao, Jing Yuan, Xiangnan Gou, Wei Jin, Zhanbo Wang, Xin Chen, Xiaohui Ding, Jinhong Liu, Chunkai Yu, Calvin Ku, Cancheng Liu, Zhuo Sun, Gang Xu, Yuefeng Wang, Xiaoqing Zhang, Dandan Wang, Shuhao Wang, Wei Xu, Richard C. Davis, and Huaiyin Shi, "Clinically applicable histopathological diagnosis system for gastric cancer detection using deep learning," *Nature Communications*, August 2020.

[25] Szegedy, Christian, Vincent Vanhoucke, Sergey Ioffe, Jonathon Shlens, and Zbigniew Wojna, "Rethinking the inception architecture for computer vision," *Computer Vision and Pattern Recognition*, June 2016.

[26] Chollet, François, "Xception: Deep learning with depthwise separable convolutions," *Computer Vision and Pattern Recognition*, October 2016.

[27] He, K., X. Zhang, S. Ren, and J. Sun, "Deep residual learning for image recognition," *IEEE Conference on Computer Vision and Pattern Recognition*, pp. 770–778, June 2016.

[28] Huang, G., Z. Liu, L. Van Der Maaten, and K.Q. Weinberger, "Densely connected convolutional networks," *IEEE Conference on Computer Vision and Pattern Recognition*, pp. 2261–2269, July 2017.

[29] Al-Sabaawi, Aiman, Hassan Muayad Ibrahim, and Zinah Mohsin, "Amended convolutional neural network with global average pooling for image classification," *20th International Conference on Intelligent Systems Design and Applications (ISDA)*, December 2020.

[30] Kingma, Diederik P. and Jimmy Lei Ba, "Adam: A method for stochastic optimization," 3rd International Conference for Learning Representations, December 2014.

[31] Zhang, Zhilu and Mert R. Sabuncu, "Generalized cross entropy loss for training deep neural networks with noisy labels," 32nd Conference on Neural Information Processing Systems, 2018.

[32] Goutte, Cyril and Eric Gaussier, "A probabilistic interpretation of precision, recall and F-score, with implication for evaluation," Proceedings of the 27th European conference on Advances in Information Retrieval Research, April 2005.

CHAPTER 3

Role of Histone Methyltransferase in Breast Cancer

Surekha Manhas and Zaved Ahmed Khan

CONTENTS

3.1 INTRODUCTION

Every year, all over the world, cancer is the dreadful mark of death for millions. Even though various drugs and therapies have been developed, a number of other associated issues should be addressed for future medical therapies. Cancer causes the generation of abnormal

DOI: 10.1201/9781003185604-3

cells due to uncontrollable growth in the body. This abnormal group of mutant cells has the potential to penetrate or pervade other body parts. These quickly, highly dividing cells are called cancer cells, malignant cells, or tumor cells. Cellular mutations in the breast tissues lead to breast cancer, including a lump in the breast, skin dimpling, changes in the breast shape, fluid discharge from the nipple, inverted shape nipple, or patches appearing on the skin that are red or scaly. Nowadays, the number of treatments available in the present market for cancer include surgery with chemotherapy and/or radiation therapy, but further research is needed to control this life-threatening disease.

During DNA packaging, basic proteins – histones – play a reported mark as a chromatin component in the nucleus of eukaryote cells, where they bind with DNA and further proceed the DNA for packaging into smaller units designated as nucleosomes that display their role in gene regulation. The unwounded chromosomal DNA length varies. Diploid cell DNA of humans is about 1.8 meters, shows wounded association on the basic proteins, and has approximately 0.09 mm (90 micrometers) of chromatin. During the mitotic process, the human diploid cell undergoes condensation and duplication, resulting in about 120 mm of chromosome. Histone modifications are directly correlated with gene regulation functions, including ADP-ribosylation, methylation, acetylation, ubiquitination, and citrullination.

Histone methyltransferases represent the class of histone-modifying enzymes whose function is to transfer the alkyl group from methyl donating molecule S-Adenosyl-L-methionine onto the residues of arginine or lysine of the H3 and H4 histones. Alteration in the histones is responsible for various insidious diseases, including cancer, by leading to pro-apoptotic protein downregulations or tumor suppressor silencing.

DNA methylation is an imperative mechanism related to the studies of epigenetic regulation that triggers reorganization of chromatin, which is highly mediated through methyl-binding motifs. Basically, it has an almost relatively elementary binary pattern like alkylated versus non-alkylated bases compared to the highly composite specific pattern associated with histone modifications represented in Figure 3.1. Also, it is more specifically amenable to inventive experimental dependent analysis. Pattern changes found in DNA methylation have been analyzed in all different forms of cancer, either hypermethylation or hypo-methylation of cancer, examined so far. Moreover, studies have clearly shown that human cancerous cells can promote alteration in epigenetic makeup due to genetic lesions. The PML–RAR leukemia-promoting fusion protein, for example, can recruit DNA-based methyltransferases to the specific site of target genes to induce the process of protein fusion and persuade epigenetic silencing [1]. These available results illustrated an important marked paradigm that shows the cooperative relationship between the genetic- and epigenetic-dependent point lesions that play a role in tumorigenesis-promoting mechanisms.

Methylation of DNA occurs through the activity of the target enzyme DNA methyltransferases (DNMTs). Solid circles (cytosine residues mostly are methylated) are bounded by histone-modifying enzymes, which subsequently recruit histone methyltransferases and histone deacetylases (HDACs). In addition, these enzymes are responsible for the induction of complex variable changes in the pattern of histone modification, which result in

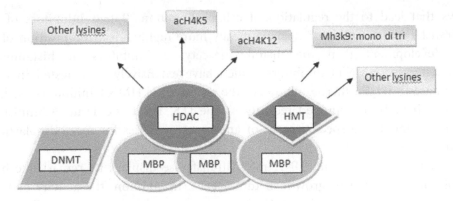

FIGURE 3.1   Epigenetic-dependent regulatory mechanism of methyltransferase [2].

repressive chromatin structure establishment. Open circles = unmethylated cytosine residues; acH4K12 < lysine 12-H4 acetylene histone; mH3K9 = lysine 9–methylated histone H3; acH4K5 = lysine 5–acetylated histone H4 and mono, di, tri = all-methylated [2].

Characterization of genomic tumor is generally carried out through distinct changes in methylation that have also been marked as the term "epimutations". Genomic instability is linked to hypomethylation, especially at the centromeric repeat sequences [2]. The other epimutation class is characterized explicitly by individual gene local hypermethylation, which has been related to deviant gene silencing [3]. The role of epimutations has been very well illustrated in various types of drastic cancer and tumorigenesis. For example, DNA mismatch inactivation is mainly associated with epigenetic silencing in sporadic colon cancer rather than gene mutation [4]. E-cadherin methylation has also played a central markable role in the process of metastasis as well as in invasion in case of issues associated with breast cancer [5]. These kinds of epimutation changes rarely appear in healthy tissue, which shows the high tumor specificity of epigenetic therapies.

Epigenetic modification reversibility provides more attractive targets in the medicinal intervention field [6]. In comparison to mutations at the genetic level, epigenetic modification reversibility is passively inherited by means of replication of DNA. Mutations at the level of epigenetic studies should be maintained actively. Correspondingly, epigenetic modification-based pharmacological inhibition could have the potential to correct faulty patterns associated with modification and consequently alter the expression pattern of genes directly along with reciprocal cellular characteristics.

Developmental progression of inhibitors associated with pharmacological studies vary widely among independent families of the enzyme. Inhibitors related to histone methyltransferase are still in a preliminary stage of preclinical studies. Various others inhibitors of histone deacetylase are presently being tested under phase I and phase II clinical trials. Although various acetylated proteins, including basic key malignant cell growth regulators, are being tested, it is not clear yet whether the inhibitors of histone deacetylase are responsible for the induction of growth inhibition results of pattern changes of histone acetylation and other certain changes in cell-signalling-based pathways that lead to the regulation of cell proliferation. Potent inhibitors of DNA methyltransferase presently are at the clinically more highly advanced position of therapeutic development than the histone deacetylase inhibitors or histamine N-methyltransferase (HMNT) inhibitors, which have extensively been tested in clinical trials of phases I–III. Further, inhibitors of the prototypical HMNT inhibitors, such as 5-azacytidine, have been approved recently by the U.S. Food and Drug Administration (FDA), represented as a specific agent of antitumor activities for myelodysplastic syndrome treatment.

The activity associated with DNA methyltransferase displays its remarkable benchmark role in the malignant growth of tumor cells. In addition, the activity of HMNT inhibitors might be easily analyzed. Various histone methyltransferase inhibitors have been highly developed from natural resources as potential therapeutic cancer agents.

Conformational changes and functions of chromatin templates associated with histone also undergo histone modifications in which they play a vital specific role [7]. Methylation at the histone residue of H3K27 is mediated through the formation of PRC2 complex that is critical for polycomb silencing, regulation at the transcriptional level, mammalian X inactivation, drosophila segmentation, and tumor formation (cancer) [7]. Interestingly, after disruption of PCR2 complex, in vivo levels of H3K27me1 always remain unaffected, which indicates the effective existence of several other varied contributing histone protein methyltransferases to H3K27me1 [8,9].

3.2 ACTIVE HISTONE MODIFICATIONS

Regulation of gene expressions in eukaryotic organisms is regulated synergistically through different transcriptional factors, including chromatin remodelers, specific histone variants, transcriptional machinery, and histone modifications but not limited to these factors. Active domains of chromatin are usually characterized by apparent series associated with histone marks. H3K4me1 and H3K27ac are connected with specific active enhancers [10]. The H3K4me3 level is high at promoter sequences of active genes, and acetylation of H4 and H3 are within specific promoters of active genes [11–13]. Active gene bodies are mostly enriched in H4 and H3 acetylation [14], H2BK120u1 [15,16] and H3K79me3 acetylation [7], and H3K36me3 acetylation increasing toward the 30 end [17]. These different histone marks might regulate transcriptional regulation of genes by generating open chromatin structures along with effector recruitment that helps to mediate competent state transcriptionally. Although the varied function of various active modifications of histone proteins is not fully recognizable and understandable, there is still an abundance of data available in the literature that shows that deposition of these histone marks is necessary for the appropriate gene expression regulation mechanism. There are various distinct positive crosstalk mechanisms found between several distinct modifications of histone proteins, which play a crucial role in maintenance and recruitment at the site of active genes through histone modifications.

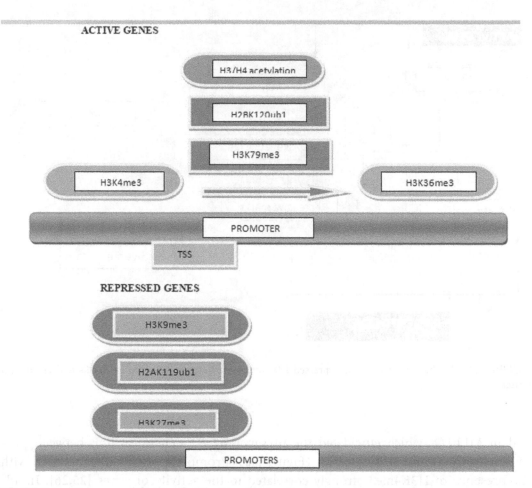

FIGURE 3.2   Histone modification distribution of overactive as well as repressed genes.

3.3   H3K4ME3: ESTABLISHMENT AS WELL AS MAINTENANCE

H3K4me3 is evolutionarily a highly conserved, effective histone modification in eukaryotes. The gene hallmark H3K4me3 is distributed across TSS and the promoter regions [13,18,19]. The work that has been done on yeast shows the association of SET1 with PAF complex. In addition, pol II initiation forms the Ser5-dependent phosphorylated that is deposited co-transcriptionally [20] (Figure 3.2). In addition, MLL and SETD1 recruitment to discrete target genes is usually mediated by means of various different cell-dependent specific transcriptional co-activators [18,19,21–23]. However, especially in higher organisms, the recruitment and establishment of more extensive H3K4me3 mechanisms are also highly at play.

Primarily, the H3K4me3 distribution is thoroughly coupled to CpG-dependent dinucleotide repeated units present in CpG islands. Predominately, unmethylated GC-dense DNA and CpG- regions are found at promoter regions in 50–70% of vertebrates [24]. The discovery of Zn-finger CxxC is usually found in SETD1A/B subunit CFP1

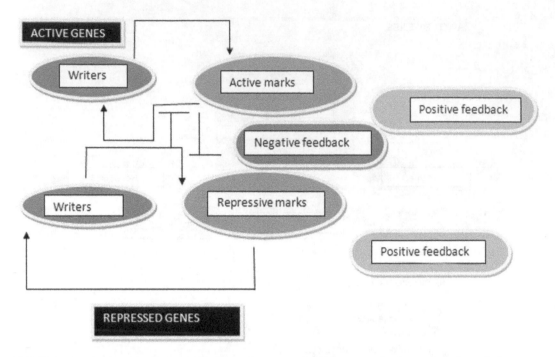

FIGURE 3.3   At the gene active and repressed sites, crosstalk between the histone marks and chromatin writers.

and in MLL1/2, which elucidated the presence of a biochemical link between promoters of CpGI and H3K4me3 [2] (Figure 3.3). Promoters of CPGI are marked with the presence of H3K4me3 strongly correlated to the activity of genes [25,26]. In addition, emerging evidence illustrates that MLL2 is highly responsible in order to maintain H3K4me3 in vivo at CpGI promoters along with reduce expression [27,28]. Although CEPI, a specific subunit of SETD1, is more preferentially enriched in the higher H3K4me3 levels and mostly found at the most of active regions of gene promoter [29]. CpGI promoters started showing linkage with them in regulated developmental genes, which possess bivalent structure and play a role in harboring the H3K4me3 repressive marks and H3K4me2 [30]. Interestingly, H3K4me3 writers' ability to sample the genome of CpGI is wide. It has also been found that H3K4me3 presence at promoters of CpGI might act as poison for the silent genes that cause rapid activation of these genes upon differentiation. The binding in between the complex of SETD1/MLL might reinforce their strong binding by means of recognition of the presence of their specific own marks, such as H3K4me3. CFP1 having PHD finger domain, known explicitly for its role in H3K4me3 read, also found that it displays its potent role in mediating the interaction between SETDI and H3K4me3 [31–33]. In Hox Locus, the recruitment of MLLI to the specific target sites is usually carried out through the presence of MLL1 containing its third domain, which is more important in the case of H3K4me3 binding [34].

3.4 CROSSTALK BETWEEN H2BK120U1, H3K4ME3, AND H3K79ME3

It has been found that a particular pattern of posttranslational modifications of histones and their crosstalk might designate as a code that determines possible outcomes generated by transcriptional machinery. Among the various distinct histone modification crosstalk pathways, the most studied one is H3K79me3 and H3K4me3 stimulation by H2BK120u1 found in yeast. In addition, another studied pathway is RAD6/BRE1, a ubiquitin ligase that established the H2BK123u1 during the ignition of the transcription process and localized to the transcription initiation site and the gene bodies that are active [35]. RAD6/BRE1 depletion or H2BK123 mutation causes severe critical loss of H3K79me3 and H3K4me3 [36,37]. The positive crosstalk among H2BK123u1, H3K79me3, and H3K4me3 is specific, which does not lead to H3K36me3 regulation designated as another transcriptional hallmark [36,37]. Both modifications lie in close proximity to the exposed surface of the nucleosome, H3K79 and H2BK123 [38]. In yeast DOT1, H3K79 methyltransferase has been observed to be influenced by mutations or deletions of histone residue on the tail portion of H2B histone protein [38]. The situation is converted into a more complex zone in humans because distribution of DOTIL and H3K79me3 is not completely dependant on H2BK120u1. Localization of DOT1L occurs locally at active genes but reaches the maximum to TSS (Transcription Start site) [39]. Moreover, it shows its binding affinity with PoL11 phosphorylated forms, including Ser2 and Ser5 [39]. Moreover, H3K79me3 is recognized as a marker of transcriptionally active genes, but the exact transcriptional mechanism is not discovered yet. In mammals, crosstalk between H2BK120u1 and H3K4me3 mostly remain conserved, as RNF20/40, BRE1 homologs result in the global reduction of H3K4me3 [40]. Recently, a study has been carried out on E3 ligase, MSL1/MSL2, which catalyzes H2BK34u1. The study revealed the crosstalk between H2BK34u1 and H3K4me3 [41]. MLL complex activity stimulates allosterically by H2BK34u1 and H2BK120u1 through binding with the ASH2L subunit [42]. The nucleosome-exposed surface of H2BK34 has ubiquitylation sites that act as a favorable substrate for binding with MLL complex or SET1 [42].

3.5 H3K4ME3: HISTONE ACETYLATION

Acetylation at lysine residues represents an abundant highlighted mark known to display its role in the regulatory mechanism of cellular processes like transcription. Acetylation at the histone residues of H/H4 is directly correlated with the expression of the gene. Bromodomain, structural motifs, act as epigenetic readers present in all different proteins that play a specific role in recognizing acetylated lysines and transcriptional regulation [41]. Despite direct effector recruitment, histone acetylation introduces certain changes in the structure of chromatin physically by neutralizing observable charge of lysines residues and disrupts the intra- and inter-nucleosomal interactions results in the open structure of chromatin, which provide the permissible environment for transcription. Acetylation of these three lysine residues on H3-based globular domains, H3K122, H3K64, and H3K56, is present on the H3–DNA interface that might disrupt nucleosomal interactions and also is directly linked with gene activation [43–45]. H3K122ac, lysine residue, has also shown its role to promote in vitro transcription by means of process stimulation of histone eviction [44]. Acetylation at the tail of H3 and H4 histone residues stimulates DNA unwrapping, whereas acetylation at H3 residues plays a role in nucleosome sensitization towards salt-induced dissociation [46]. H3/H4 and H3K4me3 acetylation generally coexist at TSS and promoter regions of specific active genes.

Moreover, there are several other studies that suggest that H3K4me3 enhances downstream H4/H3-dependent acetylation by recruiting HATs. The readers of H3K4me3 have been already identified in various HAT complexes. The complex, SAGA HAT, has a component, SGF29, that has tandem tudor methyl lysine/argnine binding domain that binds with H3K4me3 and shows overlapping with H3K4me3 at gene promoters. Deletion of SGF29 leads to H3K9ac loss along with SAGA complex loss at target points [47]. Correspondingly, yeast NuA3 [48], NuA4 [49], and mammalian HBO1 [50] all provide various other examples associated with HAT complexes, which encompass PHD fingers that bind with H3K4me3 preferentially. The dynamic turnover of lysine acetylation at H3 histone protein residues by the combinatorial HDAC and HAT CBP/p300 actions have been manifested to occur on tails of H3 histone protein residues with already pre-existing H3K4me3, except that no other modifications correlated with the expression of active genes, including H3K36me3 or H3K79me3 [51]. Specifically, H3K4me3-dependent acetylation is highly conserved in higher eukaryotes by including humans, mice, and flies. H3K4me3 loss upon the deletion of CFP1 results in CpGI-related H3K9ac loss in embryonic stem cells [26].

Furthermore, the studies using the model of Dictyostelium discoideum show that mostly upon SET1 knockout along with H3K4me3 leads to loss of dynamic acetylation at H3 histone protein was also lost [52]. The dynamic acetylation turnover in preference to the modification itself might be indicated as a basic key factor in transcriptional activation (reviewed in Ref. [53]). On the basis of that, all other members associated with H3K4me3-binding protein containing PHD fingers correlated with HATs/HDACs [54]. Moreover, H3K4me3 acts as a promoter that has been mostly found to be strongly associated before the initial transcription process, co-targeting by H3K4me3 histone residue of both HDACs and HATS that might facilitate the dynamic histone acetylation turnover. The above notable examples strongly illustrate that positive crosstalk in between histone acetylation and H3K4me is an important evolutionarily, highly conserved pathway that also shows cooperatively between hyperacetylation and H3K4me3. Further, dynamic histone acetylation turnover is important to ensure proper specific gene transcriptional regulation.

3.6 H3K36ME3: HISTONE DEACETYLATION

Methylation at H3K36 histone protein residue is recognized as an abundant mark of histone that is highly conserved in eukaryotes. In addition, mono/di/trimethylation of H3K36 residue of H3 histone exists in yeast, and all these states of H3K36 are catalyzed through SET2. In the other cases, mammals have all other H3K36 methylation multiple writers, which include SETD2, NSD (1–3) family, SMYD2, ASH1L, and SETMAR, but SETD2 is recognized as the main sole enzyme that is responsible for proceeding the process of trimethylation at H3K36 in vivo [55]). Captivatingly, uncoupling of the activity H3K36me3 from H3K36me (1–2) over evolutionary alludes towards the biologically specified variable roles associated with each state of methylation. In addition, H3K36me3 is mostly associated with the active transcribed specific regions of specific genes and H3K36me3 level increase in the direction of the 30th end of active genes [10].

Further, this specific distribution leads to set2 association with plo11 component, elongating Ser2-dependent phosphorylated CTD, basically which is highly predominant over 30 ends and bodies of functional genes [56–58]. Similarly, H3K36me3 residue has also interlinked with the regulation of specific histone protein residue acetylation. Histone residue, H3K36me3, is able to recruit HDACs from active transcription regions. In yeast, H3K36me2/3 recognition by means of EAF3 complex containing bromodomain recruits the HDAC+RPD3S complex that deacetylates histones. In addition, it also prevents spurious initiation of transcription within bodies of active genes [59–61]. At the specific region of gene promoters, histone hyperacetylation and H3K4me3 might play a particular role in the regulation of transcriptional initiation from regions of transcriptional stating sites, whereby the H3K36me2/3-mediated process related with deacetylation is needed in the wake of specific active gene transcriptional machinery to prevent transcriptional initiation from inappropriate aberrant regions present within gene structure. Mutual exclusivity between the H3K36me3 and H3K4me3 may be crucial to maintain transcriptional integrity.

Further, this above idea is preferably supported by means of work, which shows that promoters due to lack of H3K36me2/3 highlighted mark, and also KDM2A/B, H3K36me2-dependent demethylases co-localize with H3 residue, H3K4me3 at the specific CpGI promoters, which ensure the active H3K36me2 removal from TSS [62,63]. Recognition of H3K36me2/3 is accompanied by PWWP domain, a protein motif, mostly found in various nuclear-based chromatin-dependent binding proteins [64–67]. Interestingly, all three members linked with H3K36-dependent methyltransferases belong to the NSD family, which catalyses H3K36me1/2, each having 2-PWWP domains and preferentially bind with H3 peptides, which contain H3K36me3 [66,67]. This indicates that recognition of H3K36me2/3 by means of its writers could be highly important for H3K36me1 propagation. Mono-/dimethylation of protein residue, H3K36, is specifically highly pervasive compared to the H3K36me3 and is not restricted to a region's euchromatic domain or active transcription [68,69]. The recognizable biological functional role displayed by mono-/dimethylation has been unknown until now, though an H3K36me2 increase due to mutational changes in NSD2 has been directly associated with the upregulation mechanism of gene-dependent expression profiles in the case of tumors [70,71]. H3K36me2 may have crucial biological activity in its own right or may be necessary to serve the required substrate for successive SETD2-mediated trimethylation of H3K36. H3K36me3 and H3K36me2 distribution over active gene chromatin could also delay spreading and prevent silencing marks accumulation like H3K27me3 by directly inhibiting the PRC2, polycomb complex [72,73]. Histone methyltransferase, G9a, that controls in vivo functional activity of H3K9me2 predominantly represses the activity of genes at euchromatic regions [4].

3.7 EPIGENETIC REGULATION MECHANISM

Epigenetic regulation encloses the extensive range of specific mechanisms that might lead to the various heritable changes in various gene expression levels. From physical gene localization within the different regions of the nucleus up to the DNA posttranslational modification and histones posttranslational modifications, all these epigenetic mechanisms could profoundly influence the expression of active genes and introduce changes in the development and function of cellular lineage. Importantly, site-specific methylation of the CpG motif and demethylation in DNA by the TET protein family and DNMTs is perhaps the most effective ever studied associated epigenetic mechanism that directly plays a role in the gene regulation [74].

Gene expression regulation by means of histone-modifying enzymes marks a dominant mechanism that regulates the differentiation and development of cells. Posttranslationally, modifications of histones could be carried out by methylation, acetylation, phosphorylation, ubiquitination, and sumoylation [75]. In particular, methylation at lysine residues of histone protein is the chief regulator of active gene expression. MLL1-dependent H3K4me3 and EZH2-dependent H3K27me3 EZH2, H3K27me3, are the foremost well-known modifications that are strongly related to recognizable gene expression also with repression [76–80]. Various other specific histone-methylation regions have been recognized to be more critical, including H3K9 histone residue with G9a-dependent H3K9me2 and Suv39h (1–2)-mediated H3K9me3. All these display crucial functional roles in cellular differentiation and functions, too [81–84]. Available data suggest that H3K9me2 has also been found to modify euchromatin. In addition, it also is dynamically able to regulate the gene expression of many differentiating cells.

The rise in H3K9me2 marks covered the genome during the cellular differentiation or when it acquired cellular lineage specificity in ES cells (genome embryonic stem (ES) cells), although it is contentious [85,86]. Interestingly, the H3K9me2 level is high at lineage nonspecific genes, suggesting that H3K9me2 acquisition is more censorious for gene silencing throughout differentiation [87]. Nevertheless, insufficient data are available that could explain the potent G9a role in immune cells. In T cells and innate lymphoid cells (ILCs; lymphoid cells or immune cells), it is more clear that HNMT inhibitors, G9a-based H3K9me2, are highly critical in cellular lineage differentiation and simultaneously with function. However, the exact specific mechanisms differ as compared to the mechanism of ES cells.

3.8 G9A REQUIREMENT: H3K9 DIMETHYLATION

G9a (Ehmt2), histone methyltransferase was recognized as the gene was found at varied loci in leukocyte antigen in human beings and MHC loci in mice and was also recognized as BAT8 (HLA-B-associated transcript 8) [88,89]. G9a gene is located in the average range of 1.1Mb MHC in humans /~700kb (mice)/ / HLA-based Class-3rd region consists of over 60 different genes, including enzymes (steroid 21-hydroxylase Cyp21) [90]. Cytokines include TNF-α/β, heat shock proteins, and C2/C4 complement proteins. The gene Ehmt2 (G9a) consists of 28 exons, which code for approximately 1263 amino acid proteins. Although splice form lacks exon 10, it has been identified to code specifically for 34 different amino acids; moreover, functional significance is not discovered yet [91].

The associated G9a-based proteins, including GLP and EHMT1, whose gene locations are not found in the HLA/MHC locus, are able to form heterodimer in vivo along with G9a that is critically needed for H3K9me2-based methylation activity [92]. Any kind of genetic deletion associated with both of these proteins leads to a significant H3K9me2 reduction, representing that both protein subunits are very essential to enzyme-based activities [93]. Mutation at the active sites of the gene has shown to be found in in-vivo studies that indicated that HMNT activity plays an important role in H3K9me2 me-thylation [94]. However, global neuron analysis of gene expression in mice, along with specifically targeted deletions in the case of either GLP or G9a, identified the observable difference that might be created due to the differential subunit requirement in gene expression [95]. Furthermore, GLP loss is related to Kleefstra syndrome. This genetic disorder, found very rarely, is characterized by impairments in physical/social activities and intellectual disability [96]. No analysis has been done on the functional role of immune defense cells in this syndrome. Since GLP might display a specific potent role in gene regulation, it might be tested directly.

G9a is a protein that consists of 1263 amino acids with many distinct domains. Due to the lack of DNA-binding domain in G9a, it specifically relies on cofactors for its loca-lization. The C-terminal dependent SET domain must have the activity of enzyme lysine methyltransferase, which specifically defines major functions of this protein family. G9a SET domain has the potential to mono-/dimethylate H3K9; still, it is the least efficient to mediate trimethylation [97]. Consistent with this, G9a deletion results in global H3K9me2 reduction [84,93]. Unlike other members associated with the SET domain, G9a has specific domains that provide additional functions. First, G9a shows resemblance with drosophila notch because of eight series of 33-amino acid repeats [92].

Further, this marked region was designated as a highlighted domain that could spe-cifically bind with dimethylated lysine histone residues and provide protein that could produce posttranslational modifications specifically and have the potential to bind with that modification, too [98]. Interestingly, though the G9a ankyrin repeats have a higher affinity for H3K9me2, binding of GLP with H3K9me1 [98] and mice that were treated with G9a knock-in along with non-functional repeats of ankyrin develop normally, whereas in the case of mutated GLP knock-in, mice have more severe uncontrollable developmental defects, which leads to perinatal lethality [99]. Available results are further able to demonstrate in vivo overlapping roles of G9a and GLP. In addition, G9a, me-thyltransferase, also has a short stretch of 25 residues of glutamic acid and cysteine-based rich region, whose functions are still unclear.

Moreover, the role of G9a in gene repression studies has been studied predominantly by its histone methyltransferase activity; it is more clearly illustrated that G9a might play a role in active gene activation on certain specific conditions [100–102], that is markedly methyltransferase independent. In addition, this function mentioned above was clearly mapped in the N-protein terminal as 280 amino acids that present first in the protein chain as highly sufficient to promote the expression of the gene through acting as a scaffold to promote transcriptional co-activator recruitment including CARM1 and p300 [101,103]. At last, G9a is a protein with complexity that is highly involved in activating and repressing genes through specific but distinct mechanisms.

G9a structure: G9a is composed of about 1253 amino acids, which represent various distinct domains that are an N-terminal activation domain that is highly rich in glutamate, along with the following 23 glutamate residues and also with cysteine-based regions of unspecified function, repeat units of eight ankyrins (dimethylated lysine residues binding), and also a SET domain of C-terminal.

3.9 H3K9 DIMETHYLTRANSFERASE ACTIVITY

Histone methyltransferase, G9a, is marked as an enzyme responsible for introducing the H3K9 dimethylation, a hallmark of euchromatin silencing [84,93,104,105]. HP1 (heterochromatin protein 1) binds with H3K9me2, which works in the recruitment of transcriptional repressors that prevent the active gene activation [106]. Although G9a-mediated methylation leads to the production of H3K9me2, the complex of G9a/GLP has also been demonstrated to methylate H1 [107,108] and also shows its contribution to the H3K27 methylation [93,109]. Further, G9a proved to have specific marked activity against numerous non-histone-based proteins by means of including itself, too [110]. However, the most well-studied G9a biology aspect is the repression of H3K9me2-based genetic expression. Moreover, from the various biochemical-based studies, it is clearly understood that G9a-based H3K9me2 is correlated with those regions of the genome that expressed at very low levels [87]. Still, the exact mechanisms that work in dynamic methylation pattern regulation mediated by Ehmt was unclear until now.

H3K9me2, a G9a-dependent residue, is linked directly to the de novo pathway-based DNA methylation in embryonic stem cells [111,112]. DNA methylation of mobile genetic elements and a non-repetitive sequences subset, including promoters rich in CpG-islands, are reduced in the specifically observed G9a-based deficient cells and recruitment of Dnmt3a to retrotransposons, which is also declined in all these cells. Although the interaction was absent between the H3K9me2, G9a, and DNMTs observed in differentiated cells [113], the interaction between the G9a-DNMT is not properly maintained during the last past development. As per the G9a mentioned above, sustained silencing associated with pluripotency-acquired genes in G9a-deficient embryonic stem cells is impaired, resulting indirectly in state conversion in a reverse manner from the highly differentiated cellular state into a state of pluripotency in significant cellular-associated fractions [114,115]. In the induced pluripotent stem cell generation, this present effect has been exploited due to BIX01298 inclusion, a G9a-dependent specific chemical-based inhibitor that can replace SOX viral-dependent transduction in the case of fibroblasts [116]. Taken together, G9a playing a vital role in the epigenetic-silencing mechanism of disabling inappropriate genes of a particular cell type has emerged from ES cell-based studies [115,117]. However, the potent G9a role in the functions of immune cells is less poorly understood.

3.10 G9A ROLE: HISTONE AND NON-HISTONE PROTEINS METHYLATION

However, G9a displays its action as histone protein, such as lysine methyltransferase. Numerous studies have described G9a as also having the potential to methylate various other non-protein targets, which include G9a itself, p53, SIRT1, p21, Reptin, MyoD, WIZ and ACINUS, CDYL1, C/EBPβ, and range of numerous non-histone based targets, such as G9a itself [110], CDYL1, ACINUS, C/EBPβ, WIZ histone deacetylase (HDAC)1, CSB, KLF12, and mAM [118]. Moreover, the precise posttranslational methylation role on the protein's function remains unclear; non-histone protein methylation might affect protein-based interactions, protein stability, subcellular localization, and subcellular function [119].

3.11 G9A: METHYLTRANSFERASE INDEPENDENT ACTIVITY

In spite of its ability of substrate methylation, G9a also has methyltransferase-based independent activities that work through the G9a N-end domain [100,101,103]. They work usually from the Stallcup group, which showed the first time in contrast with the expectations that G9a would act as a strong nuclear co-activator of hormone-based receptor-associated activity, such as glucocorticoid receptors, estrogen, and androgen, in association with the GRIPI transcriptional coactivators p300 and CARM1 [32,100]. G9a has also been found to show its action through positively regulating the expression of specific genes at the locus of the β-globin-specific gene [102]. The specific locus of β-globin gene regulation is a very clear characterized system for examining the effective role of locus control regions (LCRs) in stage-specific and tissue-specific gene expressions [53].

In red blood cells, regulation of β-globin-specific locus is preferably carried out by the addition and also with removal of modifying structures associated with histones such as G9a. Knockdown in the erythroid progenitor stem cells of adults led to increased fetal β-globin in expression as well as significant decline in the gene expression of adult β-globin [102], also further demonstrating activating and inhibitory G9a effects. Similarly, with receptors of nuclear hormone studies, the gene expression activation by G9a is not depend on methyltransferase activity. Most importantly, the gene locus of fetal β-globin is regulated the same as type 2 response from H3K9me2 and H3K4me3 [54].

As a result, in addition to a specific role in repressive functions, in spite of all these, it is very clear that G9a might positively influence the expression of the gene at selected specific genetic loci.

3.12 G9A ROLE IN IMMUNOLOGY

In non-specific innate mechanisms, the immune cells, including macrophages. However, G9a-based H3K9me2 has mostly been correlated with repressive action of the gene during intolerance of endotoxin mechanism [56–58]. Macrophages that are stimulated chronically with lipopolysaccharide presence become unresponsive when again stimulated through the H3K9me2 acquisition at the region of repressed genetic-based loci [58]. Moreover, in the condition of tolerized macrophages, enzyme G9a shows its interaction with TF ATF7 as well as various other NF-κB family members, including NF-κB1, RelA,

RelB, and c-Rel [56–58]. Furthermore, it is suggested that these mentioned factors carry out G9a recruitment to specific genetic loci to deposit histone residue, H3K9me2, resulting in gene repression. During the period of endotoxin tolerance, the direct G9a role in macrophages tolerance is not tested properly.

Nevertheless, all these studies observed a notable G9a role in gene-based silencing during the time of cellular responses towards the inflammatory signals. Although consistent with the G9a role in promoting tolerance, it was also found to show its role in limiting cell signaling pathways, specifically the JAK/STAT mechanism of signalling, particularly in drosophila subsequent to viral infections [59]. During G9a absence, the viral infection results in heightened lethality in the case of flies. Still, it is not associated with heightened pathogen burden because of the increased expression associated with target genes linked to JAK/STAT signalling pathways. Thus, G9a also displays its crucially important, highly marked role in regulating the gene-dependent expression mechanism during innate inflammatory responses.

G9a's role also has implications in various aspects associated with T-cell-based biology. However, genome mapping studies on the G9a binding or H3K9me2 deposition in immunity-providing cells has not performed due to some technical issues. A comprehensive descriptive H3K9me2 marks genome analysis in the case of resting immune cells by means of using ChIP-on-chip based methods, which illustrate that the epigenetic H3K9me2 mark is highly enriched on those genes that are strongly associated with numerous specific pathways, such as GATA3 transcription, T-cell-dependent receptor-based signaling, and IL-4 signaling [60].

Furthermore, isolated lymphocytes from type 1 diabetic patients displayed an extremely distinct profile of H3K9me2, with certain genomic regions that had increased H3K9me2 levels (SLC17A4, CXCL3, and CTLA-4) and others that had reduced levels (TNF, RARA, and CAMK4) [61]. Thus, HMNT-mediated H3K9me2-associated T cell response regulation might be related to the functional status of T cells and inflammatory disease development, including diabetes. Recently, G9a-based cell lineage-dependent specific deletion has been introduced to delineate G9a's role in immune system cells. Three different mice strains have been generated with "floxed" G9afl/fl mice [15,62,63]. Despite that, the crossing of G9afl/fl mice with strain Cd4-Cre mice leads to the T-cell-dependent specific G9a deletion in G9aΔT mice. In addition, G9aΔT mice usually are born and develop with no observable discernable defects found in T-cell generation in lymph nodes, spleen, and thymus, suggesting that dissimilar to ES cells and HMNT inhibitors, G9a is replaceable for the proliferation of peripheral cellular naïve lymphocytes [15,64]. For in vivo/in vitro activation of T cells, G9a displayed a critically specific role in the functional regulation of T-helper cells. Despite that, consistent with G9a's ability to strongly promote and repress gene expression, G9a-deficient lymphocytes failed to generate various cytokines, while various others overproduced [14,15]. Due to distinct differentiating conditions, G9a was needed differentially either to activate or to repress particular programs of the gene.

IFN-γ produced through lymphocytes are critical for providing immunity against various intracellular damage-causing pathogens, specifically including parasites, viruses, bacteria, and protozoan [65]. Strikingly, G9a's absence in lymphocytes has shown no noticeable effect for in vivo/in vitro studies, the magnitude of development of Th1 cell-based responses [15]. No observable difference was noticed in the frequency of the Th1 cell that developed during activation of wild-type T cells or G9a-deficient T-cell activation in the presence of G9a-dependent specific inhibitors under the specific Th1 cell-based promoting conditions [15]. Thus, G9a is dispensable in the regulation of Th1 cell-based responses.

For immunity to parasitic helminths infection, like whipworm and Trichuris muris, both related to polarized type II cytokine response, IL-3, IL-5/4 production by T-helper cells resulted in the production of mucus, turnover of intestinal epithelial cells, and expulsion of parasitic worms [66]. G9aΔT mice infected with Trichuris experienced significantly reduced protective frequencies of Th2 cells; increased non-protective frequencies of Th1 cells leads to high susceptibility towards infection [15]. Consistent with the inappropriate reduction in type II cytokines, production by T-helper cells after activation of in vitro conditions. G9a's role in repressing promiscuous gene expression of type-A cytokine in lymphocytes was temporarily observed, as H3K27me3 replaced H3K9me2 at the locus of Ifng during differentiation [67]. Thus, G9a is needed in order to activate the program associated with the gene of type 11 cytokine. Transcriptional factors like STAT6 and GATA3 express at the same level in G9a-deficient Th2 cells and major Th2 cells. Still, these are unable to generate type 11 cytokines, suggesting that the central component of the transcription process for type-B cytokines is G9a. As the locus of IL-4/IL-5/IL-13 is somehow similar to structures on a genetic basis to the β-globin-based locus, perhaps it's not at all surprising that G9a has the ability to immediately transactivate the gene of type-B cytokine locus and also does not depend on its HMNT activity [15]. Taken together, all these observable results identify histone protein. G9a also acts as a critical component in regulatory machinery.

In disparity to T-helper cells, G9a also plays a crucial role in order to limit the cellular differentiation of Treg and Th17 cells, whose activity relies on its HMNT activity [14]. G9a-deficient T-helper cell activation under cell differentiation conditions of Th17 or Treg cells led to heightened frequencies within those cells that significantly express FOXP3 and IL-17A-producing cells [14]. The synthetic inhibitors BIX-01294 or UNC0638 that inhibit the methyltransferase activity of G9a led to promotion of cellular differentiation of Treg and Th cells. Contradictory to the expected G9a role in embryonic cells, deposition of H3K9me2 occurs at lineage-dependent promiscuous genes in order to properly control lineage cellular differentiation in lymphocytes. In spite of that, G9a-based H3K9me2 level is, as expected, high in undifferentiated naive lymphocytes and is lost rapidly after T-cell activation on non-specific loci or at loci of lineage [14]. H3K9me2 loss alone is clearly insufficient for the promotion of gene expression, given an appropriate explanation of phenotype lacking in the steady state. Due to this, in lymphocytes, G9a and H3K9me2 both act as an additional layer related with negative regulation in order to maintain all cells in a naive state. G9a-dependent H3K9me2 loss deals with increased chromatin accessibility to transactivating factors, resulting in increased responsiveness towards external signals like cytokines. In the Treg and Th17 cells, cellular sensitivity of G9a-deficient lymphocytes is ~40 times higher compared to TGF-β [14]. Taken together, all these results demonstrate that protein G9a, by means of H3K9me2 deposition at numerous types of genes of the immune system, is especially important in naive lymphocytes in order to repress the expression of genes, possibly by strongly limiting TFs along with co-activators and co-activators to the specific genetic point.

In contrast to lymphocytes, it has been already proposed that G9a plays a potent role in repressing CD27 and CD275 expressions, receptors present on the surface of cells related to cellular-based proliferation actions and simultaneously the activation mechanism, following viral infection in lymphocyte-based memory cells [68]. More potent PRDMI interaction displays its role in the recruitment of G9a in order to determine genetic loci leading to gene repression. In Blimp-1's absence, H3K9me2, H3K9me3, and H3K27me3 levels get reduced at some extent that is observed, indicating that G9a plays a critical role in gene-based silencing during the differentiation process and development of memory T cells. G9a is required for the generation of memory-based T cells, which has not been directly examined. However, this represents a specific active area of novel research where we need to shed light on G9a's role in the development of memory T cells since, in G9a's absence, various other, more repressive modifications, including EZH2-dependent H3K27me3 and Suv39h1/2-dependent H3K9me3, might compensate. Moreover, the available details still remain unclear. In addition, the identification related to epigenetic mechanisms in the developmental process, along with the associated function of memory T cells, would be more critical for optimal vaccine design, along with the development of health-associated therapeutic approaches, in order to target dysregulated responses of memory T cells following inflammatory diseases.

In the differentiation and development of ILCs, G9a display its potent role [69]. Hematopoietic-based cell-specific G9a deletion generated by means of crossing in between the mice with G9afl/fl and mice with vav-cre leads to the number reduction in ILCs group 2 along with simultaneously increased ILC3s frequencies in all the examining tissues. Moreover, the ILCs number is small, especially those that are present in tissues of lungs that are normal phenotypically. ILCs have failed to produce IL-3 and IL-5 effector cytokines following IL-33 cytokine stimulation or during intranasal administration of antigen of house dust mite and protease allergen papain [69].

In contrast to lymphocytes and ILCs, protein G9a was also identified to play a unique, minor role display in the development and function of B-cells [49,64]. An early study was done by using V–D–J mini locus, which suggested that G9a inhibited the machinery of germline transcription along with recombination [70]. In mice with B lymphocyte-based specificity, G9a deletion, or in other words Mb1-Cre, is unable to produce overt phenotypes that include display VDJ recombination [64]. G9a's absence resulted in the skewed κ-chain designated as light chain usage over the λ-type light chain, along with slight LPS and IL4 reduction-induced differentiation and proliferation in plasma cells. This differentiation reduction in cells, mainly plasma cells, is consistent with the study showing that G9a interacts directly with Blimp-1, a critical factor of plasma cell-based differentiation [71]. Since G9a is dispensable in the case of normal development of B cells and has shown a minor effect on cellular functions associated with B lymphocytes, it might be possible that protein G9a has a subtle identifiable role in various aspects associated with B lymphocyte-based biology that remains to be disclosed. Together, all these available results establish that G9a acts as an important, specific regulator of a defense system that promotes cellular differentiation and proliferation. Moreover, the exact mechanisms behind it are not explained yet.

3.13 G9A INTERACTIONS

For epigenetic cellular landscape establishment, G9a acts as a central regulatory junction and is also critical for shaping cellular activity clear from the above-outlined studies. However, the functional mechanism of G9a is not understood well. How G9a mediates its role is not clear yet. For localization at distinct specific genetic loci, G9a has certain additional cofactors on which it depends due to lack of a DNA-binding domain. Various G9a-interacting protein classes have been identified (Figure 1.2). Strikingly, in the development and functions of immune cells, distinct G9a cofactors play important roles, potentially explaining the phenotypes responsible for lymphoid cells. For the development and function of lymphocytes, growth factor independent 1 (GFI1) acts as a potent regulator and can bind with various enhancers and promoters and can play an essential centralized role in switching off gene expression by repressive modulator recruitment like HDAC, HMNT, and HDM [71–74,120]. According to available data, GFI1 shows direct interaction with G9a [74,121]. In addition, due to the lack of GFI1, H3K9 methylation gets decreased significantly in cells [74].

Further, in the immune system, the phenotypes associated with the deficiency of GFI1 were strikingly similar to those observed in the deficiency of G9a in mice, representing that the functions of GFI1 are correlated with the functions of G9a. During GFI1 induction in an IL-2 dependent T cell line, it was designated as a factor resulting in independent growth of IL-2 [122]. Through modulation in the cell cycle regulation of T cells, the GFI1 requirement for IL-2 gets reduced [75,76]. Furthermore, GFI1 can generate multiple effects by which it can echo those phenotypes that were found absent in mice due to the lack of G9a in T lymphocytes. In addition, it is first more critical for GFI1 to promote Th2-cell-based differentiation through several mechanisms, including inhibition of Th2-cell-differentiation, increasing the stability of GATA3, inhibiting cell-based differentiation of Th1 cellular lymphocytes, and promoting the expression of type 11 cytokines, along with enhancement of cell proliferation in STh2 cells [77–80]. Under the cell-polarizing conditions of Th2, GFI1 upregulation was carried out by IL-4 in the signal transduction mechanism and activator of lymphocyte transcription protein 6 [77].

Further, GFI1 retroviral overexpression in cells of Th2 led to an increase in the rate of cellular survival and proliferation [77]. During the infection or in vitro stimulation with parasites, including Schistosoma mansoni and helminth parasite, T cells that lack of GFI1 failed to generate IL-4 optimally [80]. Mechanistically, GFI1 works to inhibit GATA3 proteasomal degradation by targeting its SNAG domain at the N-terminal position [78]. As cellular differentiation of Th2 cells is getting impaired in the case of G9a-deficient Th2 cells, it may increase the chances of interactions between these three G9a/GFI1/GATA3 critical for transcriptional module establishment, which leads to type 11 cytokine locus activation [15]. As per G9a's role, the N-terminus of ligand activating receptors present on the nuclear hormone regulate gene expression to act as a scaffold [35]. Based on the above available results, it is very clear that in T cells, G9a N-terminus might aid in GATA3, GFI1, and the various other factors that potentially play a role in optimal Th2-cell development. In the cellular differentiation of Treg cells and Th17 cells, involvement of GFI1 has also been observed [81].

TGF-β makes it critical to express CD103 and IL-17A/F in Treg and Th17 cells by downregulation, the expression of GFI1 up to that extent [81]. Furthermore, it also inhibits CD73 and CD39 ectonucleotidase expressions [82]. For the activation reduction of methylation marks, lysine demethylae LSD1 recruitment is carried out by GFI1 to the mentioned genetic loci. Upon TGF-β stimulation, gene expression of GFI1 gets reduced, which allows the cellular differentiation of Treg and Th17 cells optimally. T cells that lack GFI1 display an increase in IL-17A production and an increase in the expression of FOXP3 in response to transforming growth factor-beta (TGF-β) that shows similarities with G9a-deficient lymphocytes, specifically T cells [14]. As dysregulated IL-17A expression was observed in Th2 cells with a lack of G9a, the same was observed with GFI1, which is basically required to silence the expression of IL-17A found in lymphocytes [15,81]. Consequently, it is very interesting to specifically hypothesize about interactions between GFI1–G9a. Specifically, they are more critical in restraining the cellular-based responses of Treg cells along with Th17 cells, resulting in repression in the transcriptional mechanism that leads to epigenetic gene inactivation or gene silencing. For the type 11 innate lymphoid cell (ILC2) development and cellular functions, GFI1 usually acts as an important potent regulator [83]. GFI1 expression is correlated to the ST2-based receptor IL-33 expression (Il1rl1, ST2), along with the expression of GATA3. GFI1 loss in ILC2s results in the impairment of GATA3 expressions and IL-17A expression upregulation, too. It is reminiscent of the specified G9a role in ILC biology, where G9a is needed to repress the actions of genes specifically related to ILC during the development of ILC2 [69], although, unlike T cells, the GFI1 effect and potentially G9a seem to be reliant on methyltransferase-dependent repressive activity of the specific gene. By analyzing all the available dates, which suggest G9a–GFI1 are critical to performing functions in ILCs and T cells, future studies defining these interactions on the basis of molecular level might open new ways for novel therapeutics that might inhibit the dysregulated responses of Th2 cell-related to other diseases like allergies and asthma.

3.14 G9A INHIBITION: BY CHEMICAL PROBES

At present, several chemical probes on the market specifically focus on G9a by targeting its methyltransferase activity. Identification of the synthetic drug BIX-01294 was first carried out in a high-throughput screen that prevented methylation by showing bonding with the domain SET of GLP along with G9a in the peptide-binding site [116,117]. Optimization of BIX-01294, the potent inhibitor, was subsequently carried out through structure–activity effective relationships to generate E72, UNC0321, and UNC0224, all specifically showing increased specificity and activity [115,118]. In addition, further improvement in the development of G9a-based inhibitors UNC0638/UNC0642 resulted to a specific, potent stability inactivity and cellular permeability [119]. Although for in vivo studies UNC0642 has shown poor pharmacokinetics, currently A-366, an additional inhibitor that targets the methyltransferase activity of G9a and acts as a potent G9a inhibitor, was identified by an independent high throughput screen, which is unrelated to UNC0642 [123,124]. For in vivo studies, A-366 showed the growth reduction of tumor xenografts with no observable toxicity [124]. However, no tests have been performed on inflammatory disease by using A-366, but rather on the basis of available data, suggesting that G9a could be a significant approach for a future perspective to modulate immunogenic actions.

The effectiveness of G9a inhibitors or DNMT inhibitors is easily recognizable in cellular-based activities for in in vitro studies. MTT assay has been used in different research approaches to evaluate drug or inhibitor effectiveness. In addition, the antitumor activity of different drugs is predictable by targeting the methyltransferase activity of G9a and DNMTs through MTS assay.

3.15 G9A TARGET DEPENDENCY IN BREAST CANCER

As per the findings, G9a might have a targetable dependency in the case of breast cancer. Around 20% of cases of breast cancer have the occurrence of ERBB2/HER2 [123]. Various advancements have been made on HER2 therapies that improved patient conditions dramatically [124]. Because of tumor recurrence, approximately 30–40% of females will lose amplification of HER2 factor by rendering them insensitive against anti-HER2 therapies, resulting in a decrease in the survival rate of patients [125,126]. Thus, new therapeutic strategies are needed to overcome the chances of therapeutic resistance in HER2 recurrent cancer. By molecular profiling of breast cancer, the studies focused on genetic alterations will lead to the increase in HER2–independent resistance, including MET amplification [127], PTEN loss [128], and PIK3CA mutations [91,129–131].

REFERENCES

[1] Di Croce L., Raker V.A., Corsaro M., Fazi F., Fanelli M., Faretta M., et al. (2002) Methyltransferase recruitment and DNA hypermethylation of target promoters by an oncogenic transcription factor. *Science* 295: 1079–1082.

[2] Ehrlich M. (2002) DNA methylation in cancer: too much, but also to little. *Oncogene* 21: 5400–5413.

[3] Jones P.A., Baylin S.B. (2002) The fundamental role of epigenetic events in cancer. *Nat Rev Genet* 3: 415–428.

[4] Herman J.G., Umar A., Polyak K., Graff J.R., Ahuja N., Issa J.P., et al. (1998) Incidence and functional consequences of hMLH1 promoter hypermethylation in colorectal carcinoma. *Proc Natl Acad Sci U S A* 95: 6870–6875.

[5] Strathdee G. (2002) Epigenetic versus genetic alterations in the inactivation of E-cadherin. *Semin Cancer Biol* 12: 373–379.

[6] Egger G., Liang G., Aparicio A., Jones P.A. (2004) Epigenetics in human disease and prospects for epigenetic therapy. *Nature* 429: 457–463.

[7] Allis C.D., Jenuwein T., Reinberg D. (2006) In: Allis C.D., Jenuwein T., Reinberg D., eds. *Epigenetics*. New York: Cold Spring Harbor Laboratory Press, 23–56.

[8] Cao R., Zhang Y. (2004) SUZ12 is required for both the histone methyltransferase activity and the silencing function of the EEDEZH2 complex. *Mol Cell* 15: 57–67.

[9] Pasini D., Bracken A.P., Jensen M.R., et al. (2004) Suz12 is essential for mouse development and for EZH2 histone methyltransferase activity. *EMBO J* 23: 4061–4071.

[10] Creyghton M.P., Cheng A.W., Welstead G.G., Kooistra T., Carey B.W., Steine E.J., Hanna J., Lodato M.A., Frampton G.M., Sharp P.A., et al. (2010) Histone H3K27ac separates active from poised enhancers and predicts developmental state. *Proc Natl Acad Sci USA* 107: 21931–21936.

[11] Barrera L.O., Li Z., Smith A.D., Arden K.C., Cavenee W.K., Zhang M.Q., Green R.D., Ren B. (2008) Genome-wide mapping and analysis of active promoters in mouse embryonic stem cells and adult organs. *Genome Res* 18: 46–59.

[12] Deckert J., Struhl K. (2001) Histone acetylation at promoters is differentially affected by specific activators and repressors. *Mol Cell Biol* 21: 2726–2735.

[13] Liang G., Lin J.C., Wei V., Yoo C., Cheng J.C., Nguyen C.T., Weisenberger D.J., Egger G., Takai D., Gonzales F.A., et al. (2004) Distinct localization of histone H3 acetylation and H3-K4 methylation to the transcription start sites in the human genome. *Proc Natl Acad Sci USA* 101: 7357–7362.

[14] Myers F.A., Evans D.R., Clayton A.L., Thorne A.W., Crane-Robinson C. (2001) Targeted and extended acetylation of histones H4 and H3 at active and inactive genes in chicken embryo erythrocytes. *J Biol Chem* 276: 20197–20205.

[15] Batta K., Zhang Z., Yen K., Goffman D.B., Pugh B.F. (2011) Genome-wide function of H2B ubiquitylation in promoter and genic regions. *Genes Dev* 25: 2254–2265.

[16] Ng H.H., Dole S., Struhl K. (2003) The Rtf1 component of the Paf1 transcriptional elongation complex is required for ubiquitination of histone H2B. *J Biol Chem* 278: 33625–33628.

[17] Pokholok D.K., Harbison C.T., Levine S., Cole M., Hannett N.M., Lee T.I., Bell G.W., Walker K., Rolfe P.A., Herbolsheimer E., et al. (2005) Genome-wide map of nucleosome acetylation and methylation in yeast. *Cell* 122: 517–527.

[18] Song Z.T., Sun L., Lu S.J., Tian Y., Ding Y., Liu J.X. (2015) Transcription factor interaction with COMPASS-like complex regulates histone H3K4 trimethylation for specific gene expression in plants. *Proc Natl Acad Sci USA* 112: 2900–2905.

[19] Katada S., Sassone-Corsi P. (2010) The histone methyltransferase MLL1 permits the oscillation of circadian gene expression. *Nat Struct Mol Biol* 17: 1414–1421.

[20] Ng H.H., Robert F., Young R.A., Struhl K. (2003) Targeted recruitment of Set1 histone methylase by elongating Pol II provides a localized mark and memory of recent transcriptional activity. *Mol Cell* 11: 709–719.

[21] Okuda H., Kawaguchi M., Kanai A., Matsui H., Kawamura T., Inaba T., Kitabayashi I., Yokoyama A. (2014) MLL fusion proteins link transcriptional coactivators to previously active CpG-rich promoters. *Nucleic Acids Res* 42: 4241–4256.

[22] Narayanan A., Ruyechan W.T., Kristie T.M. (2007) The coactivator host cell factor-1 mediates Set1 and MLL1 H3K4 trimethylation at herpesvirus immediate early promoters for initiation of infection. *Proc Natl Acad Sci USA* 104: 10835–10840.

[23] Yokoyama A., Wang Z., Wysocka J., Sanyal M., Aufiero D.J., Kitabayashi I., Herr W., Cleary M.L. (2004) Leukemia proto-oncoprotein MLL forms a SET1-like histone methyltransferase complex with menin to regulate Hox gene expression. *Mol Cell Biol* 24: 5639–5649.

[24] Deaton A.M., Bird A. (2011) CpG islands and the regulation of transcription. *Genes Dev* 25: 1010–1022.

[25] Barski A., Cuddapah S., Cui K., Roh T.Y., Schones D.E., Wang Z., Wei G., Chepelev I., Zhao K. (2007) High-resolution profiling of histone methylations in the human genome. *Cell* 129: 823–837.

[26] Guenther M.G., Levine S.S., Boyer L.A., Jaenisch R., Young R.A. (2007) A chromatin landmark and transcription initiation at most promoters in human cells. *Cell* 130: 77–88

[27] Hu D., Garruss A.S., Gao X., Morgan M.A., Cook M., Smith E.R., Shilatifard A. (2013) The Mll2 branch of the COMPASS family regulates bivalent promoters in mouse embryonic stem cells. *Nat Struct Mol Biol* 20: 1093–1097.

[28] Denissov S., Hofemeister H., Marks H., Kranz A., Ciotta G., Singh S., Anastassiadis K., Stunnenberg H.G., Stewart A.F. (2014) Mll2 is required for H3K4 trimethylation on bivalent promoters in embryonic stem cells, whereas Mll1 is redundant. *Development* 141: 526–537.

[29] Clouaire T., Webb S., Skene P., Illingworth R., Kerr A., Andrews R., Lee J.H., Skalnik D., Bird A. (2012) Cfp1 integrates both CpG content and gene activity for accurate H3K4me3 deposition in embryonic stem cells. *Genes Dev* 26: 1714–1728.

[30] Bernstein B.E., Mikkelsen T.S., Xie X., Kamal M., Huebert D.J., Cuff J., Fry B., Meissner A., Wernig M., Plath K. et al. (2006) A bivalent chromatin structure marks key developmental genes in embryonic stem cells. *Cell* 125: 315–326.

[31] Eberl H.C., Spruijt C.G., Kelstrup C.D., Vermeulen M., Mann M. (2013) A map of general and specialized chromatin readers in mouse tissues generated by label-free interaction proteomics. *Mol Cell* 49: 368–378.

[32] Shi X., Kachirskaia I., Walter K.L., Kuo J.H., Lake A., Davrazou F., Chan S.M., Martin D.G., Fingerman I.M., Briggs S.D. et al. (2007) Proteome-wide analysis in Saccharomyces cerevisiae identifies several PHD fingers as novel direct and selective binding modules of histone H3 methylated at either lysine 4 or lysine 36. *J Biol Chem* 282: 2450–2455.

[33] Murton B.L., Chin W.L., Ponting C.P., Itzhaki L.S. (2010) Characterising the binding specificities of the subunits associated with the KMT2/Set1 histone lysine methyltransferase. *J Mol Biol* 398: 481–488.

[34] Wang Z., Song J., Milne T.A., Wang G.G., Li H., Allis C.D., Patel D.J. (2010) Pro isomerization in MLL1 PHD3-bromo cassette connects H3K4me readout to CyP33 and HDAC-mediated repression. *Cell* 141: 1183–1194.

[35] Schulze J.M., Hentrich T., Nakanishi S., Gupta A., Emberly E., Shilatifard A., Kobor M.S. (2011) Splitting the task: Ubp8 and Ubp10 deubiquitinate different cellular pools of H2BK123. *Genes Dev* 25: 2242–2247.

[36] Sun Z.W., Allis C.D. (2002) Ubiquitination of histone H2B regulates H3 methylation and gene silencing in yeast. *Nature* 418: 104–108.

[37] Ng H.H., Xu R.M., Zhang Y., Struhl K. (2002) Ubiquitination of histone H2B by Rad6 is required for efficient Dot1-mediated methylation of histone H3 lysine 79. *J Biol Chem* 277: 34655–34657.

[38] Guan X., Rastogi N., Parthun M.R., Freitas M.A. (2013) Discovery of histone modification crosstalk networks by stable isotope labeling of amino acids in cell culture mass spectrometry (SILAC MS). *Mol Cell Proteomics* 12: 2048–2059.

[39] Kim S.K., Jung I., Lee H., Kang K., Kim M., Jeong K., Kwon C.S., Han Y.M., Kim Y.S., Kim D., et al. (2012) Human histone H3K79 methyltransferase DOT1L protein [corrected] binds actively transcribing RNA polymerase II to regulate gene expression. *J Biol Chem* 287: 39698–39709.

[40] Kim J., Hake S.B., Roeder R.G. (2005) The human homolog of yeast BRE1 functions as a transcriptional coactivator through direct activator interactions. *Mol Cell* 20: 759–770.

[41] Wu L., Zee B.M., Wang Y., Garcia B.A., Dou Y. (2011) The RING finger protein MSL2 in the MOF complex is an E3 ubiquitin ligase for H2B K34 and is involved in crosstalk with H3K4 and K79 methylation. *Mol Cell* 43: 132–144.

[42] Wu L., Lee S.Y., Zhou B., Nguyen U.T., Muir T.W., Tan S., Dou Y. (2013) ASH2L regulates ubiquitylation signaling to MLL: trans-regulation of H3K4 methylation in higher eukaryotes. *Mol Cell* 49: 1108–1120.

[43] Yuan J., Pu M., Zhang Z., Lou Z. (2009) Histone H3-K56 acetylation is important for genomic stability in mammals. *Cell Cycle* 8: 1747–1753.

[44] Di Cerbo V., Mohn F., Ryan D.P., Montellier E., Kacem S., Tropberger P., Kallis E., Holzner M., Hoerner L., Feldmann A., et al. (2014) Acetylation of histone H3 at lysine 64 regulates nucleosome dynamics and facilitates transcription. *Elife* 3: e01632.

[45] Tropberger P., Pott S., Keller C., Kamieniarz-Gdula K., Caron M., Richter F., Li G., Mittler G., Liu E.T., Buhler M., et al. (2013) Regulation of transcription through acetylation of H3K122 on the lateral surface of the histone octamer. *Cell* 152: 859–872.

[46] Gansen A., Toth K., Schwarz N., Langowski J. (2015) Opposing roles of H3- and H4-acetylation in the regulation of nucleosome structure–a FRET study. *Nucleic Acids Res* 43: 1433–1443.

[47] Bian C., Xu C., Ruan J., Lee K.K., Burke T.L., Tempel W., Barsyte D., Li J., Wu M., Zhou B.O., et al. (2011) Sgf29 binds histone H3K4me2/3 and is required for SAGA complex recruitment and histone H3 acetylation. *EMBO J* 30: 2829–2842.

[48] Taverna S.D., Ilin S., Rogers R.S., Tanny J.C., Lavender H., Li H., Baker L., Boyle J., Blair L.P., Chait B.T., et al. (2006) Yng1 PHD finger binding to H3 trimethylated at K4 promotes NuA3 HAT activity at K14 of H3 and transcription at a subset of targeted ORFs. *Mol Cell* 24: 785–796.

[49] Doyon Y., Selleck W., Lane W.S., Tan S., Cote J. (2004) Structural and functional conservation of the NuA4 histone acetyltransferase complex from yeast to humans. *Mol Cell Biol* 24: 1884–1896.

[50] Hung T., Binda O., Champagne K.S., Kuo A.J., Johnson K., Chang H.Y., Simon M.D., Kutateladze T.G., Gozani O. (2009) ING4 mediates crosstalk between histone H3K4 trimethylation and H3 acetylation to attenuate cellular transformation. *Mol Cell* 33: 248–256.

[51] Crump N.T., Hazzalin C.A., Bowers E.M., Alani R.M., Cole P.A., Mahadevan L.C. (2011) Dynamic acetylation of all lysine-4 trimethylated histone H3 is evolutionarily conserved and mediated by p300/CBP. *Proc Natl Acad Sci USA* 108: 7814–7819.

[52] Hsu D.W., Chubb J.R., Muramoto T., Pears C.J., Mahadevan L.C. (2012) Dynamic acetylation of lysine-4-trimethylated histone H3 and H3 variant biology in a simple multicellular eukaryote. *Nucleic Acids Res* 40: 7247–7256.

[53] Clayton A.L., Hazzalin C.A., Mahadevan L.C. (2006) Enhanced histone acetylation and transcription: a dynamic perspective. *Mol Cell* 23: 289–296.

[54] Doyon Y., Cayrou C., Ullah M., Landry A.J., Cote V., Selleck W., Lane W.S., Tan S., Yang X.J., Cote J. (2006) ING tumor suppressor proteins are critica regulators of chromatin acetylation required for genome expression and perpetuation. *Mol Cell* 21: 51–64.

[55] Wagner E.J., Carpenter P.B. (2012) Understanding the language of Lys36 methylation at histone H3. *Nat Rev Mol Cell Biol* 13: 115–126.

[56] Li B., Howe L., Anderson S., Yates J.R. 3rd, Workman J.L. (2003) The Set2 histone methyltransferase functions through the phosphorylated carboxyl-terminal domain of RNA polymerase II. *J Biol Chem* 278: 8897–8903.

[57] Kizer K.O., Phatnani H.P., Shibata Y., Hall H., Greenleaf A.L., Strahl B.D. (2005) A novel domain in Set2 mediates RNA polymerase II interaction and couples histone H3K36 methylation with transcript elongation. *Mol Cell Biol* 25: 3305–3316.

[58] Morris S.A., Shibata Y., Noma K., Tsukamoto Y., Warren E., Temple B., Grewal S.I., Strahl B.D. (2005) Histone H3K36 methylation is associated with transcription elongation in Schizosaccharomyces pombe. *Eukaryot Cell* 4: 1446–1454.

[59] Joshi A.A., Struhl K. (2005) Eaf3 chromodomain interaction with methylated H3-K36 links histone deacetylation to Pol II elongation. *Mol Cell* 20: 971–978.

[60] Carrozza M.J., Li B., Florens L., Suganuma T., Swanson S.K., Lee K.K., Shia W.J., Anderson S., Yates J., Washburn M.P., et al. (2005) Histone H3 methylation by Set2 directs deacetylation of coding regions by Rpd3S to suppress spurious intragenic transcription. *Cell* 123: 581–592.

[61] Keogh M.C., Kurdistani S.K., Morris S.A., Ahn S.H., Podolny V., Collins S.R., Schuldiner M., Chin K., Punna T., Thompson N.J., et al. (2005) Cotranscriptional set2 methylation of histone H3 lysine 36 recruits a repressive Rpd3 complex. *Cell* 123: 593–605.

[62] Blackledge N.P., Zhou J.C., Tolstorukov M.Y., Farcas A.M., Park P.J., Klose R.J. (2010) CpG islands recruit a histone H3 lysine 36 demethylase. *Mol Cell* 38: 179–190.

[63] He J., Kallin E.M., Tsukada Y., Zhang Y. (2008) The H3K36 demethylase Jhdm1b/Kdm2b regulates cell proliferation and senescence through p15 (Ink4b). *Nat Struct Mol Biol* 15: 1169–1175.

[64] Dhayalan A., Rajavelu A., Rathert P., Tamas R., Jurkowska R.Z., Ragozin S., Jeltsch A. (2010) The Dnmt3a PWWP domain reads histone 3 lysine 36 trimethylation and guides DNA methylation. *J Biol Chem* 285: 26114–26120.

[65] van Nuland R., van Schaik F.M., Simonis M., van Heesch S., Cuppen E., Boelens R., Timmers H.M., van Ingen H. (2013) Nucleosomal DNA binding drives the recognition of H3K36-methylated nucleosomes by the PSIP1- PWWP domain. *Epigenetics Chromatin* 6: 12.

[66] Maltby V.E., Martin B.J., Schulze J.M., Johnson I., Hentrich T., Sharma A., Kobor M.S., Howe L. (2012) Histone H3 lysine 36 methylation targets the Isw1b remodeling complex to chromatin. *Mol Cell Biol* 32: 3479–3485.

[67] Vermeulen M., Eberl H.C., Matarese F., Marks H., Denissov S., Butter F., Lee K.K., Olsen J.V., Hyman A.A., Stunnenberg H.G., et al. (2010) Quantitative interaction proteomics and genome-wide profiling of epigenetic histone marks and their readers. *Cell* 142: 967–980.

[68] Kim A., Kiefer C.M., Dean A. (2007) Distinctive signatures of histone methylation in transcribed coding and noncoding human beta-globin sequences. *Mol Cell Biol* 27: 1271–1279.

[69] Schneider T.D., Arteaga-Salas J.M., Mentele E., David R., Nicetto D., Imhof A., Rupp R.A. (2011) Stage-specific histone modification profiles reveal global transitions in the Xenopus embryonic epigenome. *PLoS ONE* 6: e22548.

[70] Zheng Y., Sweet S.M., Popovic R., Martinez-Garcia E., Tipton J.D., Thomas P.M., Licht J.D., Kelleher N.L. (2012) Total kinetic analysis reveals how combinatorial methylation patterns are established on lysines 27 and 36 of histone H3. *Proc Natl Acad Sci USA* 109: 13549–13554.

[71] Martinez-Garcia E., Popovic R., Min D.J., Sweet S.M., Thomas P.M., Zamdborg L., Heffner A., Will C., Lamy L., Staudt L.M., et al. (2011) The MMSET histone methyl transferase switches global histone methylation and alters gene expression in t(4;14) multiple myeloma cells. *Blood* 117: 211–220.

[72] Schmitges F.W., Prusty A.B., Faty M., Stutzer A., Lingaraju G.M., Aiwazian J., Sack R., Hess D., Li L., Zhou S., et al. (2011) Histone methylation by PRC2 is inhibited by active chromatin marks. *Mol Cell* 42: 330–341.

[73] Yuan W., Xu M., Huang C., Liu N., Chen S., Zhu B. (2011) H3K36 methylation antagonizes PRC2-mediated H3K27 methylation. *J Biol Chem* 286: 7983–7989.

[74] Schübeler D. (2015) Function and information content of DNA methylation. *Nature* 517: 321–326. doi:10.1038/nature14192.

[75] Berger S.L. (2007) The complex language of chromatin regulation during transcription. *Nature* 447: 407–412. doi:10.1038/nature0591.

[76] Chen K., Chen Z., Wu D., Zhang L., Lin X., Su J., et al. (2015) Broad H3K4me3 is associated with increased transcription elongation and enhancer activity at tumor-suppressor genes. *Nat Genet* 47: 1149–1157. doi:10.1038/ng.3385.

[77] Barski A., Cuddapah S., Cui K., Roh T.-Y., Schones D.E., Wang Z., et al. (2007) Highresolution profiling of histone methylations in the human genome. *Cell* 129: 823–837. doi:10.1016/j.cell.2007.05.009.

[78] Huang Y., Min S., Lui Y., Sun J., Su X., Liu Y., et al. (2012) Global mapping of H3K4me3 and H3K27me3 reveals chromatin state-based regulation of human monocytederived dendritic cells in different environments. *Genes Immun* 13: 311–320. doi:10.1038/genc. 2011.87.

[79] Wei G., Wei L., Zhu J., Zang C., Hu-Li J., Yao Z., et al. (2009) Global mapping of H3K4me3 and H3K27me3 reveals specificity and plasticity in lineage fate determination of differentiating CD4+ T cells. *Immunity* 30: 155–167. doi:10.1016/j.immuni. 2008.12.009.

[80] Russ B.E., Olshanksy M., Smallwood H.S., Li J., Denton A.E., Prier J.E., et al. (2014) Distinct epigenetic signatures delineate transcriptional programs during virus-specific CD8(+) T cell differentiation . *Immunity*41: 853–865. doi:10.1016/j.immuni.2014.11.001

[81] Antignano F., Burrows K., Hughes M.R., Han J.M., Kron K.J., Penrod N.M., et al. (2014) Methyltransferase G9A regulates T cell differentiation during murine intestinal inflammation. *J Clin Invest* 124: 1945–1955. doi:10.1172/JCI69592.

[82] Lehnertz B., Northrop J.P., Antignano F., Burrows K., Hadidi S., Mullaly S.C., et al. (2010) Activating and inhibitory functions for the histone lysine methyltransferase G9a in T helper cell differentiation and function. *J Exp Med* 207: 915–922. doi:10.1084/jem. 20100363.

[83] Yokochi T., Poduch K., Ryba T., Lu J., Hiratani I., Tachibana M., et al. (2009) G9a selectively represses a class of late-replicating genes at the nuclear periphery. *Proc Natl Acad Sci U S A* 106: 19363–19368. doi:10.1073/pnas.0906142106.

[84] Tachibana M., Sugimoto K., Nozaki M., Ueda J., Ohta T., Ohki M., et al. (2002) G9a histone methyltransferase plays a dominant role in euchromatic histone H3 lysine 9 methylation and is essential for early embryogenesis. *Genes Dev* 16: 1779–1791. doi:10.11 01/gad.989402.

[85] Wen B., Wu H., Shinkai Y., Irizarry R.A., Feinberg A.P. (2009) Large histone H3 lysine 9 dimethylated chromatin blocks distinguish differentiated from embryonic stem cells. *Nat Genet* 41: 246–250. doi:10.1038/ng.297.

[86] Filion G.J., van Steensel B. (2010) Reassessing the abundance of H3K9me2 chromatin domains in embryonic stem cells. *Nat Genet* 42: 4; author rely 5–6. doi:10.1038/ng0110-4

[87] Shinkai Y., Tachibana M. (2011) H3K9 methyltransferase G9a and the related molecule GLP. *Genes Dev* 25: 781–788. doi:10.1101/gad.2027411.

[88] Spies T., Bresnahan M., Strominger J.L. (1989) Human major histocompatibility complex contains a minimum of 19 genes between the complement cluster and HLA-B. *Proc Natl Acad Sci U S A* 86: 8955–8958. doi:10.1073/pnas.86.22.8955.

[89] Kendall E., Sargent C.A., Campbell R.D. (1990) Human major histocompatibility complex contains a new cluster of genes between the HLA-D and complement C4 loci. *Nucleic Acids Res* 18: 7251–7257. doi:10.1093/nar/18.24.7251.

[90] Yokochi T., Poduch K., Ryba T., Lu J., et al. (2009) G9a selectively represses a class of late-replicating genes at the nuclear periphery. *Pro Natl Acad Sci USA* 109: 19363–19368.

[91] Brown S.E., Campbell R.D., Sanderson C.M. (2001) Novel NG36/G9a gene products encoded within the human and mouse MHC class III regions. *Mamm Genome* 12: 916–924. doi:10.1007/s00335-001-3029-3.

[92] Milner C.M., Campbell R.D. (1993) The G9a gene in the human major histocompatibility complex encodes a novel protein containing ankyrin-like repeats. *Biochem J* 290(Pt 3): 811–818. doi:10.1042/bj2900811.

[93] Xie T., Rowen L., Aguado B., Ahearn M.E., Madan A., Qin S., et al. (2003) Analysis of the gene-dense major histocompatibility complex class III region and its comparison to mouse. *Genome Res* 13: 2621–2636. doi:10.1101/gr.1736803.

[94] Ogawa H., Ishiguro K.-I., Gaubatz S., Livingston D.M., Nakatani Y. (2002) A complex with chromatin modifiers that occupies E2F- and Myc-responsive genes in G0 cells. *Science* 296: 1132–1136. doi:10.1126/science.1069861.

[95] Tachibana M., Ueda J., Fukuda M., Takeda N., Ohta T., Iwanari H., et al. (2005) Histone methyltransferases G9a and GLP form heteromeric complexes and are both crucial for methylation of euchromatin at H3-K9. *Genes Dev* 19: 815–826. doi:10.1101/gad.1284005

[96] Willemsen M.H., Vulto-Van Silfhout A.T., Nillesen W.M., Wissink-Lindhout W.M., van Bokhoven H., Philip N., et al. (2012) Update on Kleefstra syndrome. *Mol Syndromol* 2: 202–212. doi:10.1159/000335648.

[97] Collins R.E., Tachibana M., Tamaru H., Smith K.M., Jia D., Zhang X., et al. (2005) In vitro and in vivo analyses of a Phe/Tyr switch controlling product specificity of histone lysine methyltransferases. *J Biol Chem* 280: 5563–5570. doi:10.1074/jbc.M410483200.

[98] Collins R.E., Northrop J.P., Horton J.R., Lee D.Y., Zhang X., Stallcup M.R., et al. (2008) The ankyrin repeats of G9a and GLP histone methyltransferases are mono and dimethyllysine binding modules. *Nat Struct Mol Biol* 15: 245–250. doi:10.1038/nsmb.1384.

[99] Liu S., Ye D., Guo W., Yu W., He Y., Hu J., et al. (2015) G9a is essential for EMT-mediated metastasis and maintenance of cancer stem cell-like characters in head and neck squamous cell carcinoma. *Oncotarget* 6: 6887–6901. doi:10.18632/oncotarget.3159.

[100] Lee D.Y., Northrop J.P., Kuo M.-H., Stallcup M.R. (2006) Histone H3 lysine 9 methyltransferase G9a is a transcriptional coactivator for nuclear receptors. *J Biol Chem* 281: 8476–8485. doi:10.1074/jbc.M511093200.

[101] Purcell D.J., Jeong K.W., Bittencourt D., Gerke D.S., Stallcup M.R. (2011) A distinct mechanism for coactivator versus corepressor function by histone methyltransferase G9a in transcriptional regulation. *J Biol Chem* 286: 41963–41971. doi:10.1074/jbc.M111.298463.

[102] Chaturvedi C.P., Hosey A.M., Palii C., Perez-Iratxeta C., Nakatani Y., Ranish J.A., et al. (2009) Dual role for the methyltransferase G9a in the maintenance of betaglobin gene transcription in adult erythroid cells. *Proc Natl Acad Sci U S A* 106: 18303–18308. doi:10.1073/pnas.0906769106.

[103] Bittencourt D., Wu D.Y., Jeong K.W., Gerke D.S., Herviou L., Ianculescu I., et al. (2012) G9a functions as a molecular scaffold for assembly of transcriptional coactivators on a subset of glucocorticoid receptor target genes. *Proc Natl Acad Sci U S A* 109: 19673–19678. doi:10.1073/pnas.1211803109.

[104] Tachibana M., Sugimoto K., Fukushima T., Shinkai Y. (2001) Set domain-containing protein, G9a, is a novel lysine-preferring mammalian histone methyltransferase with hyperactivity and specific selectivity to lysines 9 and 27 of histone H3. *J Biol Chem* 276: 25309–25317. doi:10.1074/jbc.M101914200.

[105] Rice J.C., Briggs S.D., Ueberheide B., Barber C.M., Shabanowitz J., Hunt D.F., et al. (2003) Histone methyltransferases direct different degrees of methylation to define

distinct chromatin domains. *Mol Cell* 12: 1591–1598. doi:10.1016/S1097-2765(03)004 79-9.

[106] Maison C., Almouzni G. (2004) HP1 and the dynamics of heterochromatin maintenance. *Nat Rev Mol Cell Biol* 5: 296–304. doi:10.1038/nrm1355.

[107] Trojer P., Zhang J., Yonezawa M., Schmidt A., Zheng H., Jenuwein T., et al. (2009) Dynamic histone H1 isotype 4 methylation and demethylation by histone lysine methyltransferase G9a/KMT1C and the Jumonji domain-containing JMJD2/KDM4 proteins. *J Biol Chem* 284: 8395–8405. doi:10.1074/jbc.M807818200.

[108] Weiss T., Hergeth S., Zeissler U., Izzo A., Tropberger P., Zee B.M., et al. (2010) Histone H1 variant-specific lysine methylation by G9a/KMT1C and Glp1/KMT1D. *Epigenetics Chromatin* 3: 7. doi:10.1186/1756-8935-3-7.

[109] Wu H., Chen X., Xiong J., Li Y., Li H., Ding X., et al. (2011) Histone methyltransferase G9a contributes to H3K27 methylation in vivo. *Cell Res* 21: 365–367. doi:10.1038/cr.2010.157

[110] Chin H.G., Esteve P.O., Pradhan M., Benner J., Patnaik D., Carey M.F., et al. (2007) Automethylation of G9a and its implication in wider substrate specificity and HP1 binding. *Nucleic Acids Res* 35: 7313–7323. doi:10.1093/nar/gkm726.

[111] Leung D.C., Dong K.B., Maksakova I.A., Goyal P., Appanah R., Lee S., et al. (2011) Lysine methyltransferase G9a is required for de novo DNA methylation and the establishment, but not the maintenance, of proviral silencing. *Proc Natl Acad Sci U S A* 108: 5718–5723. doi:10.1073/pnas.1014660108.

[112] Dong K.B., Maksakova I.A., Mohn F., Leung D., Appanah R., Lee S., et al. (2008) DNA methylation in ES cells requires the lysine methyltransferase G9a but not its catalytic activity. *EMBO J* 27: 2691–2701. doi:10.1038/emboj.2008.193.

[113] Feldman N., Gerson A., Fang J., Li E., Zhang Y., Shinkai Y., et al. (2006) G9a-mediated irreversible epigenetic inactivation of Oct-3/4 during early embryogenesis. *Nat Cell Biol* 8: 188–194. doi:10.1038/ncb1353.

[114] Epsztejn-Litman S., Feldman N., Abu-Remaileh M., Shufaro Y., Gerson A., Ueda J., et al. (2008) De novo DNA methylation promoted by G9a prevents reprogramming of embryonically silenced genes. *Nat Struct Mol Biol* 15: 1176–1183. doi:10.1038/nsmb.1476.

[115] Chen W.L., Sun H.P., Li D.D., Wang Z.H., You Q.D., Guo X.K. (2016) G9a – an appealing antineoplastic target. *Curr Cancer Drug Targets* 16: 1–15. doi:10.2174/156800961 6666160512145303.

[116] Gyory I., Wu J., Fejér G., Seto E., Wright K.L. (2004) PRDI-BF1 recruits the histone H3 methyltransferase G9a in transcriptional silencing. *Nat Immunol* 5: 299–308. doi:10. 1038/ni1046.

[117] Roopra A., Qazi R., Schoenike B., Daley T.J., Morrison J.F. (2004) Localized domains of G9a-mediated histone methylation are required for silencing of neuronal genes. *Mol Cell* 14: 727–738. doi:10.1016/j.molcel.2004.05.026.

[118] Carr S.M., Poppy Roworth A., Chan C., La Thangue N.B. (2015) Post-translational control of transcription factors: methylation ranks highly. *FEBS J* 282: 4450–4465. doi: 10.1111/febs.13524.

[119] Pappano N.W., Guo J., He Y., Ferguson D., et al. (2015) The Histone Methyltransferase Inhibitor A-366 Uncovers a Role for G9a/GLP in the Epigenetics of Leukemia. *PLoS One* 10(7): e0131716.

[120] Young H.A., Ghosh P., Ye J., Lederer J., Lichtman A., Gerard J.R., et al. (1994) Differentiation of the T helper phenotypes by analysis of the methylation state of the IFN-gamma gene. *J Immunol* 153: 3603–3610.

[121] Makar K.W., Wilson C.B. (2004) DNA methylation is a nonredundant repressor of the Th2 effector program. *J Immunol* 173: 4402–4406. doi:10.4049/jimmunol.173.7.4402.

[122] Makar K.W., Perez-Melgosa M., Shnyreva M., Weaver W.M., Fitzpatrick D.R., Wilson C.B. (2003) Active recruitment of DNA methyltransferases regulates interleukin 4 in thymocytes and T cells. *Nat Immunol* 4: 1183–1190. doi:10.1038/ni1004.

[123] Howlader N., Altekruse F.S., Li C., Chen W.V., Clarke A.C., et al. (2011) US incidence of breast cancer subtypes defined by joint hormone receptor and HER2 status. *J Natl Cancer Inst* 106(5). doi:10.1093/jnci/dju055.

[124] Hoque R., Ahmed A.S., Inzhakova G., Shi J., Avila C., et al. (2012) Impact of breast cancer subtypes and treatment on survival: an analysis spanning two decades. *Cancer Epidemiol Biomarkers Prev* 21(10).

[125] Hurley J., Doliny P., Reis I., Silva O., et al. Docetaxel, Cisplatin, and Trastuzumab As Primary Systemic Therapy for Human Epidermal Growth Factor Receptor 2–Positive Locally Advanced Breast Cancer. *Journal of Clinical Oncology.*

[126] Mittendorf A.E., Wu Y., Scaltriti M., Hunt K.K., et al. (2009) Loss of HER2 amplification following trastuzumab-based neoadjuvant systemic therapy and survival outcomes. *Clin Cancer Res* 15(23).

[127] Shattuck L.D., Miller K.J., Carraway L.K., and Sweeney C. (2008) Met receptor contributes to trastuzumab resistance of Her2-overexpressing breast cancer cells. *Cancer Res* 65(5).

[128] Nagata Y., Lan H.K., Zhou X., Tan M., Esteva J.F., et al. (2004) PTEN activation contributes to tumor inhibition by trastuzumab, and loss of PTEN predicts trastuzumab resistance in patients. *Cancer Cell* 6(2).

[129] Loibl S., Shaughnessy O.J., Untch M., Sikov M.W., et al. (2018) Addition of the PARP inhibitor veliparib plus carboplatin or carboplatin alone to standard neoadjuvant chemotherapy in triple-negative breast cancer (BrighTNess): a randomised, phase 3 trial. *Lancet Oncol* 19(4).

[130] From: DNA Methyltransferase Inhibitors and the Development of Epigenetic Cancer Therapies. (2005) *J Natl Cancer Inst* 97(20): 1498–1506. doi:10.1093/jnci/dji311

[131] Shi Y., Do J.T., Desponts C., Hahm H.S., Schöler H.R., Ding S. (2008) A combined chemical and genetic approach for the generation of induced pluripotent stem cells. *Cell Stem Cell* 2: 525–528. doi:10.1016/j.stem.2008.05.011.

CHAPTER 4

Breast Cancer Detection Using Machine Learning and Its Classification

Ashish Kumar and Ruchir Ahluwalia

CONTENTS

4.1 INTRODUCTION

Cancer is a broad spectrum of diseases. In all forms of cancer, the basic process of spreading and formation of the disease is the same. Cancer occurs due to the breakdown of cells in the human body. These cells divide with no end and start affecting the neighboring tissues [1].

Cancer can occur in any region of the body, which consists of billions or trillions of cells. The process of occurrence of cancer is quite simple to understand. The body has an ordered process for replenishing old and dead cells that are worn out. At times, these old cells become abnormal, and when they should die, they somehow survive. The body's components making new cells do not know of this and continue to make new cells without stopping. Thus, these cells accumulate and continue to divide without stopping

DOI: 10.1201/9781003185604-4

and may form a growth, which is known as a tumor [2]. The formation of these masses or tumors also has differences. Many masses are solid tissue, but there are cancers of the blood, such as leukemia, which do not form a solid tumor.

Cancerous tumors have the property of being malignant; that is, they can invade and attack nearby and surrounding tissues. Over the period when they grow, they can even break off and travel to a distant body part and attack that part of the body as well. They transmit through the blood or lymph system [3]. However, benign tumors do not have the ability to spread and attack nearby tissues – even though they can get quite big. These types of cancer aren't life-threatening, except for the formation of benign tumors in the brain, which are life-threatening. Generally, benign tumors do not grow back upon removal [4] (Figure 4.1).

4.1.1 Breast Cancer

Breast cancer is cancer that occurs in the breasts when cancerous cells begin to uncontrollably grow. The initiation of cancer on the breast can take place at any part.

- A higher percentage of breast cancers have their initiation at the nipples. These are known as ductal cancers [4].

- Lobular cancer starts in the glands that make milk [4].

- Other breast cancers that aren't as common are angiosarcoma and phyllodes tumor [6].

- Some cancers, such as sarcomas and lymphomas, start at other regions of the breast, and they at times aren't thought of as breast cancer [6].

Figure 4.2 represents the population (in %) affected by breast cancers versus other kinds of cancer. It has been inferred that breast cancer is the second most prominent form of cancer, its occurrence being 24% in comparison to other variants. The formation of tumors in the breasts takes place when cancerous cells enter the lymph vessels that are connected to the breasts. The lymph vessels connect various lymph nodes and contain by-products as well as immune system cells. The vessels in the breasts are used to carry away fluids from the breasts, where the cancerous cells enter the vessels and travel to other nodes of the body, and these cells start growing at other nodes [8]. Figure 4.3 illustrates the various development stages of breast cancer in lymph nodes.

4.1.2 Importance of Early Detection of Breast Cancer

One of the key factors in curing or limiting a disease such as cancer is its early diagnosis. To limit the spread and growth of cancer to other parts of the body, early detection is substantially important. It not only prevents any further damage to the body but also reduces the mortality rate. Breast cancer is no different from the rest. In addition, it is one of the diseases that doesn't have an allopathic/medicinal cure, but only its early diagnosis

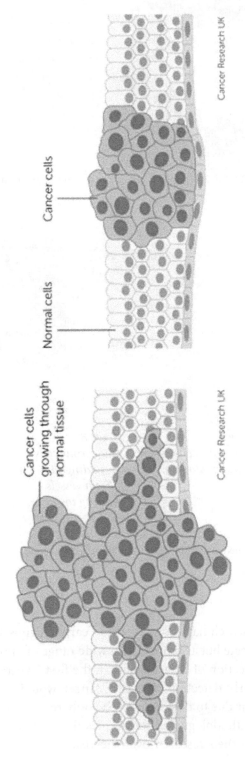

FIGURE 4.1 Spreading of cancer cells Source: Cancer Research UK [5].

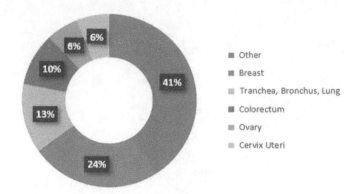

FIGURE 4.2 SEQ Figure * ARABIC 2: Various types of cancer and population affected (in %).

Source: Tahmooresi et al. [7]

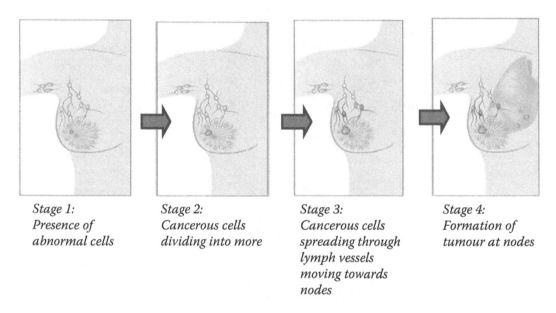

Stage 1:
Presence of
abnormal cells

Stage 2:
Cancerous cells
dividing into more

Stage 3:
Cancerous cells
spreading through
lymph vessels
moving towards
nodes

Stage 4:
Formation of
tumour at nodes

FIGURE 4.3 Different development stages of breast cancer in lymph nodes.

Source: Everyday Health [9]

can be life-saving [10]. Research has shown that the early diagnosis of breast cancer not only increases the survival rate but also provides a wide range of options for its treatment. One study showed that detection of breast cancer in the first 5 years led to a survival rate of 93% or higher [11]. Early detection of breast cancer would save a lot of lives that succumb to death every year due to this disease. The only roadblock that stands in its way is the availability of the methodology and techniques that can ease its detection. Several researchers have submitted their research over the years to uncover this roadblock that would save a lot of lives around the globe [12]. In this direction, a lot of work has been proposed in the domain of machine learning. Machine learning techniques not only ease the detection of breast cancer in the early stage but also ensure high accuracy for better treatment. The next section will elaborate on the various research works in the domain of machine learning and highlight their contribution in the detection of breast cancer.

4.2 LITERATURE REVIEW

In recent years, many researchers have investigated and proposed several studies to implement machine learning for the early detection of breast cancer. A lot of methods have been proposed in this direction to address the problem and provide an efficient solution with high accuracy.

In this direction, most of the authors have recommended state vector machine (SVM) as a classifier for the detection of cancerous cells. SVM and its sub-type classify malignant cells from non-malignant cells. For this, the authors exploited SVM to classify the results [13]. Features such as range, variance, and compactness were extracted to prove the accuracy of the method. The evaluation results were notably impressive, having a variance of 95%, range of 94%, and compactness of 86%. The results imply that SVM classifies the cells to a great extent and can be considered for breast cancer detection. However, Aminikhanghahi et al. [14] conducted a study in which wireless cyber mammography images were explored. Features were selected and extracted, and SVM and Gaussian mixture models (GMM) were utilized as a classifier. Wang and Yoon [15] selected SVM, artificial neural network (ANN), Naïve Bayes Classification, and AdaBoost (adaptive boosting) tree – methods of data mining – in their research to provide an efficient tool for the detection of breast cancer. Hafizah et al. [16] used multiple datasets that included Wisconson Breast Cancer Database (WBCD), British United Provident Association Joint National Conference (BUPA JNC) data, and ovarian for breast cancer detection. These datasets were used to repeatedly analyze the results given by SVM and ANN. The researchers concluded that both methods had high performance. However, SVM performed better in comparison to the other methods. Azar and El-Said [17] compared ST-SVM with other sub-methods of SVM. The research was intended to find the best method in terms of specified parameters. LPSVM turned out to be most effective, with an accuracy of 97.1429%, sensitivity of 98.2456%, specificity of 95.082%, and receiver operating characteristic (ROC) of 99.38%. Rehman et al. [18] extracted various features, such as phylogenetic trees, statistical features, and local binary patterns, using mammography images. A hybrid model was used, which was a combination of SVM and radial basis function (RBF) classifiers. The accuracy for each feature was checked individually. Amongst the 90 features that were chosen by taxonomic indices-based feature (TIF), 76% was the value for the highest accuracy. Avramov and Si [19] extracted features and applied correlation selection, such as T-test significance, random feature selection, and principal component analysis (PCA), along with five clas-sification models. Amongst these, the most notable results were displayed by stacking the logistic, SVM, and CSVM to increase accuracy to 98.56%. Ngadi et al. [20] tested various classification methods such as poly, RBF, and linear by the use of the neighboring support vector classifier (NSVC) algorithm. Results were compared with other classification results, such as Naïve Bayes, decision tree (DT), K-nearest neighbor (KNN), SVM, Random Forest (RF), and AdaBoost. RF came out the most accurate at 93%. This proves that NSVC is better than the other methods. In sum, it can be concluded that SVM is one of the more popular classifiers amongst researchers due to its high accuracy and fewer complications during analysis. Hence, SVM can be considered an ideal classifier for breast cancer detection.

In other lines of research, the second most popular choice for a classifier amongst the various researchers is either KNN or ANN. There are many benefits that KNN offers as a classifier. It is easy to understand and implement. It provides quick analysis and high sensitivity in results. For this, Chunqiu Wang et al. [21] exploited GMM and KNN as classifiers. According to their results, sensitivity through GMM was 67%, whereas it was 87% for KNN. GMM provided an accuracy of 75%, whereas accuracy for KNN came out to be 85% on breast cancer datasets. GMM gave a result of 48% for Matthews correlation coefficient (MCC), whereas it was 67% for KNN. As for specificity, it was 86% for GMM and 84% for KNN. These results pointed towards only one conclusion, that KNN is a better choice out of the two, giving drastically better results in terms of sensitivity, accuracy, and MCC, although GMM had slightly better specificity and precision. Mejia et al. [22] implemented a KNN classifier, which gave an accuracy of 88.8% for abnormal cases and 94.4% in the case of normal cases. Avramov and Si [19] proved that KNN stood second best in almost all aspects after SVM and its sub-types, even though KNN had an appreciable result. While KNN was popular amongst researchers due to its simplicity, ANN was popular due to its high performance and results. Wang and Yoon [15] had analyzed that ANN was marginally behind SVM in the WBCD. It performed even better than SVM in the Wisconsin Diagnostic Breast Cancer (WDBC) database. It was concluded by the research of Hafizah et al. [16] that even though the performance of ANN and SVM are neck to neck, SVM was still deemed the better of the two. In sum, both ANN and KNN are the most preferable classifiers with SVM. ANN has significantly better results and performance than KNN. In addition, KNN also provides an appreciable level of results and is much simpler in implementation in comparison to ANN. Hence, KNN has a decent level of result with quick and simple implementation. Both ANN and KNN are suitable alternatives as classifiers for the detection of breast cancer after SVM.

Amongst these traditional approaches toward the detection of breast cancer, there were some other unconventional candidates with notable results. Deng and Perkowski [23] used Weighted Hierarchical Adaptive Voting Ensemble (WHAVE). They compared the accuracy of WHAVE with seven other methods that had the highest accuracies in previous research. WHAVE came out with the highest performance with 99.8% accuracy. Ayeldeen et al. [24] used artificial intelligence and its techniques for detection. Various algorithms were tested, amongst which the RF algorithm presented the highest accuracy of 99%. Hence, the RF algorithm was adjudged to be the better algorithm. Jiang and Xu [25] used diffusion-weighted magnetic resonance image (DWI) for breast cancer detection. They used two types of features: one based on return on investment (ROI) and another one based on automatic defect classification (ADC) on data from 61 patients. Moreover, they implemented Random Forest-Recursive Feature Elimination (RF-RFE), and an RF algorithm was used. The study findings display that the accuracy of RF-RFE and RF and histogram + gray-level co-occurrence matrix (GLCM) is 77.05%, which indicates that feature-based texture has a critical role in improving performance and detection.

To summarize, SVM is the most popular choice amongst the researchers as well as the ideal classifier due to its high performance, accuracy, and easy implementation. Also, KNN and ANN is second fiddle to SVM where KNN can be adopted due to its ease of implementation, whereas ANN can be selected due to its high performance and accuracy. Out of the non-traditional approaches, the most notable result was provided by the WHAVE technique providing high accuracy.

4.3 MACHINE LEARNING-BASED CLASSIFIERS FOR BREAST CANCER DETECTION

Machine learning is the technique by which various algorithms are implemented to help computer machines understand more and more human-like concepts by sorting through huge amounts of data. This step is known as training the machine. The next part is testing, where the machines are provided with data, and they have to predict the outcome. In this chapter, we have assessed the training of various classifiers. Some of the most significant classifiers and algorithms are discussed below:

- ANN is a technique used for replicating the neural system of the human brain and giving the computer a brain of its own. In this technique, just like the human brain, the algorithm consists of several nodes, which have two values, i.e., 0 or 1. Zero here means that the node is active, whereas 1 means it is inactive. These nodes also have a weight that again has its kinds: positive and negative, which are used to adjust the strength of the node. The trained machine is supposed to look for patterns hidden in the provided data and is used to search amongst the patients' records to highlight such patterns and help to identify tumors [18].

- SVM is an algorithm that is trained to learn classification and regression rules from the acquired data [22]. It operates by creating a line or a hyperplane and hence divides groups of data into classes. Its function is to separate the data until a high minimum distance. SVM can be used to solve both linear as well as non-linear problems. It is considered one of the best general-purpose classifiers for breast cancer detection.

- KNN is a supervised learning method that is used for diagnosing and classifying cancer [24]. In this method, data points are identified, which are known as K. The number of data points can be pre-given or be established by the computer itself. The method works by checking each point's distance with all the given data points and assigning each point to the closest data point, also referred to as neighbors. In this method, it is suitable to select a vast dataset and set the value of K as an odd number.

- DT is a technique of data mining that is useful in the early diagnosis of breast cancer. In this technique, data are broken down into nodes. The representation of these nodes

TABLE 4.1
Computational Comparison of Various Machine Learning Methods For Breast Cancer Detection

Reference	Methodology	Data Base	Performance	Dataset	Comments
[13]	SVM	Mammogram	Variance: 95%, Range: 94%, Compactness: 86%	Digital Database for Screening Mammography (DDSM)	SVM is one of the top contenders for being an ideal classifier.
[21]	GMM, KNN	Microwave tomography image	Sensitivity: KNN – 87%, GMM – 67%, Accuracy: KNN – 85%, GMM – 75%, MCC: KNN – 67%, GMM – 48%	Electronics and Telecommunications Research Institute (ETRI)	Both KNN and GMM are suitable candidates, but KNN is still the better of the two.
[26]	SVM, KNN, Rough Set Data Analysis (RSDA)	Mammogram	Accuracy: Normal – 100%, Benign – 96.7%, Malignant – 94%	Mammographic Image Analysis Society (MIAS)	This method showed 94% accuracy for detecting malignant breast lesions.
[14]	SVM, GMM	Mammogram	MCC: SVM – 78.8%, GMM – 72.06%, Sensitivity: SVM – 82%, GMM –84%, Specificity: SVM – 96%, GMM – 86%	DDSM University of South Florida	SVM has a better accuracy, but GMM is safer.
[27]	Logical Regression Classifier (LRC)	Standard data	Accuracy: LRC – 99.25, B-Flow Imaging (BFI) – 95.46, Iterative Dichotomiser (ID) – 3-92.99, J48 – 98.14, SVM – 96.40	University of California, Irvine (UCI)	LRC is the most accurate of all.
[15]	SVM, ANN, NB, AdaBoost tree, PCA	Standard data	Highest accuracy: WBC – 97.47% (PCs-SVM), WDBC – 99.63% (PCj-ANN)	WBC/WDBC	PCA can be a critical factor to improve performance.
[16]	ANN, SVM	Standard data	Accuracy: SVM – 99.51%, ANN – 98.54%, Sensitivity: SVM – 99.25%, ANN – 99.25%, Specificity: SVM – 100%,	WDBC	SVM is better than ANN, even though both classifiers gave a high performance.

[17]	ST-SVM, PSVM, LSVM, NSVM, LPSVM, SSVM	Mammogram	WDBC	ANN – 97.22%, AUC: SVM – 99.63%, ANN – 98.24% Highest accuracy: LPSVM – 97.1429, Highest sensitivity: LPSVM – 98.2456, Highest specificity: SSVM, NSVM – 96.5517, Highest ROC: LPSVM-99.38	LPSVM has the highest performance.
[23]	WHAVED Neuro Fuzzy (NF) rule-based method, DT, Naive Baiyes (NB), SVM	Mammogram	WDBC	Accuracy: Disjunctive Normal Form (DNF) – 65.72, DT – 94.74, NB – 84.5, SVM – 99.54, Hybrid – 99.54, KNN – 97.14, Quadratic classifier – 97.14, WHAVE – 99.8	WHAVE proved to achieve the highest performance value of 99.8%.
[18]	SVM RBF kernel	DDSM	Mammographic Image Analysis Society (MIAS)	Highest accuracy: Model I – 76%, Model II – 68%, Model III – 80%, Highest specificity: Model I – 76%, Model II – 64%, Model III – 76%	Model III showed the best results out of the three models.
[22]	KNN	Thermogram	Federal Fluminense University Hospital	Accuracy: Normal – 94.44%, Abnormal – 88.88%	Implementation of KNN improved the accuracy: 88.88% for abnormal, whereas 94.445 for normal.
[24]	Bayes Net (BN), Multi-class classifier, DT, RBF, RF	Blood serum	Department of Biochemistry and Molecular Biology of Kasr Alainy	Highest Accuracy: 99% (RF algorithm)	RF algorithm showed the highest result, with 99% performance.
[19]		Microscope, digital image	UCI	Highest accuracy: 98.56% (SVM, CSVM)	SVM and CSVM gave the best accuracy, with *(Continued)*

TABLE 4.1 (*continued*)

Reference	Methodology	Data Base	Performance	Dataset	Comments
	Logistic regression (LR), DT.KNN, Cubic SVM (CSVM)				improved accuracy of 98.56%.
[20]	NSVC	Mammogram	Accuracy – 99%	UCI	NSVC was better than the other methods.
[25]	RF-Recursive Feature Elimination (RF- RFE) method	DWI	Highest accuracy: RF-RFE and RF, Histogram + GLCM RF, Histogram + GLCM 77.05, Highest sensitivity: RF-RFE and RF, Histogram + GLCM 84.21, Highest specificity: RF-RFE and RF, Histogram + GLCM 65.21, Highest AUC: RF-RFE and RF, Histogram + GLCM 0.76	Zhejiang Cancer Hospital	The feature-based texture is highly important in stabilizing performance and improving detection.
[28]	Fast modular artificial neural network (FM-ANN)	X-ray	Highest accuracy – 99.96% (KDD)	WBCD, KDD Cup 2008	Comparing the results, FM-ANN proved to be more accurate.
[29]	Optimized ANN	MRI	Highest accuracy – 100%, Average accuracy – 89.7%, Sensitivity – 89.08%, Specificity – 90.46%	Radiologists of the University of Bari Aldo Moro	Results were significantly improved by using the algorithm.

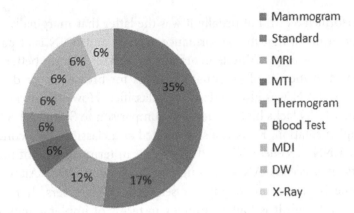

- Mammogram
- Standard
- MRI
- MTI
- Thermogram
- Blood Test
- MDI
- DW
- X-Ray

FIGURE 4.4 Various breast cancer detection methods and contribution (in %) Source: Tahmooresi et al. [7].

when put together appears to be like a tree with its branches, hence its name. Through the means of various algorithms upon scanning the available data, the tree decides on its own to form sub-nodes that can be assumed to be the branches of the tree. Upon various iterations, a result is achieved at the end of the tree [19].

- AdaBoost classifier implements classification and regression to predict the presence of breast cancer. AdaBoost adapts the weights of the various nodes with higher weights. This process is repeated until a high accuracy is obtained. This method, however, is sensitive to any noise present in the data [25].

In sum, various machine learning-based classifiers have been discussed. The research work from the various works of literature will be analyzed in the next section.

4.4 COMPUTATIONAL COMPARISON OF MACHINE LEARNING TECHNIQUES FOR BREAST CANCER DETECTION

The work from the various literature is extensively reviewed and tabulated in Table 4.1.

Figure 4.4 shows that mammogram is one of the most prevalent feature extraction techniques. This may be due to its cheaper price and high accuracy. This technique is very popular amongst researchers as it is not only faster than the other methods but also safe in its execution.

4.5 CONCLUSION

In this chapter, we briefly analyzed the various machine learning-based techniques for breast cancer detection. We deduced that breast cancer and its implications can be cured if detected at an early stage. Work from various researchers was extensively reviewed, and we concluded that in the line of machine learning, SVM – which classifies cancerous data from normal data – can be considered the best classifier. Further, ANN is a classifier that gives tough competition to SVM in terms of accuracy and performance. In certain test cases,

ANN even outperformed SVM, but usually it was the latter that marginally overshadowed the former. We determined that the performance of SVM and ANN is at par, but SVM is still preferred due to the ease of implementation as well as slightly better performance. ANN precedes SVM in the list of potential classifiers for breast cancer detection. In the next line of research, KNN was also utilized as a classifier. However, it can be concluded from the results that KNN lacks high accuracy in comparison to SVM and ANN. However, due to ease of implementation, KNN is also exploited as a classifier. We concluded that in terms of accuracy KNN precedes SVM and ANN, but in terms of ease of implementation and quick results, it succeeds ANN although still precedes SVM. After all these, the WHAVE technique is part of an unpopular selection of classifiers. It provided a high accuracy of 99.8%, although it is highly complex in terms of implementation.

To summarize, the leading candidate for breast cancer detection is SVM. For the selection of its alternative, a trade-off between accuracy and ease of implementation is needed, where you get higher results with ANN but quicker results with ease with KNN. Depending upon the problem, an informed decision can be made.

REFERENCES

[1] Rmili M., and A. El, "A Combined Approach for Breast Cancer Detection in Mammogram," *2016 13th International Conference on Computer Graphics*, Imaging and Visualization, pp. 350–353, 2016.

[2] World Health Organization, "Cancer Country Profiles 2014," *WHO*, http://www.who.int/cancer/country-profiles/en/

[3] Stalin M., and R. Kalaimagal, "Breast Cancer Diagnosis from Lowintensity Asymmetry Thermogram Breast Images Using Fast Support Vector Machine," *I-manager's Journal on Image Processing*, vol. 3, no. 3, pp. 17–26, 2016.

[4] Khan T. M., and S. A. Jacob, "Brief Review of Complementary and Alternative Medicine Use Among Malaysian Women with Breast Cancer," *Journal of Pharmacy Practice and Research*, vol. 47, no. 2, pp. 147–152, 2017.

[5] https://www.cancerresearchuk.org/about-cancer/what-is-cancer/how-cancers-grow: Accessed on:30 May 2021.

[6] Caplan L., "Delay in Breast Cancer: Implications for the Stage at Diagnosis and Survival," *Frontiers in Public Health*, vol. 2, 2014.

[7] Tahmooresi M., A. Afshar, Rad B. Bashari, K. B. Nowshath, and M. A. Bamiah, "Early Detection of Breast Cancer Using Machine Learning Techniques" *Journal of Communication, Electromic and Computer Engineering*, 2018.

[8] Richards M. A., A. M. Westcombe, S. B. Love, P. Littlejohns, and A. J. Ramirez, "Influence of Delay on Survival in Patients with Breast Cancer: A Systematic Review," *The Lancet*, vol. 353, no. 9159, pp. 1119–1126, 1999.

[9] https://www.everydayhealth.com/breast-cancer/stages-what-they-mean/; Accessed on:30 May 2021

[10] Stewart B., and C. P. Wild, World Cancer Report 2014, *International Agency for Research on Cancer*, WHO, 2014.

[11] Korkmaz S. A., and M. Poyraz, "A New Method Based for Diagnosis of Breast Cancer Cells from Microscopic Images: DWEE—JHT," *J. Med. Syst.*, vol. 38, no. 9, p. 92, 2014.

[12] Louridas P., and C. Ebert, "Machine Learning," *IEEE Softw.*, vol. 33, no. 5, pp. 110–115, 2016.

[13] Gc S., R. Kasaudhan, T. K. Heo, and H. D. Choi, "Variability Measurement for Breast Cancer Classification of Mammographic Masses," in Proceedings of the 2015 Conference on Research in Adaptive and Convergent Systems (RACS), Prague, Czech Republic, pp. 177–182, 2015.

[14] Aminikhanghahi S., S. Shin, W. Wang, S. I. Jeon, S. H. Son, and C. Pack, "Study of Wireless Mammography Image Transmission Impacts on Robust Cyber-aided Diagnosis Systems," *Proc. 30th Annu. ACM Symp. Appl. Comput. - SAC '15*, pp. 2252–2256, 2015.

[15] Wang H., and S. W. Yoon, "Breast Cancer Prediction Using Data Mining Method," *IIE Annu. Conf. Expo* 2015, pp. 818–828, 2015.

[16] S. Hafizah, S. Ahmad, R. Sallehuddin, and N. Azizah, "Cancer Detection Using Artificial Neural Network and Support Vector Machine: A Comparative Study," *J. Teknol*, vol. 65, pp. 73–81, 2013.

[17] Azar A. T., and S. A. El-Said, "Performance Analysis of Support Vector Machines Classifiers in Breast Cancer Mammography Recognition," *Neural Comput. Appl.*, vol. 24, no. 5, pp. 1163–1177, 2014.

[18] Rehman A. U., N. Chouhan, and A. Khan, "Diverse and Discriminative Features Based Breast Cancer Detection Using Digital Mammography," *2015 13th Int. Conf. Front. Inf. Technol.*, pp. 234–239, 2015.

[19] Avramov T. K., and D. Si, "Comparison of Feature Reduction Methods and Machine Learning Models for Breast Cancer Diagnosis," *Proc. Int. Conf. Comput. Data Anal. - ICCDA '17*, pp. 69–74, 2017.

[20] Ngadi M., A. Amine, and B. Nassih, "A Robust Approach for Mammographic Image Classification Using NSVC Algorithm," *Proc. Mediterr. Conf. Pattern Recognit. Artif. Intell. – MedPRAI* 2016, pp. 44–49, 2016.

[21] Wang C., W. Wang, S. Shin, and S. I. Jeon, "Comparative Study of Microwave Tomography Segmentation Techniques Based on GMM and KNN in Breast Cancer Detection," in Proceedings of the 2014 Conference on Research in Adaptive and Convergent Systems (RACS '14), Towson, Maryland, 2014, pp. 303–308.

[22] Mejia T. M., M. G. Perez, V. H. Andaluz, and A. Conci, "Automatic Segmentation and Analysis of Thermograms Using Texture Descriptors for Breast Cancer Detection," *2015 Asia-Pacific Conf. Comput. Aided Syst. Eng.*, pp. 24–29, 2015.

[23] Deng C., and M. Perkowski, "A Novel Weighted Hierarchical Adaptive Voting Ensemble Machine Learning Method for Breast Cancer Detection," *Proc. Int. Symp. Mult. Log.*, vol. 2015, pp. 115–120, 2015.

[24] Ayeldeen H., M. A. Elfattah, O. Shaker, A. E. Hassanien, and T.-H. Kim, "Case-Based Retrieval Approach of Clinical Breast Cancer Patients," *2015 3rd Int. Conf. Comput. Inf. Appl.*, pp. 38–41, 2015.

[25] Jiang Z., and W. Xu, "Classification of Benign and Malignant Breast Cancer Based on DWI Texture Features," *ICBCI 2017 Proceedings of the International Conference on Bioinformatics and Computational Intelligence* 2017.

[26] Chowdhary C. L., and D. P. Acharjya, "Breast Cancer Detection using Intuitionistic Fuzzy Histogram Hyperbolization and Possibilitic Fuzzy c-Mean Clustering Algorithms with Texture Feature-based Classification on Mammography Images," in Proceedings of the International Conference on Advances in Information Communication Technology & Computing, Bikaner, India, 2016, pp. 1–6.

[27] Durai S. G., S. H. Ganesh, and A. J. Christy, "Novel Linear Regressive Classifier for the Diagnosis of Breast Cancer," In *Computing and Communication Technologies (WCCCT)*, 2017 World Congress on 2017.

[28] Salma M. U., "Fast Modular Artificial Neural Network for the Classification of Breast Cancer Data," *Proc. Third Int. Symp. Women Comput. Informatics - WCI ' 15*, pp. 66–72, 2015.

[29] Bevilacqua V., A. Brunetti, M. Triggiani, D. Magaletti, M. Telegrafo, and M. Moschetta, "An Optimized Feed-forward Artificial Neural Network Topology to Support Radiologists in Breast Lesions Classification," *Proc. 2016 Genet. Evol. Comput. Conf. Companion - GECCO ' 16 Companion*, pp. 1385–1392, 2016.

CHAPTER 5

Diagnosis and Prediction of Type-2 Chronic Kidney Disease Using Machine Learning Approaches

Ritu Aggarwal and Prateek Thakral

CONTENTS

DOI: 10.1201/9781003185604-5

5.1   INTRODUCTION

Chronic kidney disease (CKD) is a major health issue according to global public health data. In the world's total population, approximately 10% of people are affected by this disease, but in China, the percentage factor is more, and in the United States, the range prevalence is approximately 10–20%. The term "chronic disease" means the normal and regular blood filtering process in kidney cells is slowing or has been degrading for a long time. This condition is due to the heavy buildup of fluid in the human body and collection of excessive calcium salts and other protein intake. The kidneys eventually lose renal function if the symptoms are not detected at the early stages of kidney disease [1]. The detection of poor renal function and kidney failure occurs when 28% of the kidney is damaged [2]. The right amount of salts in the body are necessary to control the activated hormones, red blood cells (RBCs), and the excessive amount of calcium, which also can rise due to sudden illness and allergies in some people, called acute kidney disease [3].

In CKD, mortality and morbidity are very high throughout the world. Patients who are suffering from kidney disease have increased risk of cardiovascular disease. Some of the diseases, such as diabetics, heart disease, kidney failure, as well as kidney injury, can be detected using machine learning (ML) algorithms. This chapter is organized as follows: Section 5.2 contains related work. Section 5.3 consists of the proposed methodology, and Section 5.4 contains various ML techniques for prediction of CKD. In Section 5.5, the framework for the CKD dataset from the University of California, Irvine (UCI), and its algorithm are explained, whereas Section 5.6 contains experiments and results. Finally, Section 5.7 contains the conclusion.

5.2   RELATED WORK

Dovgan et al. projected the method of presaging renal replacement therapy for persistent kidney disease [1]. They developed a model that is used to check the heterogeneous population and evaluate it for clinical practice. It takes the dataset from UCI/Kaggle and applies for feature selection and ML classifiers. Chen et al. [4] studied the different ML algorithms that are designed to model class prophecy as well as to detect CKD. By using K-nearest neighbor (KNN) and state vector machine (SVM) algorithms, they achieved 99.27% accuracy. Their model uses the categorical values 0 and 1 for the prediction of CKD at the initial stages and also uses the fuzzy rule for building the expert system that partially diagnoses CKD. Polat et al. [2] proposed a methodology for feature selection that improves accuracy by using ML algorithms and reduces high computational cost. It achieves an accuracy of 97.75%. Qin et al. proposed a technique for detecting data imputation by taking 400 samples for diagnosis of CKD [5]. They proposed an unsupervised imputation algorithm by using the KNN concept. They used the integrated model technique for detecting CKD and achieved satisfactory accuracy.

Are works on the category for CKD and non-CKD for the recorded pattern used in the dataset? Wickramasinghe et al. [6] proposed a method to control CKD by a proper diet plan. The classifiers used in this work were based on the different ML algorithms such as Random Forest, Mean Nearest Neighbour (MNN), Meta Decision Tree (MDT), and logistic regression. In this methodology, with the help of ML algorithms, CKD is predicted by the allowable potassium amount in the patient's body. This research predicts the potassium level in the kidney. Wibawa et al. [7] studied and evaluated kidney disease by the kernel-based extreme learning machine. They used different performance standards. The above standards and methods used different classification metrics like sensitivity, specificity, recall, etc. The Radial basis Function and Extreme Learning Machine (RBF-ELM) has been used to diagnose kidney disease with a higher showing prediction of CVD, diabetics, etc. Kaur et al. [8] proposed a methodology to detect renal disease by some data mining algorithms like Hadoop. Different ML classifiers like SVM, Random Forest, and KNN are used in this research.

This chapter focuses on research on creatinine, sodium, calcium salts, blood urea, and blood nitrogen levels in patients. With the help of these factors, kidney disease can be easily detected. To decide the chance of survival or need for kidney transplantation depends on these tests. Otherwise, diagnosis of CKD is very difficult. Revathy [3] proposed a methodology to detect kidney disease by using the different classifiers of ML – SVM, Random Forest, decision tree, and feature selection – to calculate the precision.

This chapter is proposed to distinguish CKD at an early stage. Ravindra et al. [9] used the CKD attributes and parameters using the KMM ML algorithm, which detects the patient's survival rate and accuracy with the help of clustering algorithms. The researchers identified the survival rate of a patient by dialysis. Mohamed Elhoseny [10] proposed a methodology that is based on a classification system using Density based Feature Selection (DFS) called the Ant Colony based Optimization (D-ACO) algorithm. It proposed a CKD dataset. This chapter removes the irrelevant feature in the dataset by the ACO-based learning algorithm. Comparisons between different classifiers are proposed in this research. Gunarathne et al. [11] found the concept of the missing value using an ML algorithm decision tree. With the help of this algorithm, the best accuracy and performance were achieved. The accuracy found in CKD was 99.1%. Filling with zero to extract the absent values using a decision tree classifier achieves the preeminent performance accuracy.

Ekanayake et al. [12] proposed a (CKD) or constant renal sickness has become a significant issue with a consistent development rate. An individual can get by without kidneys for a normal season of 18 days, which causes immense interest in a kidney transplant and dialysis. It is essential to have successful techniques for an early forecast of CKD. Artificial intelligence (AI) strategies are viable in a CKD forecast. These researchers introduce a work process to foresee CKD status dependent on clinical information, joining information inclining, a missing worth taking care of strategy with community sifting, and qualities determination. Out of the 11 AI techniques considered, the additional tree classifier and arbitrary woodland classifier appeared to bring about the most exact and insignificant inclination to the properties. The work inspects the capacity to recognize CKD.

Researchers Almasoud M., Ward et al. [13] proposed AI calculations while thinking about the minimal number of tests or highlights. We approach this point by incorporating four different AI classifiers: calculated relapse, SVM, arbitrary timberland, and inclination boosting on a small dataset of 400 records. To lessen the count of highlights and eliminate excess, the relationship between factors has been considered. A channel highlight choice strategy has been applied to the leftover credits and found that hemoglobin, egg whites, and explicit gravity have the most effect on anticipating CKD. The classifiers have been prepared, tried, and approved utilizing 10-crease cross-approval. Better results were accomplished with the slope boosting calculation by F1 measure (99.1%), affectability (98.8%), and particularity (99.3%). This result is the most elevated among past investigations with fewer highlights and consequently less expense. Accordingly, we reason that CKD can be recognized with just three highlights. Likewise, we found that hemoglobin has the most elevated commitment in identifying CKD, though egg whites have the most reduced utilizing Random Forest and gradient boosting models. Since the little information has been utilized in this exploration, later on we intend to approve our outcomes by utilizing a large dataset or thinking about the outcomes utilizing another dataset that contains similar highlights. Additionally, to help in decreasing the commonness of CKD, we intend to foresee if an individual with CKD has risk factors like diabetes, hypertension, and family background of kidney problems that lead to CKD by utilizing a suitable dataset.

5.3 PROPOSED METHODOLOGY

For data mining, the knowledge-based and Decision Support System (DSS) is an important area to process or detect the various stages of data processing. In data processing, various methods could be used for feature selection. In the pre-processing stage, the data are taken from the UCI dataset that is the ML repository. The key feature is set to identify the large dataset for evaluation. With the help of CKD datasets, the useful data is extracted and transformed by using data mining or ML algorithms. This chapter is implemented on four ML algorithms: Random Forest, SVM, logistic regression, and decision tree. With the help of these classifiers, we could analyze the occurrence of CKD as shown in Figure 5.1. The following methodology is used to detect CKD.

5.3.1 Classification Accuracy Metrics

The accuracy of this proposed methodology is calculated by using one of the best classifier models. This accuracy is calculated by the prediction sets: true_pos, true_neg, false_pos, false_neg. Many taxonomy precision metrics are used in ML. The accuracy is estimated by the given equation.

$$\textbf{Classification accuracy} = \frac{True_{pos} + True\_neg}{True_{pos} + True_{neg} + False_{pos} + False\_neg} \quad (5.1)$$

True_pos = If the true_pos is predicted as positive, then positive instances are called a true positive. True_neg = If the true_neg is predicted as negative, then positive instances

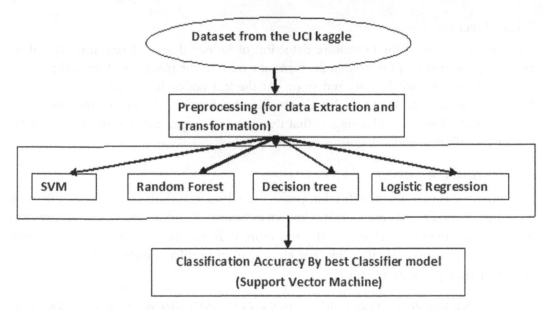

FIGURE 5.1   Methodology of CKD.

are called a true negative. False_pos = If the false_pos is predicted as positive, then a positive instance is called a true positive. False_neg = If the false_neg is predicted as negative, then a positive instance is called a true negative.

5.4   MACHINE LEARNING TECHNIQUES FOR PREDICTION OF CHRONIC KIDNEY DISEASE

Different ML classifiers are used to recognize and check renal function or CKD. These algorithms are discussed below:

5.4.1   Support Vector Machine

This classifier is used for a supervised ML approach [14] and used for classification. SVM works by finding an optimal line that performs the partitioning of the dataset into two classes. This line is called a hyperplane. The hyperplane acts as a boundary between two classes [2]. The SVM model will place the data across one of the sides of the hyperplane, producing classification [11].

5.4.2   Random Forest

This classifier is used when model quality and regularization points are highest. By using the Random Forest algorithm, the business is removed and overcomes the problem of decision trees. It is used in predictions that are used for the learned patterns. It can be used for classification and regression. Random Forest is based on an unsupervised ML method. Random Forest is a group classifier that uses a group of individual classifiers to detect kidney disease by using feature sets [3].

5.4.3 Decision Tree

This classifier is used for premature detection of kidney disease. Classification and regression problems are presented in the form of a tree. As the tree grows larger, the dataset is divided into smaller datasets and so on. At the leaf nodes, level data is analyzed, and results are produced. An internal node represents a feature, and leaf nodes represent a class label [3]. The main advantage is that it is easy to recognize and understand, handles numeric attributes, and is vigorous to missing values.

5.4.4 Logistic Regression

This classifier is used for classification problems. Given two values of variable y, 0 and 1, it predicts the value of y as 0 or 1. It is known as binary classification. It can also predict y if y has more than two values [7]. If y has more than two possible values, then classification is called multi-classification. For classification problems instead of linear regression, logistic regression is used [5].

5.5 FRAMEWORK: CHRONIC KIDNEY DATASET FROM THE UCI AND ITS ALGORITHM

For the proposed work, the following algorithm is used to analyze the CKD dataset. This dataset is taken from the online source UCI as well as Kaggle. It consists of 26 attributes for 400 different samples. As shown in Figure 5.2, the dataset used for CKD prediction is represented where the Jupyter notebook is used for its analysis. The algorithm is as below:

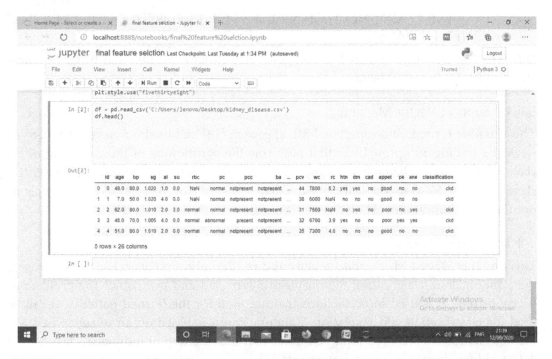

FIGURE 5.2   Dataset used for CKD.

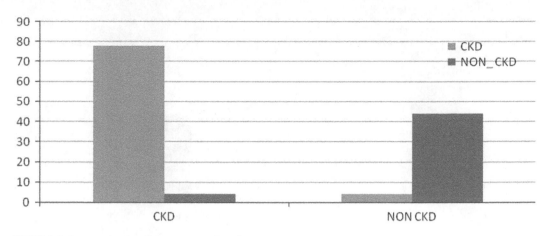

FIGURE 5.3   Results for decision tree classifier.

Step 1. Take the CKD dataset for diagnosis. (input data)

Step 2. Use classification accuracy so that the prediction gives the best performance. (output data)

Step 3. Take data from the dataset for pre-processing.

Step 4. Convert and replace the categorical values and missing values by the mean and mode method.

Step 5. Construct and select one by one each classifier model for evaluation.

Step 6. Check constructed model accuracy by their confusion matrix.

Step 7. Select the model that provides the highest accuracy performance for CKD.

5.6   EXPERIMENTS AND RESULTS

In this proposed work, the classifier models are constructed using the training dataset for the 300 instances, which is 75% of the dataset used for CKD. In this work, the data are tested or validated for 25% of the original dataset. The accuracy is calculated by test datasets along with the confusion matrix. The highest accuracy is decided by the results of the best classifier models. In the following sub-sections, the accuracy of each model is calculated for non-CKD or CKD.

5.6.1   Accuracy by Decision Tree Classifier

The test data for the decision tree model are for 130 instances. From this data, the confusion matrix is generated. It clearly defines the 9 instances are not classified properly,

TABLE 5.1
DT Classifier by Confusion Matrix

Type of Disease	CKD	NON_CKD
CKD	78	3
NON_ CKD	6	43

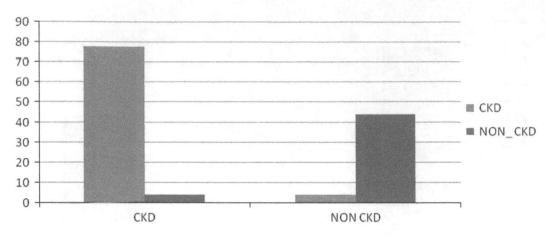

FIGURE 5.4   Results for SVM classifier.

so the accuracy of this model is 93.07%. Figure 5.3 shows the results in the form of bar charts, and Table 5.1 lists the information.

5.6.2   Accuracy by SVM Classifier

The test data for the SVM model are for 130 instances, from which the confusion matrix is generated. It clearly defines the 2 instances that are not classified properly; 128 instances are properly classified. The accuracy of this model is 98.46%. Figure 5.4 shows results for the SVM classifier in graph form, and Table 5.2 lists the information.

5.6.3   Accuracy by Random Forest Classifier

The test data for Random Forest are for 130 instances, from which the confusion matrix is generated. It clearly defines the 10 instances that are not classified properly; 120 instances are properly classified. The accuracy of this model is 92.30%, as shown in Figure 5.5 in graph form and Table 5.3 in list form.

5.6.4   Accuracy by Logistic Regression Classifier

The test data for the logistic regression classifier are for the 130 instances from which the confusion matrix is generated. It clearly defines the 8 instances that are not classified properly, whereas the remaining 122 instances are properly classified. The accuracy of this model is 93.84%. Figure 5.6 shows results by logistic regression to detect CKD, also given in Table 5.4.

TABLE 5.2
SVM Classifier by Confusion Matrix

Type	CKD	NON_CKD
CKD	80	1
NON_ CKD	1	48

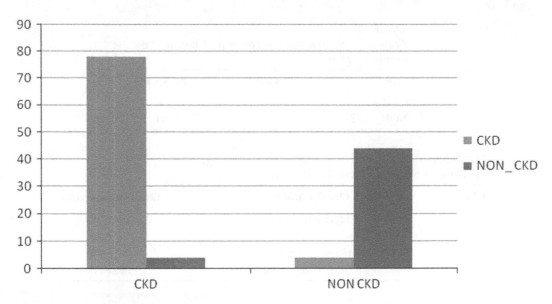

FIGURE 5.5   Results by random forest classifier.

TABLE 5.3
RF Classifier by Confusion Matrix

Type	CKD	NON_CKD
CKD	76	4
NON_ CKD	6	44

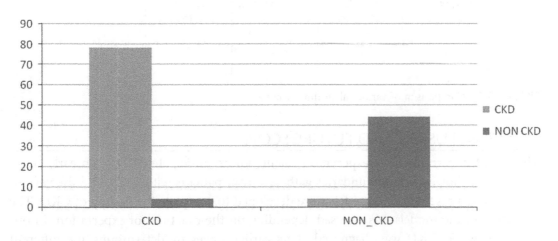

FIGURE 5.6   Results by logistic regression classifier.

5.6.5   Select the Best Classifier Model by its Classification Accuracy

SVM has been the most accurate classifier, shown in Table 5.5. SVM predicts better results to detect CKD. Results for the best model are represented by the graphs in Figure 5.7.

TABLE 5.4

Accuracy of Logistic Regression Classifier by Confusion Matrix

Type	CKD	NON_CKD
CKD	78	4
NON_ CKD	4	44

TABLE 5.5

Comparison of Various Classifier Models

S. No	Classifier Model	Classification Accuracy
1	DT (decision tree)	93.07%
2	SVM	97.46%
3	RF (Random Forest)	92.30%
4	LR (logistic regression)	93.84%

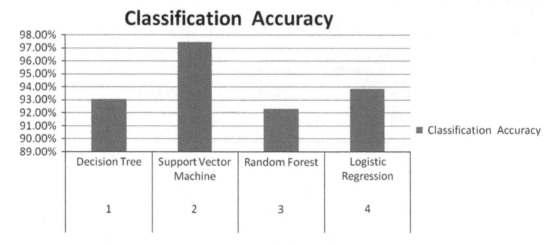

FIGURE 5.7   Comparison of various algorithms accuracy.

5.7   CONCLUSION AND FUTURE SCOPE

This chapter introduced an expectation calculation to anticipate CKD at an early stage. The dataset showed input boundaries gathered from patients with CKD, and the various models were presented. ML models were developed to complete the finding of CKD. The execution of the models was assessed depending on the exactness of expectation. In our proposed work, CKD was diagnosed at its earlier stages by determining the different attributes and instances. For implementation purposes, the CKD dataset was collected from the Machine Learning Repository (MLR) of UCI. This dataset was trained and tested to check its performance and accuracy. The different algorithms of ML were determined, and a comparison was made by their accuracy. The results found that the best accuracy classifier was SVM. This research gave the best results for early diagnosis of

CKD by performing implementation ML classifiers. The accuracy by decision tree was 93.07%. Random Forest obtained an accuracy of 92.30%. Logistic regression obtained an accuracy of 93.84%, and the SVM algorithm gave the highest accuracy of 97.46%. In the future, different feature selection and correlation sets could be implemented on this model for the best results [15–22].

REFERENCES

[1] E. Dovgan, A. Gradisek, M. Lustrek, M. Uddin, A.A. Nursetyo, S.K. Annavarajula (June 2020) "Using machine learning models to predict the initiation of renal replacement therapy among chronic kidney disease patients," *PLoS One*, vol. 15, no. 6, e0233976.

[2] H. Polat, H.D. Mehr, A. Cetin (April 2017) "Diagnosis of chronic kidney disease based on support vector machine by feature selection methods," *J. Med. Syst.*, vol. 41, no. 4, 55.

[3] S. Revathy, B. Bharathi, P. Jeyanthi, M. Ramesh (2020) "Chronic kidney disease prediction using machine learning models," *Int. J. Eng. Adv. Technol.*, vol. 9, 6364–6367.

[4] Z. Chen, et al. (April 2016) "Diagnosis of patients with chronic kidney disease by using two fuzzy classifiers," *Chemometr. Intell. Lab.*, vol. 153, 140–145.

[5] J. Qin, L. Chen, Y. Liu, C. Liu, C. Feng, B. Chen (2020) "A machine learning methodology for diagnosing chronic kidney disease," *IEEE Access*, vol. 8, 20991–21002. doi:10.1109/ACCESS.2019.2963053.

[6] M.P.N.M. Wickramasinghe, D.M. Perera, K.A.D.C.P. Kahandawaarachchi (2017) "Dietary prediction for patients with chronic kidney disease (CKD) by considering blood potassium level using machine learning algorithms," *IEEE Life Sci. Conf. (LSC)*, Sydney, NSW, pp. 300–303.

[7] H.A. Wibawa, I. Malik, N. Bahtiar (2008) "Evaluation of kernel-based extreme learning machine performance for prediction of chronic kidney disease," 2nd International Conference on Informatics and Computational Sciences (ICICoS), Semarang, Indonesia, pp. 1–4.

[8] G. Kaur, A. Sharma (2017) "Predict chronic kidney disease using data mining algorithms in Hadoop," International Conference on Inventive Computing and Informatics (ICICI), Coimbatore, pp. 973–979.

[9] V. Ravindra, N. Sriraam, M. Geetha (2014) "Discovery of significant parameters in kidney dialysis data sets by K-means algorithm," International Conference on Circuits, Communication, Control and Computing, Bangalore, pp. 452–454.

[10] Mohamed Elhoseny, K. Shankar, J. Uthayakumar (2019) "Intelligent diagnostic prediction and classification system for chronic kidney disease," *Scientific Rep.*, vol. 9, 9583.

[11] W.H.S.D. Gunarathne, K.D.M. Perera, K.A.D.C.P. Kahandawaarachchi (October 2017) "Performance evaluation on machine learning classification techniques for disease classification and forecasting through data analytics for chronic kidney disease (CKD)," Proceedings of the IEEE 17th International Conference Bioinformatics and Bioengineering, pp. 291–296.

[12] M.C. Tomas (2015) "Diabetic kidney disease," *Nat. Rev. Disease Prim.*, vol. 1, 1–20. U. Ekanayake, D. Herath (2020) "Chronic kidney disease prediction using machine learning methods," Moratuwa Engineering Research Conference (Mercon), pp. 260–265. doi: 10.1109/MERCon50084.2020.9185249.

[13] M. Almasoud, E.T. Ward (2019) "Detection of chronic kidney disease using machine learning algorithms with least number of predictors," *Int. J. Adv. Com. Sci. Appl.*, vol. 10, no. 8, pp. 89–96.

[14] E. Celik, M. Atalay, A. Kondiloglu (2016) "The diagnosis and estimate of chronic kidney disease using machine learning methods," *Int. J. Int. Sys. Appl. Eng.*, Special Issue No. 4, pp. 27–31.

[15] N.H. Cho (2018) "IDF diabetes Atlas: Global estimates of diabetes prevalence for (2017) and projections for 2045. Diabetes," *Res. Clin. Pract.*, vol. 138, 271–281.

[16] N. Sarwar (2010) "Diabetes mellitus, fasting blood glucose concentration, and risk of vascular disease: A collaborative meta-analysis of 102 prospective studies," *Lancet*, vol. 375, 2215–2222.

[17] I.A. Pasadana (2019) "Chronic kidney disease prediction by using different decision tree techniques," *J. Phys.: Conf. Ser.*, vol. 1255, 012024.

[18] R. Subashini, M.K. Jeyakumar (2017) "Performance analysis of different classification techniques for the prediction of chronic kidney disease," *Int. J. Pharm. Technol.*, vol. 9, no. 4, 6563–6582.

[19] P. Sinha, P. Sinha (2015) "Comparative study of chronic kidney disease prediction by using KNN and SVM," *Int. J. Eng. Res. Technol.*, vol. 4, no. 12.

[20] K.R. Lakshmi, Y. Nagesh, M. Veera Khrisna (2014) "Performance comparison of three data mining techniques for predicting kidney dialysis survivability," *Int. J. Adv. Eng. Technol.*, vol. 7, no. 1, 242–254.

[21] S. Ramya, N. Radha (2016) "Diagnosis of chronic kidney disease using machine learning algorithm," *Int. J. Innovat. Res. Comp. Comm. Eng.*, vol. 4, no. 1.

[22] D. Sunil, B.P. Sowmya (2017) "Chronic kidney disease analysis using data mining," *Int. J. Sci. Res. Comput. Sci. Eng. Inf. Technol.*, vol. 2, no. 4.

CHAPTER 6

Behavioral Prediction of Cancer Using Machine Learning

Ashish Kumar and Rishit Jain

CONTENTS

6.1 INTRODUCTION

Cancer, or tumors, for the past several decades have been the bane of the medical industry. Cancers are named according to the specific part of the body where they originate and the cell type of which they are made. Cancer still remains one of the leading causes of death in the world, putting the lives of millions of people in question every year. Any sort of mutation to cells or DNA is the primary cause for cancer, which poses a complex problem for medical professionals who wish to examine and treat the unforeseen and unwanted origin of cancer. The biomedical and bio-informatics field has seen remarkable and continuous evolution in the process of prognosis, diagnosis, and overall research of the different types of cancer in the past few decades. To this day, new and improved imaging techniques, such as positron emission tomography (PET) scan, micro-computed tomography (CT), and magnetic resonance imaging (MRI), are being developed to ease this process and make sure that numerous lives can be saved from the verge of death. The emergence of new technology has facilitated the process of research and implementation of such techniques by trained professionals, due to copious amounts of data being analyzed, collected, and made available to the entire biomedical and bio-informatics community for further research and understanding.

Machine learning (ML), although not a new approach in the field of cancer prediction, still provides a vast array of possibilities to expedite and ease the process. Much research has been conducted that has radically changed the way cancer is treated. For cancer prediction, three prescient points of focus are taken into consideration by pathologists: (a) the prognosis of how susceptible the cancer bodies are, (b) the prognosis of how likely the cancer is to recur, and (c) the prognosis of the survivability of the cancer [1]. As seen in Figure 6.1, the initial classification of cancer begins with analyzing the data to predict whether the tumor under consideration is benign (non-carcinogenic) or malignant (carcinogenic). The data obtained from certain imaging techniques, such as PET scan or MRIs, are given as input, from which several features can be extracted such as clump thickness, uniformity of cell shape, rate of mitoses, uniformity of cell size, marginal adhesion, etc. Taking a deeper dive into diagnosis, cancer can be classified into different types, associating with the different parts of the body, such as a bladder, lungs, skin, or even the immune system.

The ultimate goal is to facilitate the process of prediction and prognosis of cancer in a way that the procedure is somewhat autonomous and accurate to a large scale. This would not only ensure a timely planned course of treatment, but it would also allow researchers to work on the eradication of the tumor from the point of origination. Several ML techniques can be used to design algorithms and models to achieve this task. The primary objective of any ML technique would be to design a model that is capable of performing classification and prediction based on the copious amounts of sample data

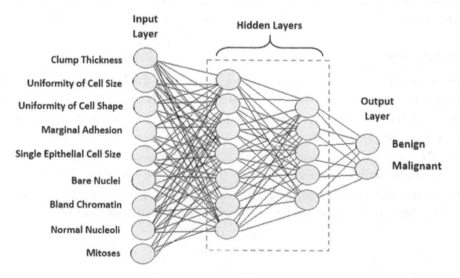

FIGURE 6.1   Representation of an ANN model to classify cancer as benign or malignant [2]

given to it [3]. Classification being the opening gambit for any model, it may pose some problems when it comes to the generalization of results based on the different test cases. An ideal classification model would be one that accurately classifies the indexes in a test set, fitting them with the data in the training set and providing the lowest generalization error. The performance of the classification model can be judged in terms of its accuracy, area under the curve (AUC), sensitivity, and specificity.

The primary objective of this chapter is to present a detailed comparative study of the various machine learning and deep learning techniques [4–8] that have been proposed in several research works conducted over the past two decades for the prediction and detection of cancer. Considering the ever-growing need for predictive medicines and a growing reliance on modern technology to facilitate diagnosis and prognosis, it's only fitting to draw out a descriptive comparison of the pros and cons of each prediction technique. Each model has its unique features and employs a unique algorithm to identify the key features from the data available and define a pattern based on it. The key trends identified from the training data can be used to classify the data into different types of cancer based on the previously mentioned predictive foci. The prediction procedure for any model largely is based on the four different types of input data: clinical data, proteomic data, genomic data, or any combination of these three types [9].

Over the last few decades, several research studies have been conducted to tackle the problem of cancer prediction using data obtained from test cases through different imaging techniques. Before we move on and discuss the best approach to tackle the prediction of different types of cancer, we must understand what ML brings to the table. ML can be broadly categorized into supervised, unsupervised, and semi-supervised learning (SSL). In supervised learning, the specifically designed algorithm is made to learn using a well-labeled and sorted dataset, alongside a set of results, in order to allow the algorithm to evaluate its accuracy based on the training set. On the other hand, unsupervised learning algorithms are largely used in self-sustaining neural networks to identify hidden patterns in the unlabeled dataset [10]. Deep learning is a branch of ML that bases how models work on the human brain, which involves neurons and neural networks. Neural networks include autonomous learning from examples and datasets and then providing an outcome based on the accuracy and specificity achieved. For the purpose of the behavioral prediction of cancer, several ML and deep learning methods such as ANNs, BNs, SVMs, DTs, etc., are usually employed.

6.1.1 Machine Learning-Based Methods for Cancer Prediction

ANNs are capable of handling a vast variety of pattern identification and classification complications. These models comprise multiple layers that generate an output based on the combination and refining of the input data [2,11]. Even though ANN is one of the most commonly used techniques, it still has certain drawbacks. Figure 6.1 is a simple representation of how ANNs are used to classify a cancer type as benign or malignant based on several input features. BN is a probabilistic model that uses a graphical approach to represent the set of variables and their dependencies via a directed acyclic graph [11,12]. BNs are extensively used as classifiers as they provide an intelligible representation of all features and the probabilistic dependencies of the data, which is why they are also known as belief networks. SVMs are another frequently used supervised learning technique that distinctly classifies a certain number of data points in an N-dimensional space, where N refers to the number of features. The hyperplane, thus defined, is where the data points are classified into two classes [13]. The classifier obtained is capable of achieving a considerable generalization level and can be used as a reliable classification model [14]. Figure 6.2 depicts how a decision boundary separates the N features. Based on the age of the patient and the size of the tumor, a graph was plotted for the several test cases, and they were classified into malignant or benign.

DTs employ a tree-like representation to map out the decisions and possible outcomes for varying scenarios. In this method, the nodes or roots represent the input variables while the leaves or the end-nodes represent the decision output [15].

This technique is also extensively used for classification purposes as it is a fairly simple model to interpret and the training process is not nearly as tedious as an ANN. Figure 6.3 contains an illustration of the structure of a DT. In the DT drawn below, T1, T2, T3, and T4 represent the thresholds or the conditions compared with the next decisions to be made. Nodes A, B, C, and D are input features that were obtained through data mining from the dataset. These features may be the uniformity of cell size or shape, the thickness of clumps, or even the rate of mitoses.

6.1.2 Comparison of Existing Cancer Prediction-Based Methods

In this chapter, we discuss descriptive comparison of the different ML and deep learning techniques used over the past two decades, to predict the behavior of the various types of cancer. Cancer prediction can be broadly categorized so that it covers the three primary aspects of its behavior – the susceptibility of cancer, the recurrence rate of cancer, and the survival rate of cancer. To predict the susceptibility of cancer, several common techniques such as SVMs, ANNs, DTs, and even RFs were used to construct efficient classification models. These different models were extensively explored by several authors. For instance, Listgarten et al. [16] and Waddell et al. [17] both used models based on SVM to assess the risk for breast cancer. Meanwhile, Ayer et al. [11] used an ANN model and worked with mammographic imagery to assess the level of risk of breast cancer.

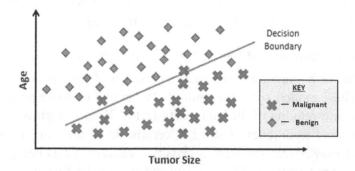

FIGURE 6.2 Illustration of a linear SVM classification model where the hyperplane comprises of two features – age and tumor size [1].

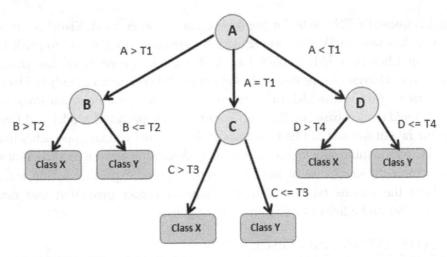

FIGURE 6.3   Illustration of a decision tree where the nodes A, B, C, and D are inputs, and based on those inputs, decisions are made in different branches, and ultimately classification is made into Class X and Class Y. T1, T2, T3, and T4 represent the classification thresholds to classify the input variables [15].

Stojadinovic et al. [18] used Bayesian Belief Networks to predict the risk of colon carcinomatosis. Dom et al. [19] designed multiple classification models based on fuzzy logic to predict oral cancer.

To predict the recurrence of cancer, multiple comparative studies were conducted over the past few decades to study the behavior of different types of cancer and how they might recur in a patient. Kim et al. [20] and Ahmad et al. [21] employed several models such as SVMs, ANNs, DTs, and even a Cox-Proportional Hazard Regression model to assess the recurrence pattern of breast cancer. Exarchos et al. [22] designed and compared models on many different techniques using clinical and genomic data to predict how oropharyngeal squamous cell cancer (OSCC) may recur. Park et al. [23] used a graph-based SSL model to study the behavior of colon and breast cancer. Asadi et al. [24] used models based on ANNs, SVM, and DTs to predict the recurrence pattern of cervical cancer. Moreover, Tseng et al. [25] designed an SVM model and a C5.0 classifier to tackle the prediction of cervical cancer. Shi et al. [26] developed SSL models to study and predict how colorectal and breast cancer can recur in a patient's body. Ho et al. [27] studied different models, such as long short-term memory (LSTM) and convolutional neural networks (CNN), and even developed an extensive model to predict the recurrence of colorectal cancer.

To predict the survival rate of cancer, generalized studies were conducted on different types of cancer, which enabled researchers to identify the behavior of each type of cancer cell. Such results can be very fruitful, as they can greatly ease the process of plotting out a course of treatment for the patient. A lot of work has been proposed to assess the survival rate of cancer. For instance, Delen et al. [28] used ANNs and DTs to study the behavior of breast cancer using the SEER Cancer Database [29]. Similarly, Kim et al. [30] tackled the same problem using an SSL co-training algorithm. Park et al. [31] employed several models based on ANNs, SVMs, and even a graph-based SSL model to study breast cancer using the SEER Cancer database. Also, Gevaert et al. [32] studied breast cancer exploiting the ITTACA 2006 dataset and employed a BN model for prediction. On the other hand, Xiaoyi Xu et al. [33] used genomic data with an SVM-based recursive feature elimination model to predict breast cancer survival. Chen et al. [34] employed an ANN model on gene expression and clinical data to study the behavior of lung cancer. Rosado et al. [35] conducted a study to identify the survival of OSCC. An SVM model was used on some clinical and molecular imagery. Kim et al. [36] explored models based on Random Forest, Cox Proportional Model, and DeepSurv to predict the rate of survival of OSCC. Kumar et al. [37] used regular approaches like Cox, Regularized Cox, and multi-task logistic regression to determine survival prediction of kidney and breast cancer. In sum, a lot of work has been proposed exploiting ML to make predictions about the various types of cancer. ML-based cancer prediction and detection techniques are fast and efficient to provide early diagnosis.

6.2   RELATED WORK AND DISCUSSION

The past few decades have seen an exponential growth in the employment of ML for more and more medical prognoses/prediction procedures. Cancer, to this day, being one of the most fatal and common causes of death in the world, means it was nothing short of essential to employ ML and deep learning in the prognosis of cancer to facilitate this procedure. Considering the vast number of genus and types of cancer cells discovered until now, specific ML algorithms have been employed to analyze patterns from the clinical, genomic, or proteomic data to identify the type of cancer. The most commonly employed algorithms include SVMs, RF, DTs, ANNs, and even BNs. These algorithms are trained using the extensively available imaging data obtained from several research studies and treatments of cancer originating in different parts of the human body. The predictive accuracy of these models was then computed from the test set, which gave an approximate estimation of the generalization errors in the algorithm. Additionally, specific attributes such as the accuracy, sensitivity, and even the receiver operating characteristic (ROC) curve were also calculated to allow an efficient comparison between the employed classification methods.

As mentioned previously, three predictive foci are taken into consideration by pathologists for the purpose of cancer prognosis/prediction: (i) the prediction of cancer susceptibility or assessment of risk, (ii) the prediction of cancer recurrence, and (iii) the prediction of cancer survival [3]. Several research studies and papers suggest that there is a growing trend of ML being used to predict the susceptibility of cancer, the rate or chance of its recurrence, and the chance of survival of the cancer type. In this chapter, we will not only briefly discuss the methodologies proposed by various researchers but also a variety of results that were obtained from the work done by them on the above-mentioned points of focus.

6.3   MACHINE LEARNING-BASED PREDICTION OF CANCER SUSCEPTIBILITY

Every year, millions of patients are diagnosed with cancer, of which only a fraction of people are treated properly and are completely rid of the disease. The first step towards the identification and prediction of cancer is to discriminate the underlying tumor as malignant or benign. This section, as it can be seen in Table 6.1, comprises a brief

TABLE 6.1
Representative Work For the Prediction of Cancer Susceptibility

Authors	Technique Used	Type of Cancer	Type of Data Used	AUC/Accuracy
Listgarten et al. [16]	Support vector machines	Breast cancer	Single nucleotide polymorphisms	69%
Stojadinovic et al. [18]	Bayesian network	Colon carcinomatosis	Clinical and pathological results	0.71
R. M. Dom et al. [19]	Fuzzy logic prediction models	Oral cancer	Clinical data from oral cancer cases in Malaysia	FuReA – 0.799; FL – 0.631; FNN – 0.803
Waddell et al. [17]	Support vector machines	Multiple myeloma	Single nucleotide polymorphisms	71%
T. Ayer et al. [11]	Artificial neural network	Breast cancer	Mammographic imaging	0.965
Jayadeep Pati [38]	Multilayer – perceptron (MLP), random sub-space (RSS), and support vector machines (sequential minimal optimization classifier, SMO)	Lung cancer	Kent ridge bio-medical dataset repository	MLP – 86.66%; RSS – 68.33%; SMO – 91.66%

overview of the many different ML approaches that were used to identify the severity or susceptibility of the cancer cells.

In the research done by Listgarten et al. [16], predictive models for breast cancer susceptibility were studied and developed, wherein the single nucleotide polymorphisms (SNPs) were identified for over 45 genes of breast cancer [16]. In this study, multiple SVM models were employed, of which the SVM quadratic kernel yielded an accuracy of 69%. On the other hand, Waddell et al. [17] also used SVMs to develop predictive models for the study of the overall susceptibility of multiple myeloma. The proposed model explored the single positions of variation in DNA, i.e., single nucleotide polymorphisms. It has been inferred that the exploration of the patterns in SNPs may make it easier to identify markers for genetic predisposition to disease [17]. Also, a maximum accuracy of 71% was achieved through this research in the risk assessment of multiple myeloma.

Stojadinovic et al. [18] explored and employed a Bayesian Belief Network (BBN) model to predict the susceptibility of colon carcinomatosis. Their classification model was trained and tested using relevant clinical, pathological, and oncological data variables, which allowed the prediction of the overall survival rate of the patients and the malignancy of the cancer cells present. Through the BBN model, an AUC of 0.71 was obtained. Dom et al. [19] used a unique approach and conducted extensive research on the different ML models based on fuzzy logic. They listed the pros and cons of every model – be it the fuzzy regression adapted (FuReA) model, the fuzzy logic (FL) prediction model, or the fuzzy neural network (FNN) prediction model with experimental analysis. It was predicted that the FNN model achieved the highest AUC, i.e., 0.803. On the other hand, Ayer et al. [11] exploited an ANN model, which was trained using a large dataset of consecutive mammographically obtained imagery from the Wisconsin State Cancer Reporting System. The aforementioned model was a three-layer feedforward ANN model that gave an AUC of 0.965. In 2018, Jayadeep Pati [38] employed the multilayer perceptron (MLP) classifier model, random sub-space classifier model, and the sequential minimal optimization classifier (SMO) model. He used the Kent Ridge Bio-Medical Dataset Repository [2] containing the lung cancer test samples, to train and test the models. As a result, it was discovered that the SMO model gave the highest accuracy of 91.66%.

6.4 MACHINE LEARNING-BASED MODELS TO PREDICT CANCER RECURRENCE

Despite the prolonged treatment of cancer, it cannot be guaranteed that the cancer cells or the tumor will be completely eradicated from the body. The leftover cancer bodies might cause a recurrence of cancer, putting the patient at risk yet again. Thus, several studies have been conducted to identify and predict the recurrence or proneness of cancer in the human body, using several ML techniques. In this section, as drawn out in Table 6.2, we will compare the performance of a few different techniques that provided the best results for the prediction of recurrence of breast, oral, colon, and cervical cancer.

Kim et al. [20] predicted the recurrence of breast cancer utilizing SVM, ANN, and a Cox-Proportional Hazard Regression Model. Clinical and pathological data of 679

TABLE 6.2
Representative Work Related to the Prediction of Cancer Recurrence

Authors	Technique Used	Type of Cancer	Type of Data Used	AUC/Accuracy
W. Kim et al. [20]	SVMS, ANN, and Cox-Proportional Hazard Regression Models	Breast cancer	Clinical, pathological, epidemiological	SVM – 0.85; ANN – 0.80; Cox Model – 0.73
Ahmad et al. [21]	Decision trees, artificial neural networks, support vector machines	Breast cancer	Clinical	DT – 0.936; SVM – 0.957; ANN – 0.947
Exarchos et al. [22]	BNs, SVMs, ANNs, DTs, and RF models	Oral squamous cell carcinoma	Clinical and imaging tissue (genomic)	BN – 69.6%; DT – 66.1%; SVM – 69.6%; ANN – 66.1; RF – 58.9%
C. Park et al. [23]	Graph-based SSL model	Colon and breast cancer	Gene expression, Protein-Protein Interactions (PPIs)	76.7%
Asadi F. et al. [24]	Artificial neural networks, decision trees, support vector machines	Cervical cancer	Imaging data of 145 patients in Iran	DTs – 95.55%; ANNs – 95.45%; SVMs – 93.33%
M. Shi et al. [26]	SSL models	Colorectal and breast cancer	Imaging data for breast and colorectal cancer	0.57
Tseng et al. [25]	Support vector machines and C5.0 classifier	Cervical cancer	Clinical, pathological	C5.0 – 92.44%; SVM – 74.44%
D. Ho et al. [27]	MLP, CNN, LSTM, transformer-based model	Colorectal cancer	National Cancer Center Singapore imaging data	LSTM-MLP – 0.884; TCN-MLP – 0.913; T-MLP – 0.916

patients who underwent breast cancer treatment in a local Korean hospital were used. Amongst all the methods used, the SVM-based model gave the highest AUC of 0.85. On the other hand, Ahmad et al. [21] employed three different ML techniques, namely DTs, SVMs, and ANNs, to predict breast cancer recurrence rates. The ICBC dataset was used for this research, which is a collection of incidence and survival data from 1997 to 2008 [21]. Among the three techniques used, the ANN model provided the highest accuracy of 95.7%, whereas Exarchos et al. [22] conducted research to use BNs, ANN, DTs, RF, and even SVM models to predict the recurrence of OSCC. Clinical and genomic data were used with these models, and different accuracies were obtained with the different techniques. The BN model and SVM model provided the highest accuracy of 69.6%.

Park et al. [23] took a very unique approach and employed a graph-based SSL model to analyze the recurrence of colon and breast cancer. A set of gene expression data was used for this research in a graph structure. A regularization approach was applied to the constructed graph in order to predict the recurrence rate of cancer. The aforementioned model used gave an accuracy of 76.7%. On the other hand, Asadi et al. [24] employed several supervised learning algorithms, such as ANNs, SVMs, and DTs, to develop prediction models for recurrence of cervical cancer. For this research, imaging data of over 140 patients was used from a local hospital in Iran. The data comprised over 23 unique attributes. Amongst the three approaches employed, the model based on ANN provided the highest accuracy of 95.45%. Shi et al. [26] used SSL models to predict the recurrence of colorectal and breast cancer. Imaging data for CRC and breast cancer were used, which comprised almost a 1000 samples. From the SSL model employed, an AUC of 0.57 was obtained.

Tseng et al. [25] used SVM and C5.0 classifier models to study and predict recurrent cervical cancer. The research was conducted using medical records accessible by Chung Shan medical university hospital [25]. This study suggested that the C5.0 classification model was more robust and efficient than the SVM model, which is evident from its accuracy of 92.44%, whereas the accuracy of the SVM model was only 74.44%. In a study conducted by Ho et al. [27], they developed an extensive model to assess the recurrence of colorectal cancer. This model employed a (1) transformer model to extract high-quality features from multiple modalities, and (2) MLP for feature integration and classification. This model yielded an AUC of 0.95. In sum, a substantial amount of work has been proposed in the domain of ML to predict and diagnose the various types of cancer at an early stage. Out of the various available methods, SVM and ANN prove to be the most popular techniques used in research due to their ease of implementation, faster convergence, and better accuracy in comparison to other techniques.

6.5 MACHINE LEARNING-BASED MODEL TO PREDICT CANCER SURVIVAL

After the diagnosis of cancer, the primary objective is to determine the course of treatment and the survival of cancer. Each patient has a different tolerance to the cancer cells and the course of treatment, due to which their bodies might react differently to the progression of cancer and the treatment. Predicting the way one's body will react to the

TABLE 6.3

Representative Work Related to the Prediction of Cancer Survival

Authors	Technique Used	Type of Cancer	Type of Data Used	AUC/Accuracy
Delen et al. [28]	Artificial neural network and decision trees	Breast cancer	SEER Cancer Database	DTs – 93.6%; ANNs – 91.2%
Gevaert et al. [32]	Bayesian Network	Breast cancer	ITTACA 2006 dataset	0.851
Xiaoyi Xu et al. [33]	Support vector machine-based recursive feature elimination	Breast cancer	Genomic	97%
Y-C. Chen et al. [34]	Artificial neural network	Lung cancer	Clinical, gene expression	93.5%
J. Kim et al. [30]	SSL co-training algorithm	Breast cancer	SEER Cancer Database	0.965
P. Rosado et al. [35]	Support vector machines	Oral squamous cell carcinoma	Clinical and molecular imagery	98%
K. Park et al. [31]	ANNs, SVMs, and graph-based SSL model	Breast cancer	SEER Cancer Database	ANNs – 0.61; SVM – 0.46; SSL – 0.71
D.W. Kim et al. [36]	DeepSurv, Random Survival Forest, and Cox Proportional Hazard Model	Oral squamous cell carcinoma	Custom data from 255 patients from 2000 to 2017	DeepSurv – 0.81; RSF – 0.77; Cox model – 0.756
L. Kumar et al. [37]	Cox, Regularized Cox, and multi-task logistic regression model	Breast and kidney cancer	METABRIC and KIPAN datasets	Cox – 0.8062; RCox – 0.8401; MTLR – 0.8495

type of cancer cells present and the underlying treatment procedure might give pathologists an advantage towards saving countless lives. As can be seen in Table 6.3, several research studies have been conducted using different ML techniques to predict the survival rate of different cancer types.

Owing to the availability of copious amounts of clinical and genomic data for breast cancer, several studies have been conducted to predict the survival rate of cancer using the data. In the paper by Delen et al. [28], data mining algorithms such as ANN and DTs were used to develop prediction models to identify the survival rate of breast cancer. The SEER Cancer Database was used to train these models, which comprises imagery from over 200,000 cases. The DT model gave an accuracy of 93.6%; meanwhile, the second model, designed using ANN, gave an accuracy of 91.2%. Moreover, a tenfold cross-validation technique was used to measure the unbiased estimate of the models [28]. Olivier Gevaert et al. [32] employed BNN models to facilitate the prediction of the survival rate of breast cancer. Clinical data from the ITTACA 2006 [29] dataset was used, which comprised laboratory analysis and ultrasound parameters. Their use of the BN model explored the full, partial, and decision integration of data sources with the model. Overall, the AUC given by this model was 0.851, which indicates its fairly efficient performance. On the other hand, Xiaoyi Xu et al. [33], developed an SVM-based recursive feature elimination model to identify the gene signature for breast cancer prognosis and identify its survivability rate. This method provided a training accuracy of about 97%. Also, an AUC of 0.78 with 70 gene signatures and an AUC of 0.99 with 50 gene signatures were obtained.

Among the studies conducted for breast cancer were two more significant ones, by Park et al. [30] and Kim et al. [30], who employed unique classification models and achieved great levels of accuracy. Kim et al. [30] used SSL algorithms trained with labeled, unlabeled, and pseudo-labeled patient data to predict the survivability rate of breast cancer. The dataset used is called the SEER Cancer Database, which was created and used by Noone et al. [39] in their research. The SSL Co-Training model, developed for this research, gave an accuracy of 76% and an AUC of 0.81. In the research conducted by Park et al. [31], different ML techniques, such as ANN, SVM, and the SSL model, were used that employ a graphical representation approach to classify the given data from the SEER Cancer Database [29]. Among the three methods used, the graph-based SSL model gave the highest mean accuracy of 0.71 and sensitivity of 0.76.

In the research by Chen et al. [34], an ANN model was used with gene expression data for the risk classification of lung cancer survival [34]. The non-small cell lung cancer patients' gene expression dataset [40] was used in this research, which is an extensive repository of gene expression data and microarrays. Chen et al. [34] claimed to have an accuracy of 93% through their approach. Pablo Rosado et al. [35], used an SVM model to predict the survivability of OSCC based on clinical and pathological features and variables. The classification and prediction model thus built gave a training accuracy of 98% for a dataset with data of 69 OSCC patients. Kim et al. [36] proposed to predict the survival of OSCC using DeepSurv, which is a deep learning-based survival prediction algorithm and compared it with a Random Survival Forest (RSF)-based model and a Cox Proportional Hazard model. The models were trained and tested using a custom dataset made from the test results of over 250 patients, and DeepSurv yielded the best c-index of all the models. On the other hand, Kumar et al. [37] explored standard approaches like the Cox and Regularized Cox models and developed a multi-task logistic regression model to predict the survival of breast and kidney cancer. METABRIC breast cancer cohort and the pan-kidney cohort KIPAN was used to train the aforementioned models and predict the survival of breast and kidney cancer, respectively.

These studies conclusively proved that several ML and deep learning techniques, such as ANNs, DTs, BNs, SVMs, and other SSL methods, can yield flawless results when it comes to the prediction of cancer survival.

6.6 CONCLUSION

In this chapter, we briefly analyzed the proposed work in the field of ML and deep learning to facilitate the process of diagnosis and prognosis of different types of cancer. The pros and cons of various predictive models were analyzed and compared using various performance metrics. We concluded that different ML models work on the three primary predictive foci in cancer prediction – prediction of cancer susceptibility or risk assessment, prediction of cancer recurrence, and prediction of cancer survival. Most of the aforementioned studies were performed in the past two decades, and they contain descriptive accounts of how the different supervised, unsupervised, and semi-supervised learning methods can be used to tackle the problem of cancer prediction. From a comparative and detailed overview of these works, we can finally conclude that a combination of copious amounts of labeled and unlabeled clinical, genomic, and proteomic data, when taken into consideration for the application of different ML techniques, can provide promising results. The results so obtained can be helpful in the early prediction and detection of the underlying disease and can save countless lives.

REFERENCES

[1] K. Kourou, T. P. Exarchos, K. P. Exarchos, M. V. Karamouzis, and D. I. Fotiadis, "Machine learning applications in cancer prognosis and prediction," *Comput. Struct. Biotechnol. J.*, vol. 13, pp. 8–17, 2015.

[2] A. K. Jain, J. Mao, and K. M. Mohiuddin, "Artificial neural networks: A tutorial," *Computer (Long. Beach. Calif).*, vol. 29, no. 3, pp. 31–44, 1996.

[3] J. A. Cruz and D. S. Wishart, "Applications of machine learning in cancer prediction and prognosis," *Cancer Inform.*, vol. 2, pp. 59–77, 2006.

[4] S. Pandey and A. Solanki "Music instrument recognition using deep convolutional neural networks" *Int. J. Inf. Technol.*, vol. 13, no. 3, pp. 129–149, 2019.

[5] R. Rajput and A. Solanki, "Real-time analysis of tweets using machine learning and semantic analysis" In: *International Conference on Communication and Computing Systems (ICCCS2016), Taylor and Francis, At Dronacharya College of Engineering, Gurgaon*, 9–11 Sept, vol. 138(25), pp. 687–692, 2016.

[6] R. Ahuja and A. Solanki, "Movie recommender system using K-means clustering and K-nearest neighbor" In: *Accepted for Publication in Confuence-2019: 9th International Conference on Cloud Computing, Data Science & Engineering, Amity University, Noida*, vol. 1231, no. 21, pp. 25–38, 2019.

[7] A. Tayal, U. Kose, A. Solanki, A. Nayyar, and J. A. M. Saucedo, "Effciency analysis for stochastic dynamic facility layout problem using meta-heuristic, data envelopment analysis and machine learning" *Comput. Intell.*, vol. 36, no. 1, pp. 172–202, 2019.

[8] A. Tayal, A. Solanki, and S. P. Singh, "Integrated frame work for identifying sustainable manufacturing layouts based on big data, machine learning, meta-heuristic and data envelopment analysis" *Sustain. Cities Soc.*, vol. 62, 102383. 10.1016/j.scs.2020.102383

[9] Y. Xiao, J. Wu, Z. Lin, and X. Zhao, "A deep learning-based multi-model ensemble method for cancer prediction," *Comput. Methods Programs Biomed.*, vol. 153, pp. 1–9, 2018.

[10] R. Sathya and A. Abraham, "Comparison of Supervised and Unsupervised Learning Algorithms for Pattern Classification," *Int. J. Adv. Res. Artif. Intell.*, vol. 2, no. 2, pp. 34–38, 2013.

[11] T. Ayer, O. Alagoz, J. Chhatwal, J. W. Shavlik, C. E. Kahn, and E. S. Burnside, "Breast cancer risk estimation with artificial neural networks revisited: Discrimination and calibration," *Cancer*, vol. 116, no. 14, pp. 3310–3321, 2010.

[12] S. Tschiatschek, K. Paul, and F. Pernkopf, "Integer Bayesian network classifiers," *Lect. Notes Comput. Sci. (including Subser. Lect. Notes Artif. Intell. Lect. Notes Bioinformatics)*, vol. 8726 LNAI, no. PART 3, pp. 209–224, 2014.

[13] L. Saitta, "Support-Vector Networks," vol. 297, pp. 273–297, 1995.

[14] J. C. Platt, M. Way, and J. Shawe-Taylor, "nipsFinal.dvi," pp. 1–7, 2004.

[15] S. R. Safavian and D. Landgrebe, "A Survey of Decision Tree Classifier Methodology," *IEEE Trans. Syst. Man Cybern.*, vol. 21, no. 3, pp. 660–674, 1991.

[16] J. Listgarten et al., "Predictive Models for Breast Cancer Susceptibility from Multiple Single Nucleotide Polymorphisms," *Clin. Cancer Res.*, vol. 10, no. 8, pp. 2725–2737, 2004.

[17] M. Waddell, D. Page, and J. Shaughnessy, "Predicting cancer susceptibility from single-nucleotide polymorphism data: A case study in multiple myeloma," *Proc. ACM SIGKDD Int. Conf. Knowl. Discov. Data Min.*, pp. 21–28, 2005.

[18] A. Stojadinovic, A. Nissan, J. Eberhardt, T. C. Chua, J. O. W. Pelz, and J. Esquivel, "Development of a Bayesian belief network model for personalized prognostic risk assessment in colon carcinomatosis," *Am. Surg.*, vol. 77, no. 2, pp. 221–230, 2011.

[19] R. M. Dom, B. Abidin, S. A. Kareem, S. M. Ismail, and N. M. Daud, "Determining the critical success factors of oral cancer susceptibility prediction in Malaysia using fuzzy models," *Sains Malaysiana*, vol. 41, no. 5, pp. 633–640, 2012.

[20] W. Kim et al., "Recurrence Prediction Model for Breast Cancer," vol. 15, no. 2, pp. 230–238, 2012.

[21] A. Lg and E. At, "Using Three Machine Learning Techniques for Predicting Breast Cancer Recurrence," *J. Heal. Med. Informatics*, vol. 04, no. 02, pp. 8–11, 2013.

[22] K. P. Exarchos, Y. Goletsis, and D. I. Fotiadis, "Multiparametric decision support system for the prediction of oral cancer reoccurrence," *IEEE Trans. Inf. Technol. Biomed.*, vol. 16, no. 6, pp. 1127–1134, 2012.

[23] C. Park, J. Ahn, H. Kim, and S. Park, "Integrative gene network construction to analyze cancer recurrence using semi-supervised learning," *PLoS One*, vol. 9, no. 1, pp. 1–9, 2014.

[24] F. Asadi, C. Salehnasab, and L. Ajori, "Supervised algorithms of machine learning for the prediction of cervical cancer," *J. Biomed. Phys. Eng.*, vol. 10, no. 4, pp. 513–522, 2020.

[25] C. J. Tseng, C. J. Lu, C. C. Chang, and G. Den Chen, "Application of machine learning to predict the recurrence-proneness for cervical cancer," *Neural Comput. Appl.*, vol. 24, no. 6, pp. 1311–1316, 2014.

[26] M. Shi and B. Zhang, "Semi-supervised learning improves gene expression-based prediction of cancer recurrence," *Bioinformatics*, vol. 27, no. 21, pp. 3017–3023, 2011.

[27] D. Ho, I. B. H. Tan, and M. Motani, *Predictive models for colorectal cancer recurrence using multi-modal healthcare data*, vol. 1, no. 1. Association for Computing Machinery, 2021.

[28] D. Delen, G. Walker, and A. Kadam, "Predicting breast cancer survivability: A comparison of three data mining methods," *Artif. Intell. Med.*, vol. 34, no. 2, pp. 113–127, 2005.

[29] L. J. Van't Veer et al., "Gene expression profiling predicts clinical outcome of breast cancer," *Nature*, vol. 415, no. 6871, pp. 530–536, 2002.

[30] J. Kim and H. Shin, "Breast cancer survivability prediction using labeled, unlabeled, and pseudo-labeled patient data," *J. Am. Med. Informatics Assoc.*, vol. 20, no. 4, pp. 613–618, 2013.

[31] K. Park, A. Ali, D. Kim, Y. An, M. Kim, and H. Shin, "Robust predictive model for evaluating breast cancer survivability," *Eng. Appl. Artif. Intell.*, vol. 26, no. 9, pp. 2194–2205, 2013.

[32] O. Gevaert, F. De Smet, D. Timmerman, Y. Moreau, and B. De Moor, "Predicting the prognosis of breast cancer by integrating clinical and microarray data with Bayesian networks," *Bioinformatics*, vol. 22, no. 14, pp. 184–190, 2006.

[33] X. Xu, Y. Zhang, L. Zou, M. Wang, and A. Li, "A gene signature for breast cancer prognosis using support vector machine," *2012 5th Int. Conf. Biomed. Eng. Informatics, BMEI* 2012, no. Bmei, pp. 928–931, 2012.

[34] Y. C. Chen, W. C. Ke, and H. W. Chiu, "Risk classification of cancer survival using ANN with gene expression data from multiple laboratories," *Comput. Biol. Med.*, vol. 48, no. 1, pp. 1–7, 2014.

[35] P. Rosado, P. Lequerica-Fernandez, L. Villallain, I. Pena, F. Sanchez-Lasheras, and J. C. De Vicente, "Survival model in oral squamous cell carcinoma based on clinicopathological parameters, molecular markers and support vector machines," *Expert Syst. Appl.*, vol. 40, no. 12, pp. 4770–4776, 2013.

[36] D. W. Kim, S. Lee, S. Kwon, W. Nam, I. H. Cha, and H. J. Kim, "Deep learning-based survival prediction of oral cancer patients," *Sci. Rep.*, vol. 9, no. 1, pp. 1–10, 2019.

[37] L. Kumar and R. Greiner, "Gene expression based survival prediction for cancer patients-A topic modeling approach," *PLoS One*, vol. 14, no. 11, pp. 1–30, 2019.

[38] J. Pati, "Gene expression analysis for early lung cancer prediction using machine learning techniques: An eco-genomics approach," *IEEE Access*, vol. 7, pp. 4232–4238, 2019.

[39] A. M. Noone et al., "Cancer incidence and survival trends by subtype using data from the surveillance epidemiology and end results program, 1992-2013," *Cancer Epidemiol. Biomarkers Prev.*, vol. 26, no. 4, pp. 632–641, 2017.

[40] K. Shedden et al., "Gene expression-based survival prediction in lung adenocarcinoma: A multi-site, blinded validation study," *Nat. Med.*, vol. 14, no. 8, pp. 822–827, 2008.

CHAPTER 7

Prediction of Cervical Cancer Using Machine Learning

Ashish Kumar, Revant Singh Rai, and Mehdi Gheisari

CONTENTS

7.1 INTRODUCTION

As modern medicine progresses, humans have been able to live longer and healthier lives. The human species, which was once petrified by simple bacterial infections, has now easily triumphed over them with the invention of antibiotics. But as modern medicine advances, we are still not able to overcome a roadblock called cancer. Cancer can be classified as a class of diseases that are caused by abnormal formation of cells in the human body. Generally, cells grow, multiply, and die in a continuous cycle. This continuous process helps the body to repair itself when wounded and grow. But sometimes cells do not grow, multiply, and perish in a conventional way. This can lead to the creation of abnormal blood or lymph fluid in the body, which can further develop into a lump or a tumor.

DOI: 10.1201/9781003185604-7

Tumors are further divided into three main categories: benign, premalignant, and malignant. Benign tumors contain cells that are restricted to one area and are not able to spread further throughout the body, but malignant tumors contain cancerous cells that are able to freely move and spread through the lymphatic system or bloodstream in the human body.

An estimated 9.6 million people died due to cancer in 2018. It has become the second largest cause of death in the world and affects one in six people [1]. Some of the most common types of cancer for women worldwide are thyroid, breast, colorectal, cervical, and lung cancer [2]. Cancer trouble keeps on increasing worldwide, applying huge physical, emotional, and monetary strain on people, families, networks, and healthcare systems. People living in developing and low-paying countries, where the health infrastructure is not good, have been especially affected [3]. A good number of missions have been deployed to help these countries to battle cancer effectively. In already developed countries, where the healthcare infrastructure is strong, the living standard of patients and survivability has increased due to early discovery and quality development of treatments (Figure 7.1).

7.2 OVERVIEW OF CERVICAL CANCER

The cervix is an important part of the female reproductive system, along with the fallopian tubes, uterus, ovaries, vagina, and vulva. It forms the lower part of the uterus, which is why it is also called the neck of the uterus. It is shaped like a cone-shaped wedge, separating the uterus from the vagina.

Cervical cancer starts when anomalous cells cultivate and multiply in the inner lining of the cervix. Cancer can spread to the areas around cervix and into tissues of the vagina and/or the lymph nodes. This generally occurs after cancer starts developing in the cervix, called the transformation zone.

7.2.1 Types of Cervical Cancer

Cervical cancer cells are classified into two different categories and are named after the cells in which they propagate. Squamous cell carcinoma and adenocarcinoma cells are the cells where cervical cancer can grow. Aden squamous carcinomas are cells that showcase glandular cells and squamous cells. Small cell carcinoma and cervical sarcoma are other types of cancer that start in the cervix.

Cervical cancer is currently one of the most dangerous forms of cancer that women face worldwide, representing 7.5% of all female cancer fatalities. It is the fourth most malevolent type of cancer confronted by woman globally, with an estimated 570k new cases in 2018 [5]. According to an estimation, every year more than 311k women succumb to cervical cancer, out of which 85% or more cases tend to materialize in impoverished and low-income countries that are very vulnerable due to their developing nature [5].

7.3 CERVICAL CANCER DIAGNOSIS AND TREATMENT IN INDIA

In a country like India, cervical cancer is the second most probable type of cancer, forming around 16.5% of outright cancer cases in the country. It is forecasted that around 160 million Indian women between the ages of 30 and 59 are in jeopardy of developing cervical cancer [6].

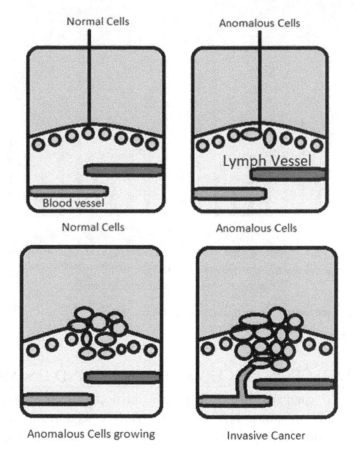

FIGURE 7.1   Growth of cancer in a human body.

Source: Cancer Council Victoria [4].

Woman living in urban areas are more aware of the process and early screening for cervical cancer in comparison to woman living in rural areas. In addition to this, a national screening campaign for cervical cancer is still lacking in the country, curtailing awareness and knowledge that should have spread across the country. As a result, Indian women have little knowledge regarding cervical cancer, its prevention, and its screening.

But in recent years, the government of India has taken an active role in screening for cervical cancer and has launched a new scheme under the National Program for Prevention and Control of Cancer, Diabetes, CVD and Stroke of the National Health Mission. All woman aged 30–64 should be screened every 5 years. The program states that a visual inspection should be done with the help of acetic acid [7].

Cervical screening across India is very inconsistent. In states like Kerala and Maharashtra, the cervical screening rate is very prevalent. It has been observed to be greater than 40% because women are aware of cervical screening. In states like Uttar Pradesh, Bihar, and Uttarakhand, the prevalence of cervical screening is very low, as 10–20% [8] (Figure 7.2).

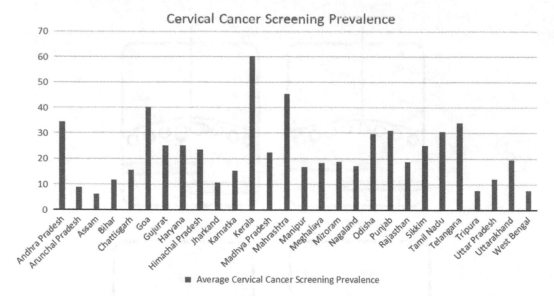

FIGURE 7.2   State-wise average of cervical cancer in India.

Source: Monica, Mishra R. [8].

7.4   EARLY DETECTION OF CERVICAL CANCER AND ITS IMPORTANCE

In underprivileged countries that lack proper medical infrastructure, this malicious disease can be highly noxious. This makes the early detection of cancer much more difficult than in more developed counterparts. Early detection of cancer is a must to prevent it efficiently.

Cancer is one of the toughest enigmas to crack in modern society, and clearly, the human brain is not enough to solve this riddle. That is why humans are employing machines that can calculate complex problems efficiently and quickly. Machine learning is being used to forecast the recurrence-proneness for cervical cancer.

7.4.1   HPV and Types of Screening

The main culprit triggering cervical cancer is called HPV, or human papillomavirus. Although the immune system can tackle the virus, in some cases, the virus can lay dormant inside the cervix, which causes the cells to become cancerous. The HPV test is one effective way to test for it. Cancer can be easily averted if an early screening is able to identify the cause as an HPV contamination.

Cervical screening helps in the early detection of cancer. It can take years for pre-cancerous lesions to form, and they can be left undiscovered. This is the reason why women above the age of 30 should regularly get screened.

There are three types of cervical screening tests that females can apply for. They are: the visual inspection test with the use of acetic acid, the conventional PAP test and liquid-based cytology, and the HPV DNA test for the dangerous HPV virus [9].

It has been observed that the population prevalence of HPV infection is highest around the age of late teens among young adults. The pre-cancer stage starts at mid-20s, showing low population prevalence, and grows steadily until the age of 30. The cancer stage shows up around 30 years, with a slight increase until the age of 45 [10].

Throughout this chapter, we compare various deep learning and machine learning techniques that are being used by researchers now and have been used in the past. Seeing the grave importance of predicting diseases like cancer in the early stages, where they have considerably low risk, and an increase in dependency on cutting edge modern technology that helps doctors to screen and diagnose these diseases, it is right to find out the differences between various models and explore their pros and cons. In the modern world, many new machine learning models are formed by combing old models or taking inspiration from them. Although they may sometimes seem similar, every model has distinct features, practicing a different set of rules to follow and algorithms to run.

In last few years, researchers have been looking into machine learning to help them tackle the problem of cervical cancer in woman. They have been using various machine learning and deep learning (neural network) methods for early detection of cancer to prevent any harm or relapse in patients.

7.5 MACHINE LEARNING-BASED METHODS TO PREDICT CERVICAL CANCER

Lin et al. (2009) [11] devised a mechanism that would investigate used pap smear images of cervical cells for detection of cytoplasm and nucleus, which would further help in segmentation of them. They used a Gaussian filter to remove noise. A two-group enhancement technique was put into the process for further reinforcement of the object relative to the pixels. They further proceeded to use a Sobel operator for computation of gradients found in the pixels in the image and used non-maximum suppression. They found contours to be more accurate than other methods.

Tseng et al. (2014) [12] used support vector machine (SVM), C5.0, and extreme learning machine (ELM) machine learning techniques to find a solution to the problem of recurrence of cervical cancer cells. They processed the data from the database of cervical cancer patients with the help of these machine learning techniques to find out different patterns. They derived patterns that were important to predict different risk groups among patients. They found the correct classification rate of 93.14% being showcase by the ELM model, which had the highest average. Meanwhile, the C5.0 model was only able to generate the average correct classification rate of 91.27%. They concluded that the maximum accuracy rate overall was 92.44% and was showcased by the C5.0 model. A decision tree model was used, and it determined that there was not a relationship with risk factors compared to others. They concluded that the decision tree method was a good method.

William et al. (2018) [13] used an approach of sequential elimination for debris rejection. This was also accompanied with a Weka segmentation classifier. They used a simulated annealing integrated for feature selection with an add-on wrapper filter. They also used a fuzzy C means (FCM) algorithm for classification while also using three different methods to evaluate their classifiers. They were able to attain accuracies of 98.88%, 97.64%, and 95.00%, respectively, for the different types of methods used.

Song et al. (2014) [14] worked to segment cervical cancer cells using convolutional neural network (CNN) and the super pixel method. They were able to use deep learning to detect the region of interest with the help of CNN. An accuracy of 94.50% was achieved for nucleus detection. Their technique could be further developed for automatic detection of cervical cancer in females.

Lu et al. (2016) [15] used the approach of segmenting the nuclei from the cytoplasm that is present in the overlapping cervical cells of the body. Their method works by dark staining the nuclei material, which allows them to identify the nuclei. This is then pursued by identifying the perimeter of cytoplasm by using geometrical constructs. It is divided into four stages. They used a complex dataset, which contained over 900 images of cervical cytology. They used AutoCyte PREP technology to prepare the specimens.

Genctav et al. (2012) [16] used an unsupervised machine learning technique that allowed them to segment and classify cervical cells. Their method was able to differentiate cell regions from the surrounding background by using automatic thresholding. The separated homogeneity and circularity used a hierarchical segmentation algorithm. In the end, they separated the nuclei from cytoplasm using a binary classifier. Their results showed that their approach was very competent and had an accuracy of 96.71%.

Asadi et al. (2020) [17] used various machine learning classifiers to predict cervical cancer and to identify its significant indicators. They used data of more than 145 patients having 23 attributes. The accuracy while using Quest was found to be around 95.5%. Similarly, the accuracy observed by C&R tree was found to be around 95.2%. The accuracy of radial basis function (RBF) was 94.5%. The accuracy of SVM was 93.3%. The accuracy of multilayer perceptron network (MLP) was 90.9%.

Sreedevi et al. (2012) [18] showcased a new algorithm that was used to classify cervical cells as anomalous or normal. They worked on pap smear images and developed an approach for segmentation of the images using the thresholding method. The approach showed sensitivity, specificity, and acceptable overall error rates of 100%, 90%, and 5%, respectively, which were further corroborated by a benchmark database.

Meiquan et al. (2018) [19] used a Faster R-CNN object detection framework, which was developed from R-CNN and Fast R-CNN. Using this, they were able to create an advanced neural network (ANN) that could in turn be used for detecting the target cells and further could be used for classification. Their model was adept at finding out about the five different types of target cells. The model gives a positive precision rate of 0.91. It gives accuracy of 78% for a two-class model, whereas the accuracy for a four-class model is 70%. They concluded that it could automatically diagnose a squamous intraepithelial lesion with good precision and reliability.

Chankong et al. (2014) [20] used FCM for automatic classification and segmentation of cervical cancer cells. Using the ERUDIT dataset, they were able to achieve an accuracy of 97.83%. They used the watershed technique and the hard C-means clustering techniques to compare various classification results with the segmented data. Their result showed that their algorithm can be employed to achieve better accuracy and to retrieve a much better set of features.

Tareef et al. (2017) [21] worked on the segmentation of cytoplasm and nuclei present in a cluster of cervical cells using a method that would automatically segment them. They employed numerous local features and used guide sparse shape deformation. With their approach, they were able to tackle problems like image noise and differentiating complex backgrounds. These methods were also useful when trying to solve the problem of overlapping and fuzzy cells. They used SVM, which allowed them to differentiate the given images into separate nuclei, background, and cellular clusters. They further used Spare Coding theory to develop a cytoplasmic shape for every overlapping cell. To enhance the quality and shape of the subject, they employed the DRLSE model. They concluded that the model was able to obtain nuclear boundaries while outperforming other models very accurately in segmenting overlapping cells.

Plissiti et al. (2011) [22] introduced a robotized strategy for the discovery and limit assurance of cell cores in pap-smear pictures. Watershed transform was applied to attain segmentation of the nuclei boundary, which allowed them to work on reconstruction of morphological dataset images, due to which they were able to identify the candidate nuclei. They were able to find out meticulous nuclei boundaries in the 90 pap-smear images that they used as an evaluation dataset by employing a Gradient Vector Flow (GVF) and active contour model (ACM) model for finding out correlations with their division aftereffects.

Van Belle et al. (2011) [23] compared different SVM-based models to each other, evaluating their regression, ranking, and approaches to further look into survival data. They used five datasets for their experiments. The first one contained data of 129 patients who had leukemia. The second one contained data received from the veteran's administration lung cancer trial (VLC). The third one contained around 500 patients suffering from prostatic cancer, and the fourth one had lung cancer data from the Mayo Clinic, which contained information on around 160 patients suffering from advanced-stage lung cancer. They used data from 720 breast cancer patients for their last dataset. Their experiments showed that the combined approach lagged the regression approach in regards to performance, and it should be chosen when taking performance into consideration.

Athinarayanan and Srinath et al. (2016) [24] worked on classification of cervical images using the SVM method. They started by using normal techniques for processing the image. Then, in the next stage they tried segmentation of cell organelles. After successfully extracting features, they then went on to train SVM to classify normal and anomalous cells. In their algorithm, the color test images of pap smears were turned into greyscale. The researchers then removed noise from the images by using smooth filter. This allowed them to remove noise with blurring edges. Their algorithm showed 86% accuracy for identifying anomalous cells and normal cells. They also used K-nearest neighbor (KNN) and ANN for comparative analysis.

Su et al. (2016) [25] used a two-tier cascade integration system that contained two classifiers. They proposed a system that would automatically detect cervical cancer from extracted pap-smear images. They observed that while using C4.5 and a logical regression classifier, the accuracy rate for anomalous cells was 92.7% and 93.2%, respectively, and while using the two-tier cascade integrated classifier system, the accuracy went as high as 95.6%.

Sharma et al. [26] used KNN for classification of a clinical dataset. They used Gaussian filters to remove noise from the images and improved the quality of the images by utilizing histogram equalization. They used the min-max technique and detection methods for feature normalization. They achieved classification accuracy of 82.9%.

Kwang Balk Kim et al. [27] used a fuzzy RBF network to showcase a new method allowing nucleus segmentation. The method allowed the extraction of cell area from the uterine cervical region. The image obtained was processed through a k means clustering algorithm, which was used to define RGB as its respective R, G, and B channels. It then used different layers to classify different cells and to finally find the abnormal cancer cells.

Mustafa et al. [28] used ANN to extract new and different features of cells. The ANN technique was used to specify abnormal and normal cervical cells that could turn into cancerous cells. This was achieved by using pap-smear images where different colors were specified to different intensity levels.

Babak Sokouti et al. [29] used multi-layer perceptron or a multi-layer neural network that works in two phases. The first phase consists of pre-processing the image, and the second state is used for feedforward of MPL neural networks. Using Levenberg-Marquardt feedforward MLP, the normal cells can be differentiated from the abnormal cancerous cells. This approach shows a very high accuracy.

TABLE 7.1
Comparison of Machine Learning-Based Approach to Predict Cervical Cancer

Authors	Technique Used	Type of Dataset	Accuracy
Tseng [12]	ELM	Chung Shan Medical University Hospital	93.14%
T. Chankong [10]	FCM	Herlev University Hospital, Denmark	97.38%
A. Genctav [16]	Decision tree, SVM, Naïve Bayes	Herlev University Hospital	96.71%
M. Sharma [26]	KNN	Fortis Hospital Punjab	82.9%
Asadi [17]	Quest, C&R tree, SVM, RBF, MLP	Shohada Hospital Tehran	Quest – 95.5%; C&R – 95.2%; RBF – 94.5; SVM – 93.3%; MPL – 90.9
Meiquan [19]	Faster R-CNN	Shenzhen Second People's Hospital	78%
Athinarayanan and Srinath [24]	SVM	Herlev University Hospital	86%
J. Su [25]	C.45 and logical regression	Epithelial cells from liquid-based cytology slides	95.6%
Kwang Balk Kim [27]	Fuzzy RBF network	Samples of cervical cells	80%
N. Mustafa [28]	ANN	Hospital University Sains	94%
Babak Sokouti [29]	Multi-layer perceptron	Aizahra Hospital	90%
Zati Athiar Ramli [30]	Hybrid multi-layered preceptor	Hospital University Sains	89.23%

Zati Athiar Ramli et al. [30] used hybrid multi-layered preceptor, which is a one-hidden-layered neural network. It is made up of different layers consisting of input, hidden, and output layers. Every layer has its own nodes. The first layer, which forms the network, is made of input nodes that are then connected to a hidden layer. Meanwhile, the output layer is connected to the hidden layer using weighted connections forming a non-linear model. The HMLP network input layer acts as the data holder, which further distributes the input to the output layer. It also reduces the false positive rate of cervical cancer while also lowering the sensitivity of the results (Table 7.1).

7.6 CONCLUSION

In this chapter, we gathered and reviewed recent work in which machine learning helped to predict and detect cervical cancer. Machine learning provides a new and innovative way to detect cancer with the amalgation of new learning models and old imaging knowledge. Based on the reviewed work, SVM was found to be one of the most prominent methods in machine learning for detecting cervical cancer in females. The SVM algorithm-based classifier is very prominent among researchers for cervical cancer prognosis. It is also complemented by various algorithms like KNN and fuzzy networks, which can further be used to improve the performance of the results obtained. From a detailed review of the works, we can see that the application of machine learning in the field of cancer prediction is very encouraging. To finish up, the issue of building up a calculation for robotized screening of cervical cells has seen remarkable specialized improvements over the past few years, and in the future these methodologies can be deployed worldwide to help people from every category of society. Broad examination calls attention to different issues that prompt the improvement of a sample-based multistage technique where a specific technique is used to build conclusions of a superior level. Researchers are taking the help of machine learning models not only to predict cancer but also to prevent it from reoccurring in patients.

REFERENCES

[1] Bray F., Ferlay J., Soerjomataram I., Siegel R. L., Torre L. A., Jemal A. Global cancer statistics 2018: GLOBOCAN estimates of incidence and mortality worldwide for 36 cancers in 185 countries. *CA Cancer J. Clin.* 2018 Nov; 68(6):394–424. doi:10.3322/caac.21492. Epub 2018 Sep 12. Erratum in: CA Cancer J Clin. 2020 Jul;70(4):313. PMID: 30207593.

[2] World Health Organization. Cancer country profiles 2014. WHO, https://www.who.int/cancer/country-profiles/en

[3] Jemal A., Center M. M., DeSantis C., Ward E. M. Global patterns of cancer incidence and mortality rates and trends. *Cancer Epidemiol. Biomarkers Prev.* 2010; 19(8): 1893–1907.

[4] https://www.cancervic.org.au/cancer-information/what-is-cancer

[5] Ferlay J., Ervik M., Lam F., Colombet M., Mery L., Piñeros M., Znaor A., Soerjomataram I., Bray F. (2018). *Global Cancer Observatory: Cancer Today.* Lyon, France: International Agency for Research on Cancer.

[6] Bobdey S., Sathwara J., Jain A., Balasubramaniam, G. Burden of cervical cancer and role of screening in India. *Ind. J. Med. Paediat. Oncol.* 2016; 37(4): 278–285. doi:10.4103/0971-5851.195751

[7] Mishra Monica R. An epidemiological study of cervical and breast screening in India: district-level analysis. *BMC Women's Health* 2020; 20: 225.

[8] Module for MOs for Prevention, Control & PBS of Hypertension, Diabetes & Common Cancer.pdf (nhsrcindia.org).

[9] Richardson L. A., Tota J., Franco E. L. Optimizing technology for cervical cancer screening in high-resource settings. *Expert Rev. Obstet. Gynecol.* 2011; 6(3): 343–353. doi: 10.1586/eog.11.13.

[10] Stelzle D., Tanaka L. F., Lee K. K., et al. Estimates of the global burden of cervical cancer associated with HIV. *Lancet Glob Health* 2020; published online Nov 16. DOI:S2214-109X(20) 30459-9 https://www.thelancet.com/journals/langlo/article/PIIS2214-109X(20)30459-9/fulltext.

[11] Lin C. H., Chan Y. K., Chen C. C., "Detection and segmentation of cervical cell cytoplasm and nucleus," *Int. J. Imaging Syst. Technol.* 2009; 19(3): 260–270.

[12] Tseng, C. J., Lu, C. J., Chang, C. C. et al. Application of machine learning to predict the recurrence-proneness for cervical cancer. *Neural Comput. Applic.* 2014; 24, 1311–1316.

[13] William W., Ware A., Basaza-Ejiri A. H., Obungoloch J. A review of image analysis and machine learning techniques for automated cervical cancer screening from pap-smear images. *Comput Methods Programs Biomed.* 2018 Oct; 164: 15–22. doi:10.1016/j.cmpb. 2018.05.034. Epub 2018 Jun 26. PMID: 30195423.

[14] Song Y. et al., A deep learning based framework for accurate segmentation of cervical cytoplasm and nuclei. *Conf. Proc. Annu. Int. Conf. IEEE Eng. Med. Biol. Soc. IEEE Eng. Med. Biol.*

[15] Lu Z. et al., Evaluation of three algorithms for the segmentation of overlapping cervical cells. *IEEE J. Biomed. Health Inf.* 2016; 21(2): 441–450.

[16] Gençtav A., Aksoy S., Önder S. Unsupervised segmentation and classification of cervical cell images. *Pattern Recognit.*, 2012; 45(12): 4151–4168.

[17] Asadi Farkhondeh, Salehnasab Cirruse, Ajori Ladan, Supervised algorithms of machine learning for the prediction of cervical cancer. *J. Biomed. Eng.* 2020; 10. doi:10.31661/ jbpe.v0i0.1912-1027.

[18] Sreedevi M.T., Usha B.S., Sandya S. Article: papsmear image based detection of cervical cancer. *Int. J. Comp. App.*, May 2012; 45(20): 35–40.

[19] Meiquan X. et al. (2018) Cervical cytology intelligent diagnosis based on object detection technology. 1st Conference on Medical Imaging with Deep Learning (MIDL 2018), Amsterdam, The Netherlands (2018).

[20] Chankong T., Theera-Umpon N., Auephanwiriyakul S. Automatic cervical cell segmentation and classification in Pap smears. *Comput. Methods Programs Biomed.* 2014; 113(2): 539–556.

[21] Tareef A. et al., Automatic segmentation of overlapping cervical smear cells based on local distinctive features and guided shape deformation. *Neurocomputing* 2017; 221: 94–107.

[22] Plissiti M. E., Nikou C., Charchanti A. Combining shape, texture and intensity features for cell nuclei extraction in Pap smear images. *Pattern Recognit. Lett.* 2011; 32(6): 838–853.

[23] Van Belle V., Pelckmans K., Van Huffel S., Suykens J. A. K. Support vector methods for survival analysis: a comparison between ranking and regression approaches. *Artif. Intell. Med.* 2011; 53(2): 107–118.

[24] Athinarayanan S., Srinath M. V. Classification of cervical cancer cells in PAP smear screening test. *ICTACT J. Image Video Process* 2016; 6(4): 1234–1238.

[25] Su J., Xu X., He Y., Song J. Automatic detection of cervical cancer cells by a two-level cascade classification system. *Anal. Cell. Pathol. (Amst).* 2016; 2016: 9535027.

[26] Sharma M., Kumar Singh S., Agrawal P., Madaan V. Classification of clinical dataset of cervical cancer using KNN. *Indian J. Sci. Technol.* 2016; 9(28).

[27] Kim K., Song D. H., Kim G. Nucleus segmentation and recognition of uterine cervical pap-smears using region growing technique and fuzzy RBF network. *Image (Rochester, N.Y.)*, pp. 153–160, 2007.

[28] Mustafa N., Isa N. A. M., Mashor, M. Y., Campus, (E.n.d.). *New features of cervical cells for cervical cancer diagnostic system using neural network*, pp. 2–5.

[29] Sokouti B., Haghipour S., Tabrizi A. D. A Framework for Diagnosing Cervical Cancer Disease Based on Feedforward MLP Neural Network and ThinPrep Histopathological Cell Image Features. *Neural Comput. Applic.* 2014; 24(1): 221–232.

[30] Ramli Dzati, Kadmin Ahmad Fauzan, Mashor Mohd, Mat Isa Nor Ashidi. Diagnosis of cervical cancer using hybrid multilayered perceptron (HMLP) network 2004: 591–598. doi:10.1007/978-3-540-30132-5_82.

CHAPTER **8**

Applications of Machine Learning in Cancer Prediction and Prognosis

Geetika Sharma and Chander Prabha

CONTENTS

8.1 INTRODUCTION

Machine learning (ML) has done tremendous work in cancer research. For the past 20 years, decision trees (DTs) and artificial neural networks (ANNs) have been applied to predict cancer and its prognosis. Nowadays, different ML methods are being employed to detect and classify tumors with the help of X-ray and CRT images as being benign or malignant. According to the latest research statistics, 2000+ papers have been published in the field of ML and its application in the field of cancer. Out of these, most of the papers are based on ML methods for detecting, identifying, classifying, or distinguishing cancers and other malignancies. To put it aptly, ML is being widely applied for cancer

DOI: 10.1201/9781003185604-8

119

prediction and prognosis. It has been observed that many cancer researchers have been applying ML towards cancer prediction and prognosis [1], but the literature survey in the domain of ML and predicting cancer and its prognosis is inadequate.

In predicting cancer and its prognosis, the focus is mainly on (1) predicting susceptibility of cancer, (2) predicting whether cancer will reoccur or not, and (3) predicting survivability of cancer. In the first scenario, the attempt is regarding the prediction of the possibility of occurrence of cancer before the development of disease. In the next scenario, the likelihood of reoccurrence of cancer after the cure of the disease is predicted. In the third case, after the diagnosis of the cancer, one is trying to predict the survivability in terms of life expectancy progression or tumor drug sensitivity [2]. In both the 2nd and 3rd cases, the success of prognostic prediction depends upon the quality and accuracy of the diagnosis. But the prognosis of any disease is possible after a prognostic prediction, and medical diagnosis must take into consideration more in comparison with just a simple diagnosis.

The primary aims of predicting cancer and its prognosis are different from the aims of detecting cancer and its diagnosis. In cancer prognosis, many factors play a major role, like clinical factors such as age, the patient's health, the type and place where cancer has occurred, along with the grade and size of the tumor. Multiple physicians from different specialties use diverse biomarkers.

The attending physician should do the prognosis based on demographic (population-based), histological (cell-based), and clinical (patient-based) information, and all this information should be cautiously assimilated, which is not a very easy job. Also, there are many challenges for both patient and physician while doing the cancer prevention and cancer susceptibility predictions. Many factors like age, obesity, bad habits (like smoking, excessive drinking), diet, family history, and any type of environmental exposure (like UV radiation, PCBs, radon, or asbestos) play a vital factor in predicting the probability of developing cancer individually. With the advancement in various technologies like positron emission tomography (PET) scans, micro-computed tomography (CT), magnetic resonance imaging (MRI), DNA sequencing, microarrays, and immune history, any kind of molecule information about patients or tumors is easy to obtain. Many molecular biomarkers also play a major role in prognosis or predictive indicators like the chemical environment of the tumor, the somatic mutation in certain genes, or the appearance of tumor proteins. Moreover, combining these molecular biomarkers has proved to be more predictive. And if these biomarkers are combined with various clinical factors like the type of tumor, family history, or risk factors, then the accuracy of cancer prognosis will be increased. Previously, due to fewer variables like tumor, patient, environment, and population data, and even with the physician's own intuition, cancer prediction was a very difficult job. But at present, with various imaging technologies and high throughput diagnostics, physicians are overwhelmed with hundreds of clinical cellular and molecular parameters [3]. For this reason, we can rely intensively on computational approaches such as ML without the intervention of human intuition. The use of ML in predicting cancer and its prognosis has gained popularity in the medical field. This has helped patients (in terms of quality-of-life decisions) and physicians (in terms of treatment decisions) and also health economists and policy planners for preventing cancer or treatment strategies.

With ever-increasing reliance on ML in predicting cancer, it would be interesting to identify various types and applications of ML methods being used for predicting cancer and its prognosis and also to study the various forms of training data that are assimilated to make various kinds of endpoint predictions and, in the end, the study of various forms of cancers and the overall performance of ML methods in prediction of cancer susceptibility. While predicting cancer and its prognosis, we found that emphasis is mainly on (1) predicting susceptibility of cancer, (2) predicting whether cancer will reoccur or not, and (3) predicting survivability of cancer. Genomic, proteomic, and clinical data are used to make almost all predictions. While doing this survey, we noted many trends, like increasing use of ML methods for predicting cancer and its prognosis by using protein markers and microarray data as well as employing both proteomic and clinical data and dependency on ANN (i.e., an older technology) [4]. Many problems that are commonly noted are too many parameters, overtraining, and a smaller amount of external validation or testing. In the end, it leads to the irresistible conclusion that ML has enhanced the accuracy of cancer prediction and susceptibility and has played an important role in predicting cancer and its prognosis.

8.2   MACHINE LEARNING TECHNIQUES

ML is a subfield of artificial intelligence that learns from the data sample for solving any kind of problem [5–7]. This learning process comprises two steps: (1) identifying the various unknown dependencies in the system by using the dataset, and (2) using these dependencies to produce new outputs of the system. The main focus of ML is on system design, and the knowledge gain from this helps in making predictions that are based on experiences, for example, data in the case of machines. Also, instead of being explicitly programmed for performing certain tasks, ML helps computer systems to perform on their own and also to make data-driven decisions. When these programs are exposed to a new set of data, then they can learn on their own and also produce improved results. In the biomedical field, ML has helped a lot and achieved the desired output by utilizing different algorithms.

ML is categorized into two common types. (1) In supervised learning, each instance of a dataset (i.e., training) is made up of a different input attribute and the desired output, where the input attribute can be taken from any kind of data (for example, any subpart of an image or any database row value or any audio frequency histogram) and desired outputs are generated for each input instance (these values are discrete, real, or continuous in nature) [8–12]. After training the algorithm, it can predict the desired output for a new input dataset, i.e., not being used earlier for training. Examples of supervised learning algorithms are linear regression, support vector machine (SVM), Random Forest, etc. (2) Unsupervised learning is another approach in which different patterns are identified depending on the various input features because the training dataset has no associated desired output. An example is clustering, in which similar data are grouped to identify clusters of data. Examples of this type of algorithm are K-means algorithm, apriori algorithm, hierarchical clustering, etc. The goal of ML is to develop a correlation between input features and one output variable, where features of input data are called "independent variables" and output features are known as "dependent variables" i.e., dependent on input features. Likewise, three other common ML models are classification, regression, and clustering. In classification, which is a supervised learning model, data are classified into one of the trained classes. The model takes separate training data that will act as a key-value pair in the form of data and class labels. The model is trained to classify the new data into classes from the training data (Note: the prediction output will be only amongst the classes present in the training data.) Regression is also a supervised learning algorithm where the model takes in the same training data as used by the classifier, but the output is continuous, unlike classification. Clustering is an unsupervised learning method that takes in a set of data and creates separate clusters. Then, when a new data point is given, it will place it in the corresponding cluster. The model detects the features and clusters the new data based on these features. Also, all the data points with relatively closer features will be placed together in a cluster. There is one more type of ML method. Semi-supervised learning combines the features of supervised learning and unsupervised learning. This model is used when the amount of data that is not labeled is greater than the amount of data that is labeled. Also, for designing an accurate model, labeled and unlabeled data are combined.

On applying any ML method, we have a large number of data samples, each of which constitutes basic components, and these samples are described by various features that further consist of different types of values. For better analysis and the right selection of a method, we should know the type of data being used well in advance. Some common problems that occurred in the analysis were data-related issues and the missing pre-processing steps. Data-related issues can be noise, biased data unrepresentative, duplicate data, missing data, and outliers. By focussing on these issues, we can improve the data quality and hence can improve the quality of the resulting analysis. Also, for making raw data more efficient, we can execute pre-processing step for making some data modifications. Also, other techniques focus on data alteration, i.e., (1) dimensionality reduction, (2) feature selection, and (3) feature extraction. Dimensionality reduction is used to eliminate noise and irrelevant features to make the learning model more robust by decreasing the number of features. For feature selection, three main approaches are followed: embedding, filtering, and wrapper approach. In feature extraction, new features are extracted for making the model work more effectively [13–16]. While developing any model based on ML methods, one has to perform various tasks like classification, prediction, or other tasks that are similar in nature. Classification is a learning function that is employed for classifying data items into classes (predefined classes). A classification model is good enough to fit the training set and should classify all instances accurately. Using any ML method when a classification model is developed may produce a training error, i.e., an error produced on training data, and it also may produce a generalization error, i.e., an error produced on testing data. If the number of occurrences of test error rates of a model is increasing in comparison with training error rates (that are decreasing in number), then this is known as an overfitting problem. The bias variance decomposition method is used to analyze the testing error rates of a learning algorithm, i.e., the error rate of any algorithm can be measured by the bias component of a particular learning algorithm. Other sources of error are known as the variance of the learning method. Above all, the combination of both bias and variance is known as bias-variance decomposition, which is used to determine the overall expected error for any classification model. Since any classification model is obtained by applying one or more ML methods, we need to check the performance of our classification model.

There are various performance analysis parameters used for analyzing the performance of any classification model like precision, specificity, sensitivity, and area under the curve (AUC). Accuracy means the total number of correct or accurate predictions. This accuracy is predicted from the testing set. Sensitivity is defined as the total number of true positives, whereas specificity is defined as the total number of true negatives. In the end, the model's performance is measured in terms of AUC, which is based on the graph drawn for the trade-offs between specificity and sensitivity, known as the ROC curve (Figure 8.1). For analyzing the performance and to obtain more reliable results, we should have large training and testing datasets and should have good knowledge about all the labels of the testing dataset.

There are a few most commonly used methods for performance evaluation like (1) the hold-out method, (2) random sampling, (3) bootstrap, and (4) cross-validation. In the first method, i.e., hold out method, the dataset is divided into training and testing sets, where the training set is applied to develop the classification model, and the testing set is used for analyzing the model's performance. Another method, i.e., random sampling, is almost akin to the hold-out method, wherein the only distinction is that the steps followed in the hold-out method are repeatedly carried out several times for estimating better accuracy. In cross-validation and bootstrap, the datasets are categorized into training and testing sets and then again replaced into the original dataset after they have been chosen for training.

There are ample numbers of ML methods that exist, but we will discuss here only those ML methods that are widely applied for cancer prediction and prognosis, like ANN, DT, SVM, Bayesian network (BN), etc. Also, along with the various ML methods, we will study the different types of integrated data and the methods used for evaluating various ML methods used in predicting and prognosis of cancer based on their performance. The ANN algorithm is a kind of neural network with multiple hidden layers for handling various classification or pattern recognition problems and also for obtaining output as a

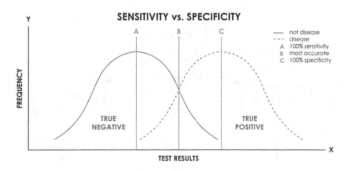

FIGURE 8.1   Sensitivity v/s specificity [17].

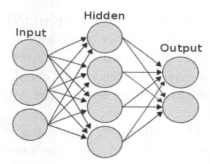

FIGURE 8.2   ANN architecture [18].

combination between the input variables (Figure 8.2). In many research areas [14], ANN has proved to be a gold standard method as a classifier but still has some drawbacks. For example, it is very time-consuming because of its layered structure, which results in low performance. Also, it is very difficult to identify sometimes why ANN did not work or a processing/classification was done. That is why it is classified as a "black box".

Next, the most common ML method and one of the oldest is known as DT, which is a classification technique that looks like a tree in which nodes are input variables and leaf nodes are output. Because of this tree-like structure (Figure 8.3), it is very easy to learn and interpret. We also consider it to be an appealing technique because the outcomes allow for adequate reasoning. Also, when classifying a new sample, we can have complete knowledge about its class by traversing the tree.

Another ML method, i.e., SVM, is a recent approach applied for the prediction of cancer and its prognosis (Figure 8.4). In SVM, the input vector is mapped into a feature space. Then, the hyperplane is recognized for dividing data points into two categories. After that, the distance between the hyperplane and the closest instances to the boundary, which are a lot less, are then increased to make them maximum. This results in making the SVM classifier achieve generalizability and in classifying new samples for obtaining probabilistic output. Bayesian algorithm (i.e., BN) uses a directed acyclic graph for representing the probabilistic dependencies in the variables. It is widely used for reasoning purposes and also used for representing knowledge.

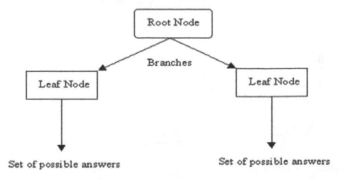

FIGURE 8.3   Decision tree architecture [18].

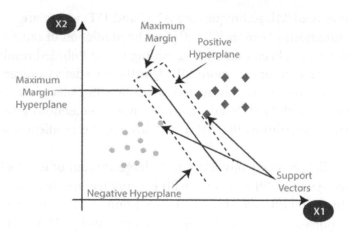

FIGURE 8.4 Support vector machine architecture [19].

8.3 CANCER PREDICTION/PROGNOSIS USING MACHINE LEARNING

For the last two decades, many different ML algorithms have been widely used in the prediction of cancer and its prognosis. These ML methods are used for modeling the progression of cancer, and also various informative factors are being identified that are used in the classification process. Roughly amongst the entire study, available histological parameters, gene expression profiles, and clinical variables are taken as an input in the prognostic procedure. Figure 8.5 shows the total published research papers that use ML in predicting cancer susceptibility, cancer recurrence, and survival. Prognostic prediction is reliant more on medical diagnosis quality. That is why this prognostic prediction is preferably considered than the simple diagnostic decision. Cancer prognosis/prediction deals with three basic predictive tasks: (1) cancer risk assessment, (2) prediction of cancer recurrence, and (3) cancer survival prediction. The first case deals with the probability of developing cancer, and the second case deals with the probability of redevelopment of cancer. Also, the survival outcome prediction is done in terms of disease-specific or overall survival after the diagnosis of cancer or after cancer treatment is done.

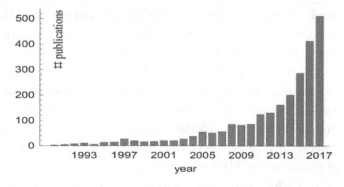

FIGURE 8.5 Distribution of published studies, that employ ML techniques for cancer prediction.

The commonly used ML techniques are ANN and DT, which are widely used in the prediction and prognosis of cancer [20–23]. For the prediction of cancer using ML, more than 10,000 articles have been published according to the PubMed results. Most of these research papers have used one or more ML algorithms to detect cancer. For prediction/ prognosis of cancer type, many researchers used the integrated data from various heterogeneous sources. In the last decade, there has been tremendous growth in the use of supervised learning algorithms like SVM and BN for the prediction and prognosis of cancer [24–27].

For cancer prediction, many physicians use a large amount of topological, clinical, and population-based data [28,29] and along with it many features like weight, age, diet, bad habits, family history, and any exposure to environmental health hazards; these altogether play a major role in the prediction of cancer [30–32]. However, for making our decisions more robust, we require much more information apart from the above macro scale information. With the tremendous use of genomic, proteomic, and various imaging technologies, a unique type of molecular information was delivered. Few factors play a major role in cancer prediction like cellular parameters, gene expressions, and molecular biomarkers. The most challenging task for any physician is to predict any disease outcome more accurately. For this purpose, ML techniques have become an important and popular technique among many researchers. These ML techniques can predict the future outcome of any cancer type very effectively by discovering and identifying patterns from any complex dataset. Apart from this, many feature selection techniques and their applications are published in the literature survey of many research papers [33–35]. Nowadays, based on various genetic defects and different clinical outcomes, a single cancer has been divided into many subgroups. Since genetic defects have different treatment approaches, one needs to identify less costly and effectively small groups of patients. The Cancer Genome Atlas Research Network (TCGA) is a community resource project that provides a large amount of genomic data about specific tumor types and also provides the ability for a better understanding of cancer with the use of high throughput genome technologies.

8.4 USE OF MACHINE LEARNING APPLICATION IN THE CANCER FIELD

Tremendous work has been done due to the application of various ML methods in the field of cancer susceptibility, cancer survivability, and cancer recurrence prediction. Since a large number of research articles are present on the web, we had to select only those articles that are relevant to our interest. Most of these research works have used different types of data like clinical data, genomic data, histological data, demographic and epidemiological data, or any combination of these input data. As it was very difficult to get the survey done for all the papers, a few relevant papers are extracted and reviewed. Specifically, the papers that make use of data from heterogeneous sources and also make use of ML techniques are used in this review in the form of Tables 8.1, 8.2, and 8.3 for cancer susceptibility, recurrence, and survival prediction, respectively. In the following subsections, a survey is made on various objectives of prediction (1) susceptibility, (2) survival, and (3) recurrence by using ML techniques.

TABLE 8.1
Research Publication on Cancer Susceptibility

Research Publication	Cancer Type	Approach Used	Accuracy Achieved	Method Used for Validation	Selected Features
Alagoz O et al. [36]	Breast	ANN	AUC = 96.5% approx.	10-fold CV	Age factor, mammography findings
Shaughnessy Jr J et al. [19]	Multiple myeloma	SVM	0.71 approx.	1-out CV	Single-nucleotide polymorphism-739514, 521522, 994532
Damaraju S et al. [37]	Breast	SVM	0.69 approx.	20-fold CV	Single-nucleotide polymorphism CY11B2
Nissan A et al. [38]	Colon	BN	AUC = 71% approx.	CV (cross-validation)	Tumor history, nodal stages, peritoneal cancer

8.4.1 Cancer Susceptibility Prediction

Out of 61 papers reviewed in this chapter, relatively 45 papers used ML for predicting cancer risk susceptibility. One of these papers piqued our interest (Andres M. Bur et al., 2019), in which the author used an ML algorithm named Decision Forest Algorithm to predict occult nodal metastasis in clinically node-negative oral cavity squamous cell carcinoma (OCSCC). Also, in the end, comparison is made to check algorithm performance with a model based on tumor depth of invasion (DOI). The dataset is taken from the National Cancer Database (NCDB) of the patients who have undergone primary tumor extirpation and non-obligatory neck dissection from 2007 to 2015. By using clinical data from among 700+ patients, many ML algorithms were designed to predict pathologic nodal metastasis. Out of this data, data of 600 patients were applied for validation, and data of 100 patient's data were applied for testing at a single academic institution. Performance was assessed in terms of AUC, i.e., (receiver characteristics). Then, for the two related ROC curves, the performance of the ML algorithm and DOI model were contrasted by using Delong's test. As a result of this test, ML has achieved higher performance in terms of AUC, i.e., 0.840, in comparison with the DOI model, i.e., AUC = 0.657. Also, the ML algorithm has reduced the recommendation of neck dissections, and the sensitivity and specificity have also increased. In cancer diagnosis, treatment planning, and outcome evaluation, brain tumor segmentation has become a vital factor in cancer prediction (Xiaomei Zhao et al., 2018). Fully convolutional neural network (FCNN) and conditional random fields (CRFs) can coalesce in a unified framework for developing a brain tumor segmentation method (novel method) for obtaining segmentation results qua appearance and spatial consistency. Training of these models using 20 image patches and image slices involves the following steps: (1) by using image patches, FCNN is trained; (2) by using image slices with fixed FCNN parameters,

TABLE 8.2
Research Publication on Cancer Survivability

Research Publication	Cancer Type	Approach Used	Accuracy Achieved	Validation Method	Features
Iliyan Mihaylov et al. [39]	Breast	SVR-linear, lasso, kernel ridge, K-Nearest Neighbors (KNN), and Decision Tree (DT)	0.83	5-fold CV	Tumor stage, tumor size, and age
Mogana Darshini Ganggayah et al. [40]	Breast	Decision tree, Random Forest	0.82	Hold-out	Size of a tumor, number of auxiliary lymph nodes which are removed, positive lymph nodes, primary treatment types
Ke W.-C. et al. [41]	Lung	ANN	0.83	CV	Age, sex, node_stage, Tumor_stageERBB2 and **LCK** Proto-Oncogenes
Ali A. et al. [42]	Breast	SSL algorithm	0.71	5-fold CV	Size of tumor, age at the time of diagnosis, total number of nodes
Abdul-Kareem S. et al. [25]	Oral	SVM	0.75	CV	p63 gene, bad habits (drinking, smoking), invasion
Zhang Y. et al. [43]	Breast	SVM	0.97	1-out CV	50-gene signature
Gevaert O. et al. [44]	Breast	BN	0.851	Hold-out	Age, angioinvasion, gradeMatrix metallopeptidase 9 (MMP9), HRASLA and RAB27B (member RAS oncogene family)
Lequerica-Fernández P. al. [45]	Oral	SVM	0.98	CV	TNM_stage (tumor, node, metasis)
Walker G. et al. [46]	Breast	DT	0.93	CV	Age at the time of diagnosis, size of the tumor, total number of nodes
Shin H. et al. [26]	Breast	SSL Co-training algorithm	0.76	5-fold CV	Age at diagnosis, tumor size, total number of nodes, an extension of tumor

CRFs are trained as recurrent neural networks (CRF-RNNs); and (3) the FCNNs and CRF-RNN are refined by using image slices. With this case study, it was proved that SVM achieved an accuracy of approximately 86%, whereas ANN achieved an accuracy of 92%. These results are approximately 10–15% better than chance. Extensive levels of

TABLE 8.3
Research Publication on Cancer Recurrence

Research Publication	Cancer Type	Approach Used	Accuracy Achieved	Method	Features
Goletsis Y. et al. [24]	Oral	BN	0.82 (imaging data), 0.78 (clinical data) and 0.91 (genomic data)	10-fold CV	Smoking habit, tumor thickness, and p53 strain.
Kim K.S. et al. [47]	Breast	SVM	0.89	Hold-out	Invasion of tumor
Ahn J. et al. [48]	Colon	SSL algorithm	0.76	10-fold CV	Breast cancer gene1 (BRCA1), Cyclin D1 (CCND1), Signal transducer and activator of transcription (STAT1), Cyclin B1 (CCNB1)
Lu C.-J. et al. [49]	Cervical	SVM	0.68	Hold-out	Pathologic_S, Pathologic_Tumor
Beheshti et al. [50]	Breast	ANN	0.80	Hold-out	CAPSO-MLP, PSO-MLP, GSA-MLP and ICA-MLP
Yucan Xu et al. [51]	Colorectal	Gradient boosting and gradient boosting machine (GBM) model	0.88	Hold-out	Chemo-sessions, age, **carcinoembryonic antigen** (CEA) and total time duration for anesthesia

cross-validation and confirmation performed are some noteworthy characteristics of this study. The prediction of each method was authenticated in the following manner: 1) 20-fold cross-validation was used to assess and monitor the training of various models. To reduce the stochastic element present in the partitioning of samples, cross-validation was performed five times and taken average of the results for employing a bootstrap re-sampling. 2) The selection process was performed 100 times to minimize the bias factor. 3) Finally, the results were compared with any ML algorithm, and accuracy was calculated. In brief, this chapter illustrates that proper designing, proper data selection, implementation, and validation can produce an efficient cancer risk prediction tool.

8.4.2 Prediction of Cancer Survivability

Along with cancer prediction, nearly half of all research studies on ML were also focused on the prediction of patient survivability (1 or 5-year survival rates).

In Park et al. [42], breast cancer prediction is done, and its survival in woman has also been diagnosed. For this, a predictive model was developed. A comparison was made among three methods: i.e., SVM, ANN, and SSL (secure socket layer); 1,62,500 records are being used as a dataset with 16 different features. For evaluating survivability, a class variable (survivability) was considered that referred to the patients who had survived or the patients who had not survived. A few features were also diagnosed, like the size of the tumor, age, and number of nodes. For evaluation of the performance of these three classifiers, 5-fold cross-validation was employed, and for collecting the most informative features, no preprocessing steps were specified by the author. The whole process of evaluation was proceeded on SEER datasets, and for evaluating performance box-whisper-plot was used, where a small box area of any specific model proves that the model is more stable and robust. After evaluating the accuracy calculated for SVM (51%), ANN (65%), and SSL (71%), the author found that SSL was the best classification model for survival analysis. Also, Chen et al. [41] carried out a study for predicting survival of patients with non-small cell lung cancer (NSCLC) with the usage of ANN as a classifier. For dataset NCI, carry database [52] was used for obtaining clinical data, and gene expression raw data were extracted from NSCLC patients. First, the pre-processing step was done. Then, the author selected genes, namely LCK and ERBB2 (that are considered as most informative survival-associated gene signature). After that, this information was used for training the classifier, i.e., ANN. The ANN model used variables like age, sex, T-stage, and N-stage for calculating an overall accuracy of 83% and for achieving this accuracy. Also, to find an optimal solution for cancer prediction, the author used different ANN architectures. As all the patients were divided into different groups, the study proved that 50% of them had not survived. In another paper, Yucan et al. [51] did extensive research on the survival of prostate cancer patients. For this dataset, approx. 400+ metastatic prostate cancer patients' data was gathered and analyzed from an Indian tertiary care center. The survivability was calculated by analyzing the treatment given to the patients as it affected the patient's overall survival and also the time taken and the difference between the time taken by each method of treatment. Also, the information regarding the time at which medication needed to be changed helped in finding the survival outcome of the patient. The overall accuracy of 84.5% and 0.89 AUC was calculated in this work.

8.4.3 Prediction of Cancer Recurrence

After reviewing so many research papers, we present here the most relevant papers in which the author used ML techniques for the prediction of cancer recurrence.

Exarchos et al. [24] studied OSCC for cancer recurrence prediction. A total of 86 patients were taken as a dataset, out of which cancer had degenerated in 13 patients and the rest were disease free. For this study, decision support system was used to analyze the emergence of OSCC. The authors used clinical, imaging, and genomic data for predicting the degeneration of OSCC with its recurrence. CFS [53] (correlation-based feature selection) and wrapper algorithm [54] were used for feature selection. While selecting any feature from the dataset, bias can be ignored. After applying the feature selection technique i.e., CFS on clinical data (65), imaging (17), and genomic (40), these were reduced to clinical (8), imaging (6), and genomic (7), which were used as the classifiers. When the CFS algorithm was applied, the most informative variables derived among clinical variables were smoking habit, tumor thickness, and p53 strain. The most informative variables among imaging and genomic features were extra tumor spreading; number of lymph nodes; and OXCT2, TCAM, and SOD2 genes. Basically, five classification algorithms, namely BN, ANN, SVM, DT, and Random Forest, were used to identify patients with disease relapse and patients without it. Ten-fold cross-validation was used for evaluating the performance of each ML method. Also, these methods were evaluated on various performance parameters like accuracy, sensitivity, specificity, and ROC curve. The prediction was also made based on the categorization of data after performing the feature selection algorithm and without applying the feature selection method. In the end, the authors declared that the BN classifier without performing a feature selection algorithm on clinical and imaging data had 78.6% and 82.8% accuracy, respectively. When the BN classifier was combined with the feature selection algorithm, then 91.7% accuracy was obtained on genomic-based data. The final stage for the differentiation between patients with OSCC relapse and without it was identified when the authors combined BN with CFS. To prove that the result was robust, the authors used more than one classification method. Also, a comparison of this method was made with other ML classifiers, which shows that the authors' assumption produces more accurate results in the prediction of cancer reoccurrence. Kim et al. [47] predicted breast cancer reoccurrence, called BCRSVM, by using an SVM-based model. The basic idea behind this research was to find or develop a predictive model that tells the possibility of reoccurrence of breast cancer after a survey within 5 years. This author divided the cancer patients into high risk or low risk for better treatment and follow-up planning. The author used three models, namely SVM, ANN, and cox-proportional hazard regression. After making a comparison between these models, the authors found SVM to be the optimal one based on accuracy. Initially, 193 variables were identified in the dataset (clinical, epidemiological, and pathological) of 733 patients. These features were taken as an input to the three classification models. For the performance evaluation, the data were divided into testing and training datasets, and the evaluation was done in the form of accuracy, specificity, and sensitivity. In this evaluation, BCRSVM achieved 84.6% of accuracy, ANN was 81.4%, and Cox-regression was 72.6%. Therefore, in comparison, BCRSVM outperformed. Also, in the end, the authors realized that the most significant factor was the local invasion of tumor in the breast cancer reoccurrence prediction. In Yucan et al. [51], the authors used logistic regression, DT, gradient boosting, and light GBM for predicting reoccurrence of cancer in stage IV colorectal cancer patients. The dataset was divided into training and testing phases for the evaluation of different ML methods. In this study, the author identified that age, chemotherapy, LogCEA, CEA, and anaesthesia time were the five major influential risk factors that played a major role in the reoccurrence of cancer in stage IV colorectal cancer patients. Out of all four ML methods, gradient boosting and GBM performed the best. As in the training group, GBM achieved the highest AUC value of 0.881, and the logistic model achieved the lowest AUC value, i.e., 0.734. Also, gradient boosting achieved the highest F1-score, i.e., 0.912. In the testing phase, the GBM model achieved the highest AUC value, i.e., 0.761, and also it achieved the highest F1-score, i.e., 0.974. That is why the authors claimed that gradient boosting and the GBM model outperformed the other two models, i.e., logistic regression and DT.

8.5 CONCLUSION AND FUTURE SCOPE

ML is widely used to detect cancer of various types, like skin, oral, breast, lung, brain, etc., at an early stage by using different algorithms. In this chapter, many such cases were discussed. First, we introduced cancer and its various types, followed by various ML techniques and their application. After that, an analysis was carried out about the work done so far in this field by various researchers, followed by the various ML techniques used for the prediction of various types of cancer. Then, the process of how cancer is predicted or prognosed using ML was discussed. After that different usage of ML in the field of cancer by discussing its susceptibility, survivability, and recurrence was explained. For the same, an analysis was also done in a tabular form in which different research papers on cancer prediction based on different parameters were compared. As there are many other techniques like deep learning, data mining, etc., for cancer prediction, we can also discuss the applications of these techniques in predicting cancer in the future, which may help us to compare all these methods based on survival rates [55–58].

REFERENCES

[1] Koscielny S. Whymost gene expression signatures of tumors have not been useful in the clinic. *Sci Transl Med* 2010; 2.

[2] Madhavan D., Cuk K., Burwinkel B., Yang R. Cancer diagnosis and prognosis decoded by blood-based circulating microRNA signatures. *Front Genet* 2013; 4.

[3] Polley M.-Y.C., Freidlin B., Korn E.L., Conley B.A., Abrams J.S., McShane L.M. Statistical and practical considerations for clinical evaluation of predictive biomarkers. *J Natl Cancer Inst* 2013; 105: 1677–1683.

[4] Hanahan D., Weinberg R.A. Hallmarks of cancer: the next generation. *Cell* 2011; 144: 646–674.

[5] Witten I.H., Frank E. *Data mining: practical machine learning tools and techniques.* Burlington, MA: Morgan Kaufmann; 2005.

[6] Bishop C.M. *Pattern recognition and machine learning.* New York: Springer; 2006.

[7] Mitchell T.M. *The discipline of machine learning: Carnegie Mellon University.* Pittsburgh, PA: Carnegie Mellon University, School of Computer Science, Machine Learning Department; 2006.

[8] Pandey S., Solanki A. Music instrument recognition using deep convolutional neural networks. *Int. J. Inf. Technol.* 2019; 13(3): 129–149.

[9] Rajput R., Solanki A. Real-time analysis of tweets using machine learning and semantic analysis. In: *International Conference on Communication and Computing Systems (ICCCS2016), Taylor and Francis, at Dronacharya College of Engineering, Gurgaon, 9–11 Sept 2016;* 138(25), pp. 687–692.

[10] Ahuja R., Solanki A. Movie recommender system using K-means clustering and K-nearest neighbor. In: *Accepted for Publication in Confuence-2019: 9th International Conference on Cloud Computing, Data Science & Engineering, Amity University, Noida* 2019; 1231(21), pp. 25–38.

[11] Tayal A., Kose U., Solanki A., Nayyar A., Saucedo J.A.M. Efficiency analysis for stochastic dynamic facility layout problem using meta-heuristic, data envelopment analysis and machine learning. *Comput. Intell.* 2019; 36(1), 172–202.

[12] Tayal A., Solanki A., Singh S.P. Integrated frame work for identifying sustainable manufacturing layouts based on big data, machine learning, meta-heuristic and data envelopment analysis. *Sustain. Cities Soc.* 2020; 62, 102383. doi:10.1016/j.scs.2020.102383

[13] Drier Y., Domany E. Do two machine-learning-based prognostic signatures for breast cancer capture the same biological processes? *PLoS One* 2011; 6:e17795.

[14] Dupuy A., Simon R.M. A critical review of published microarray studies for cancer outcome and guidelines on statistical analysis and reporting. *J Natl Cancer Inst* 2007; 99:147–157.

[15] Ein-Dor L., Kela I., Getz G., Givol D., Domany E. Outcome signature genes in breast cancer: is there a unique set? *Bioinformatics* 2005; 21:171–178.

[16] Ein-Dor L., Zuk O., Domany E. Thousands of samples are needed to generate a robust gene list for predicting outcome in cancer. *Proc Natl Acad Sci* 2006; 103:5923–5928.

[17] https://www.genomenon.com/blog/machine-learning-enhances-specificity-of-variant-search.

[18] Madanan Mukesh, Venugopal Anita, C. Nitha. Designing an artificial intelligence model using machine learning algorithms and applying it to hematology for the detection and classification of various stages of blood cancer. *Int. Conf. Innovat. Tech. Adv. Dis. Manag*, July 2020.

[19] Waddell M., Page D., Shaughnessy Jr. J. Predicting cancer susceptibility from single-nucleotide polymorphism data: a case study in multiple myeloma. *ACM* 2005: 21–28.

[20] Cicchetti D. Neural networks and diagnosis in the clinical laboratory: state of the art. *Clin Chem* 1992; 38: 9–10.

[21] Bottaci L., Drew P.J., Hartley J.E., Hadfield M.B., Farouk R., Lee P.W.R., et al. Artificial neural networks applied to outcome prediction for colorectal cancer patients in separate institutions. *Lancet* 1997; 350: 469–472.

[22] Maclin P.S., Dempsey J., Brooks J., Rand J. Using neural networks to diagnose cancer. *J Med Syst* 1991; 15: 11–19.

[23] Simes R.J. Treatment selection for cancer patients: application of statistical decision theory to the treatment of advanced ovarian cancer. *J Chronic Dis* 1985; 38: 171–186.

[24] Exarchos K.P., Goletsis Y., Fotiadis D.I. Multiparametric decision support system for the prediction of oral cancer reoccurrence. *IEEE Trans Inf Technol Biomed* 2012; 16: 1127–1134.

[25] Chang S.-W., Abdul-Kareem S., Merican A.F., Zain R.B. Oral cancer prognosis based on clinicopathologic and genomic markers using a hybrid of feature selection and machine learning methods. *BMC Bioinforma* 2013; 14: 170.

[26] Kim J., Shin H. Breast cancer survivability prediction using labeled, unlabeled, and pseudo-labeled patient data. *J Am Med Inform Assoc* 2013; 20: 613–618.

[27] Eshlaghy A.T., Poorebrahimi A., Ebrahimi M., Razavi A.R., Ahmad L.G. Using three machine learning techniques for predicting breast cancer recurrence. *J Health Med Inform* 2013; 4: 124.

[28] Cochran A.J. Prediction of outcome for patients with cutaneous melanoma. *Pigment Cell Res* 1997; 10: 162–167.

[29] Fielding L.P., Fenoglio-Preiser C.M., Freedman L.S. The future of prognostic factors in outcome prediction for patients with cancer. *Cancer* 1992; 70: 2367–2377.

[30] Bach P.B., Kattan M.W., Thornquist M.D., Kris M.G., Tate R.C., Barnett M.J., et al. Variations in lung cancer risk among smokers. *J Natl Cancer Inst* 2003; 95: 470–478.

[31] Domchek S.M., Eisen A., Calzone K., Stopfer J., Blackwood A., Weber B.L. Application of breast cancer risk prediction models in clinical practice. *J Clin Oncol* 2003; 21: 593–601.

[32] Gascon F., Valle M., Martos R., ZafraM, Morales R., Castano M.A. Childhood obesity and hormonal abnormalities associated with cancer risk. *Eur J Cancer Prev* 2004; 13: 193–197.

[33] Ren X., Wang Y., Chen L., Zhang X.-S., Jin Q. EllipsoidFN: a tool for identifying a heterogeneous set of cancer biomarkers based on gene expressions. *Nucleic Acids Res* 2013; 41: e53.

[34] Ren X., Wang Y., Zhang X.-S., Jin Q. iPcc: a novel feature extraction method for accurate disease class discovery and prediction. *Nucleic Acids Res* 2013: gkt343.

[35] Wang Y., Wu Q.-F., Chen C., Wu L.-Y., Yan X.-Z., Yu S.-G., et al. Revealing metabolite biomarkers for acupuncture treatment by linear programming-based feature selection. *BMC Syst Biol* 2012; 6: S15.

[36] Ayer T., Alagoz O., Chhatwal J., Shavlik J.W., Kahn C.E., Burnside E.S. Breast cancer risk estimation with artificial neural networks revisited. *Cancer* 2010; 116: 3310–3321.

[37] Listgarten J., Damaraju S., Poulin B., Cook L., Dufour J., Driga A., et al. Predictive models for breast cancer susceptibility from multiple single nucleotide polymorphisms. *Clin Cancer Res* 2004; 10: 2725–2737.

[38] Stojadinovic A., Nissan A., Eberhardt J., Chua T.C., Pelz J.O.W., Esquivel J. Development of a Bayesian belief network model for personalized prognostic risk assessment in colon carcinomatosis. *Am Surg* 2011; 77: 221–230.

[39] Mihaylov Iliyan, Nisheva Maria, Vassilev Dimitar. Application of machine learning models for survival prognosis in breast cancer studies. *Information* 2019.

[40] Ganggayah Morgana Darshini, Taib Nur Aishah, Har Yip Cheng, Lio Pietro, Dhillon Surinder Kaur. Predicting factors for survival of breast cancer patients using machine learning techniques. *BMC Med Inf Decis Mak*. https://bmcmedinformdecismak.biomedcentral.com/articles/10.1186/s12911-019-0801-4

[41] Chen Y.-C., Ke W.-C., Chiu H.-W. Risk classification of cancer survival using ANN with gene expression data from multiple laboratories. *Comput Biol Med* 2014, 48:1–7.

[42] Park K., Ali A., Kim D.A.Y., Kim M., Shin H. Robust predictive model for evaluating breast cancer survivability. *Engl Appl Artif Intell* 2013; 26:2194–2205.

[43] Xu X., Zhang Y., Zou L., Wang M., Li A. A gene signature for breast cancer prognosis using support vector machine. *IEEE* 2012: 928–931.

[44] Gevaert O., De Smet F., Timmerman D., Moreau Y., De Moor B. Predicting the prognosis of breast cancer by integrating clinical and microarray data with Bayesian networks. *Bioinformatics* 2006; 22: e184–e190.

[45] Rosado P., Lequerica-Fernández P., Villallaín L., Peña I., Sanchez-Lasheras F., de Vicente J.C. Survival model in oral squamous cell carcinoma based on clinicopathological parameters, molecular markers and support vector machines. *Expert Syst Appl* 2013; 40: 4770–4776.

[46] Delen D., Walker G., Kadam A. Predicting breast cancer survivability: a comparison of three data mining methods. *Artif Intell Med* 2005; 34: 113–127.

[47] Kim W., Kim K.S., Lee J.E., Noh D.-Y., Kim S.-W., Jung Y.S., et al. Development of novel breast cancer recurrence prediction model using support vector machine. *J Breast Cancer* 2012; 15: 230–238.

[48] Park C., Ahn J., Kim H., Park S. Integrative gene network construction to analyze cancer recurrence using semi-supervised learning. *PLoS One* 2014; 9: e86309.

[49] Tseng C.-J., Lu C.-J., Chang C.-C., Chen G.-D. Application of machine learning to predict the recurrence-proneness for cervical cancer. *Neural Comput & Applic* 2014; 24: 1311–1316.

[50] Beheshti Z., Shamsuddin S.M.H., Beheshti E., Yuhaniz S.S. Enhancement of artificial neural network learning using centripetal accelerated particle swarm optimization for medical disease diagnosis. *Soft Computing* 2014; 18(11): 2253–2270.

[51] Yucan Xu, Lingsha Ju, Jianhua Tong, Cheng-Mao Zhou*, Jian-Jun Yang. Machine learning algorithms for predicting the recurrence of stage IV colorectal cancer after tumor resection. *Department of Anesthesiology, Pain and Perioperative Medicine, The First Affiliated Hospital of Zhengzhou University, Henan, China, Scientific Reports* 2020.

[52] Bian X., Klemm J., Basu A., Hadfield J., Srinivasa R., Parnell T., et al. *Data submission and curation for caArray, a standard based microarray data repository system* 2009.

[53] Hall M.A. Feature selection for discrete and numeric class machine learning 1999.

[54] Kohavi R., John G.H. Wrappers for feature subset selection. *Artif Intell* 1997; 97: 273–324.

[55] Cruz J.A., Wishart D.S. Applications of machine learning in cancer prediction and prognosis. *Cancer Informat* 2006; 2: 59.

[56] Fortunato O., Boeri M. , Verri C., Conte D., Mensah M. , Suatoni P., et al. Assessment of circulating microRNAs in plasma of lung cancer patients. *Molecules* 2014; 19: 3038–3054.

[57] Heneghan H.M., Miller N., Kerin M.J. MiRNAs as biomarkers and therapeutic targets in cancer. *Curr Opin Pharmacol* 2010; 10: 543–550.

[58] Zen K., Zhang C.Y. CirculatingmicroRNAs: a novel class of biomarkers to diagnose and monitor human cancers. *Med Res Rev* 2012; 32: 326–348.

CHAPTER 9

Significant Advancements in Cancer Diagnosis Using Machine Learning

Gurmanik Kaur and Ajat Shatru Arora

CONTENTS

9.1   INTRODUCTION

Medical image evaluation is critical in detecting abnormalities in various organs. Most organ abnormalities result in rapid tumor growth, which is the most significant reason for mortality globally. As per GLOBOCAN statistical data, there were approximately 19.3 million hospital admissions as well as 10 million cancer deaths worldwide in the year 2020. As per statistics, lung cancer was the major cause of mortality, followed by colon cancer, liver cancer, abdomen cancer, and breast cancer, with mortality rates of 18%, 9.4%, 8.3%, 7.7%, and 6.9%, respectively. According to the report, Asia, Europe, and

DOI: 10.1201/9781003185604-9

America accounted for 50%, 22.8%, and 20.9% of all cancer cases, respectively. Cancer deaths in these countries accounted for 58.3%, 19.6%, and 14.2% of total cancer mortality, respectively. The global cancer burden is expected to be 28.4 million new cases in 2040, a 47% increase over 2020 [1].

Magnetic resonance imaging (MRI) [2], positron emission tomography (PET) [3], mammography [4], and computed tomography (CT) [5] are widely used to determine organ abnormalities in humans.

The human brain is a complex organ in the body. An abnormal mitosis mechanism affects the process of morphological cells in the human brain. Cancer cells with various morphological features, such as size and intensity, are formed during this process. There are two kinds of brain tumors: low grade (develops slowly) and high grade (grows quickly and disrupts blood-brain supply). As a result, the vast majority of malignant brain tumor cells have been referred to as neuroepithelial cancer cells. Glioblastoma is a common brain tumor, with 5% prevalence and a patient survival rate of less than 5 years [6]. When compared to neighboring cells, the majority of cancerous cells have low contrast. As a result, accurately detecting brain tumors is a crucial step. The most commonly utilized modality for detecting brain tumors is MRI, a pain-free method that aids in tumor analysis from various perspectives and viewpoints. As a result, MRI analysis is the most effective method for identifying brain tumors [7].

A malignant pulmonary nodule is an indication of lung cancer. Because malignant nodules' fast expansion can impact other organs, it's indeed critical to treat them at an early stage to save patients' lives. Because malignant nodules develop quickly and can significantly impact other parts of the body, it's critical to cure malignancy early [8]. CT scans are the most widely utilized screening methodology for lung cancer. Additional tests are required after a CT scan to diagnose irregularities within the lung [9,10].

Breast cancer is the most common cause of mortality among women. The majority of breast cancer victims are over the age of 50. The World Health Organization (WHO) states that nearly 6,85,000 females across the world passed away from breast cancer in the year 2020 [1]. Breast irregular cells are categorized into two types: (i) non-cancerous or benign, and (ii) cancerous or malignant. Malignant cells have the ability to penetrate and kill adjacent tissues. Malignant tumors are harder to predict at the beginning of the procedure because of their small dimensions and incidence of fatty and thick tissue. Breast tumor end match recognition is also required by advanced automatic or computerized technologies [11].

Skin cancer, abnormal development of unusual skin cells, is among the most common illnesses in the world. It is categorized into two categories: i) melanoma, and ii) non-melanoma. The more dangerous of the two categories of skin cancer is melanoma. It starts on the skin and appears as a dark patch [12,13]. Early recognition and treatment of melanoma may result in a 5-year survival rate of up to 95% [14].

Acute lymphocytic leukemia (ALL) is induced by immature cells within the stem cells. Leukemia cells spread quickly throughout the body and can impact a large portion of the blood and bone-forming cells. Although repetitive and myeloid leukemia are uncommon in children, active childhood leukemia is the most common type. The pathology of leukemic cell development and progeny has been lengthened using particular biological methodologies. This type of hematogenic cell increase is referred to as leukemia. Acute leukemia causes more than 20% of bone marrow blasts. If not treated and managed promptly, it could progress quickly and take one's life within months [15,16].

The liver is an important part of the body that operates necessary functionalities such as drug detoxification, protein production for blood, and blood waste filtering. Despite this, the fact that a human body can be afflicted without warning is remarkable, specifically in the context of a diagnosis of cancer. It is by far the most severe as well as aggressive disease, classified as hepatic cancer. The most prevalent type of liver cancer is hepatocellular carcinoma (HCC) [17]. As per the GLOBOCAN study, it is the sixth primary factor of death in males and the seventh in females. A few possible causes for liver cancer are smoking, excessive body fat, fibrosis, alcohol addiction, and hepatitis B and C [18–20].

A recent scientific field for cancer screening has emerged as a result of various forms of cancer identification and tracking using computer assistance, demonstrating the potential to reduce human system impairments. This review includes state-of-the-art methodologies, research, and comparisons based on benchmark datasets for diagnosis of various types of cancers from the perspective of performance measurement.

9.2   BENCHMARK DATASET

This section presents benchmark datasets that have been used in several trials, analyses, comparative analysis of state-of-the-art cancer diagnosis, and categorization techniques.

- *BRATS 2015*

The BRATS 2015 dataset includes 274 instances, with 192 training instances as well as 82 validation instances. With ground truth, the training examples include both high- and low-grade glioma [21].

- *BRATS 2016*

BRATS 2016 dataset contains 431 data instances, with 285 training instances as well as 146 validation instances.

- *BRATS 2018*

The databases have been modified with even more regular diagnostically obtained 3 T multi-modal MRI scans, as well as all ground truth labels are updated by certified neuroradiologists. There are 476 instances in total, with 285 training instances as well as 191 validation instances.

- *Lung Image Database Consortium image collection and Image Database Resource Initiative (LIDC-IDRI)*

The LIDC-IDRI contains images of nodule illustrations as well as qualitative nodule distinctive ratings. The database, which contains 244,617 images, was created to aid in the research of lung nodules.

- *Wisconsin Breast Cancer Dataset (WBCD)*

The WBCD contains 699 records from human breast tissue Fine Needle Aspirates (FNA). There are nine attributes in each record. The database contains 444 (65%) non-cancerous specimens and 239 (35%) cancerous specimens. It contains 201 instances from one category and 85 instances from the other.

- *Full-Field Digital Mammography (FFDM) database*

The FFDM dataset contains 739 mammograms with 100×100 μm pixel sizes and a 12-bit quantization. It has 287 biopsy-proven mass nodules, with 148 (412 images) being cancerous and 139 (327 images) being non-cancerous. There seem to be 287 tumors, 148 of which are cancerous and 139 are non-cancerous.

- *Mammographic Image Analysis Society (MIAS) Mammographic Database*

The dataset includes 322 encoded films, each with a 1024×1024 image.

- *Digital Database for Screening Mammography (DDSM)*

The DDSM database is a major source of digital mammograms. There are 2,500 sets in the database. Each set includes four images of breast (two for each breast) as well as patient information like age at onset, American College of Radiology (ACR) breast density rank, subtlety rank for complications, ACR keyword explanations of disorders, and image data.

- *International Skin Imaging Collaboration (ISIC) Dataset*

ISIC created open access dermatoscope skin lesion images. It describes the difficulties in classifying nodules, identification of trends in diagnosis, and lesion categorization, as well as verified high-resolution testing and a training dataset of nearly 3000 CC-0 certified pictures.

- *DermNet or Atlas*

DermNet or Atlas is a freely available dataset containing over 23,000 images. It ensures an early detection for 23 types of illnesses, which is further subdivided into 642 sub-types based on taxonomy.

- *PH2 dataset*

The PH2 skin lesion database was created for optimization and scientific work, allowing for comparative studies both on categorization and segmentation algorithms of image information. The dataset consists of 200 RGB-colored images (having a resolution of 768 × 560), 80 of which are benign lesions, another 80 are suspicious lesions, and the remaining 40 are malignant lesions [22–24].

9.3 BRAIN TUMOR

A brain tumor is a clustering of unusual cells that can be categorized into four categories. Brain tumors in grades 1 and 2 grow slowly, whereas tumors in grades 3 and 4 are malignant (malignant), keep growing, and thus are more difficult to manage [25–30]. There are a few initial requirements in tumor diagnosis. The pre-processing step removes the noise as well as non-brain cells first from source images [31]. Non-brain cells are extracted using brain surface extractor (BSE) methods. Otsu threshold, fuzzy C-means, and k-means grouping techniques are by far the most widely used brain tumor segmentation techniques. Likewise, a well-known convolutional neural network (CNN) framework utilized for segmentation of brain tumors is the U-Net architecture. Following the segmentation process, handcrafted features are obtained in order to convert the segmented images into reference points. Histogram orientation gradient (HOG), local binary patterns (LBP), Gabor Wavelet Transforms (GWT), and morphology-based characteristics are among the well-known feature extraction techniques. Furthermore, for optimal feature selection, several feature selection and reduction techniques like principal component analysis (PCA) and genetic algorithm (GA) have been employed. Currently, CNN architecture is thought to be an influential technique for detecting brain tumors. Figure 9.1 illustrates a generalized framework for brain tumor detection.

Vaishnavee and Amshakala [32] proposed self-organizing map (SOM) clustering for brain image segmentation. Histogram equalization was used to extract features before segmentation, which improved the accuracy. The following segmentation procedure,

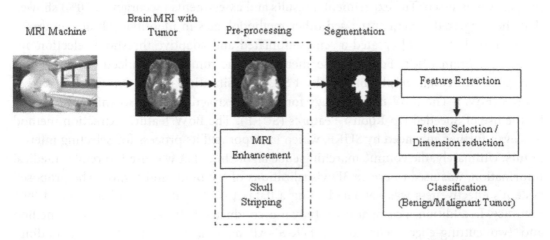

FIGURE 9.1 A generalized framework for brain tumor diagnosis using machine learning.

feature extraction with the gray level co-occurrence matrix (GLCM) was utilized to prevent the presence of mis-clustered areas. To improve classification performance, the PCA approach was employed for selecting features. Furthermore, proximal support vector machine (PSVM) was utilized to detect tumors in the MRI database. Under noisy or poor intensity normalization circumstances, the PSVM-GLCM-PCA method is a trustworthy strategy. The presented system is highly efficient for classification, with good accuracy (92%), sensitivity (94%), and specificity rate (93%) in classifying normal or abnormal brain images.

Nie et al. [33] presented deep learning approaches in order to extract features from a multimodal pre-operative image database of high-grade glioma patients. In particular, three-dimensional (3D) CNNs were used, as well as a newly developed network structure that uses multi-channel data to learn supervised features. SVM was used in addition to the key clinical features to estimate the subject's survival time. The test findings showed that the presented approaches can attain accuracy of up to 89.9%.

Ellwaa et al. [34] implemented an iterative random tree-based automated segmentation technique for MRI-detected brain tumors. Iteratively, the accuracy of the subject was improved with precise information employed using Random Forest categorization. The method was put to the test at BRATS-2016. The screening criteria for the person with the most knowledge resulted in positive results. However, hardly any justification for the selection criteria was supplied, so accuracy findings were presented.

Abbasi and Tajeripour [35] presented a fully automatic technique for identifying brain tumors in 3D images. The bias field adjustment and histogram comparison were employed for image pre-processing during the first stage. The region of interest was then segregated from the backdrop of the Flair image in the following step. The learning features were indeed an LBP in three orthogonal pPlanes (LBP-TOP) and a HOG in three orthogonal planes (HOG-TOP). Because 3D images were being used in the said study, the authors extended histogram direction gradients for 3D data using the concept of an LBP in three different directions. After that, the Random Forest (RF) approach was used to section tumorous areas. The effectiveness of the algorithm on BRATS 2013 glioma images was assessed. The experimental results and assessments (accuracy of 70%) showed that the suggested system surpassed other methodologies in identifying brain tumors.

Mehmood et al. [36] created a semi-automated and adaptive threshold selection approach for brain MRIs. Following segmentation, the tumor was indeed categorized as malignant or benign, employing a robust SVM classification model driven using Bag of Words (BoW). The BoW methodology for feature extraction was also enhanced further by the use of Speeded Up Robust Features (SURF). The BoW feature extraction method was even further enhanced by SURF, which incorporated its process for selecting interest points. Ultimately, the volume marching cube algorithm, that was used to render medical information, was used to create 3D visualizations of the brain and tumor. The proposed system's effectiveness was validated using a dataset of 30 patients, and it attained 99% accuracy. In addition, a comparative study was conducted between the developed method and two cutting-edge technologies, ITK-SNAP as well as 3D-Doctor. The findings indicate that the suggested framework outperformed current frameworks in terms of assisting radiologists in assessing the size, structure, and position of the brain tumor.

Das et al. [37] used texture-based features to distinguish between healthy and unhealthy biological samples. The researchers used 80 images of healthy and diseased tissue acquired from Gauhati Medical College and Hospital (GMCH), Guwahati Hospital. The features included 172 features from five texture communities: GLCM, Grey Run Length Matrix (GRLM), Tamura, HOG, and LBP. Each feature set's performance was evaluated individually and collaboratively utilizing quadratic discriminant, linear discriminant, logistic regression, SVM, and K-nearest neighbor (KNN) models. Each feature set's performance was assessed individually and collaboratively utilizing quadratic discriminant, linear discriminant, logistic regression, SVM, and KNN classification models. Tamura's feature, local second order GLCM, and global low order histogram outperformed LBP and GRLM's local texture metrics. Using a combination of five textural characteristics in 80 cancerous and non-cancerous images at 10x magnification, an optimized accuracy (100%) was achieved. They came to the conclusion that the computerized framework could result in improved detection because childhood brain tumors are extremely dangerous. Using multiple classifiers slows down the system and increases the computational cost.

Iqbal et al. [38] utilized long short-term memory (LSTM) and CNN to present deep learning techniques for effective tumor demarcation from reference image data. The CNN and LSTM networks, as well as their ensembles, were trained using the MICCAI BRATS 2015 brain tumor database, which included MRI images from four different modalities. Numerous variations of pre-processing methodologies, like removal of noise, histogram equalization, and texture features, were developed to increase the input images quality, and the best performer combination was used. Class weighting was used in the developed model to tackle the issue of class imbalance. The trained models were evaluated on authentication datasets derived out of the same image set, and the results of every model were confirmed. The accuracy of the CNN, LSTM-based, and ensemble models was found to be 75%, 80%, and 82.29%, respectively.

Saba et al. [39] employed the Grab cut technique in the presented design for automatic identification of actual lesion health conditions, whereas the transfer learning prototype Visual Geometry Group (VGG-19) was great to obtain the characteristics, that were prefixed with shape and texture created with a serial-based model. These characteristics were enhanced utilizing entropy for faster and more efficient categorization, and classification models were given a fusion vector. The framework described here was verified using the leading benchmark datasets in 2015, 2016, and 2017, which include multimodal tumor segmentation (BRATS). The Dice Similarity Co-efficient (DSC) test findings obtained were 0.99 in BRATS 2015 and BRATS 2017; however, it was 1.00 in BRATS 2016. They also does not test the feasibility of their method using another classification model or their hybrid to test the feasibility of developed method.

Ramzan et al. [40] efficiently informed end-to-end modeling among MRI volumes and voxel-level brain sections using 3D CNN with residual learning and substantial convolution. Using information from various sources, mean dice scores of 0.879 and 0.914 were obtained for three and nine regions of the brain, respectively. Comparative analysis revealed that proposed system performed better than the state-of-the-art in certain regions of the brain. Furthermore, the mean dice score of 0.903 acquired for eight brain areas differentiation using the MRBrains18 dataset was better than the previous work's 0.876.

Nayak et al. [28] proposed an intelligent deep CNN dependent architecture for diagnosing a variety of brain disorders. The model was tested on MD 1 and MD 2 databases, and it achieved accuracy rates of 100.00% and 97.5%, respectively. On the same databases, four skilled CNN models using the transfer learning approach were evaluated. The proposed method was found to be superior to existing schemes in a comparative study.

For Gliomas classification, a CNN ResNet with pyramid dilated convolution was proposed by Lu et al. [27]. ResNet's base included the pyramid dilated convolution to boost the original network's dynamic range and enhance predictive accuracy. Following the addition of pyramid dilated convolution framework, the receptive field of the current infrastructure underpinning convolution had been significantly enhanced. The developed model was tested using a clinical database. Studies were conducted out on a local set of data, and the glioma recognition rate achieved was 80.11%. However, they really do not have a benchmark dataset in their experimental studies.

The aforementioned approaches used to detect brain tumors, the methodologies used, the dataset, and their findings are summarized in Table 9.1.

TABLE 9.1
An Overview of the Methods Used to Detect Brain Tumor

Reference	Method	Dataset	Outcome
Vaishnavee and Amshakala [32]	PSVM	BRATS 2015	– Accuracy 92% – Sensitivity 94% – Specificity 93%
Nie et al. [33]	3D-CNN with SVM	Self-created	– Accuracy 89.9% – Sensitivity 92.19% – Specificity 88.22 – Positive predictive rate 84.44% – Negative predictive rate 95.57%
Abbasi and Tajeripour [35]	Random Forest (RF)	BRATS 2013	– Accuracy 70%
Mehmood et al. [36]	BoW-SURF based SVM	Lady Reading Hospital	– Accuracy 99.9% – Sensitivity 96% – Specificity 99% – False positive rate 0.05 – False negative rate 0.099 – F-measure 0.98
Das et al. [37]	Fusion of multiple classifiers	GMCH	– Accuracy 100%-AUC 1.00
Iqbal et al. [38]	CNN	BRATS 2015	– 82.29%
Saba et al [39]	VGG 19	BRATS 2015; BRATS 2016; BRATS 2017	– Accuracy 98.78% – Accuracy 99.63% – Accuracy 99.67%
Ramzan et al. [40]	3D CNN	From various sources	– Mean dice score 0.903
Nayak et al. [18]	CNN	Multi-class brain MRI databases, MD-1 and MD-2	– Accuracy 100.00% (on MD 1 dataset) – Accuracy 97.5% (on MD 2 dataset)
Lu et al. [17]	CNN	Local medical dataset	– Accuracy 80.11%

9.4 LUNG CANCER

Lung cancer is among the top causes of mortality worldwide. If the nodule is relatively small, a wide range of medical treatments would then benefit a number of patients. Unfortunately, because a few people have no symptoms in the initial stages of disease, detecting progressive sickness, neual advancement, and metastases illness emerges later in 75% of lung cancer cases. According to an Australian study, people with cancer have a 15% chance of survival [41]. Many other studies have revealed their findings in classifying and detecting lung nodules employing the LIDC-IDRI dataset. The dataset includes over 2,40,000 nodule pictures.

By processing image data created using artificial intelligence techniques, machine learning methodologies aid in the initial diagnosis and assessment of lung nodules. These systems are referred to as decision support systems, and they evaluate images using pre-processing, segmentation, extraction of features, and categorization phases.

Multi-CNN (MCNN) was utilized for extracting the discriminative information from stacked layers in order to obtain nodular heterogeneity. Lung nodule test and annotation were utilized to verify the proposed technique. Three CNNs were utilized in the MCNN framework in this technique, with nodule patches that run parallel, of various sizes arranged as input data. The researchers used the LIDC-IDRI dataset, and the segmentation technique had a 97% accuracy rate. Figure 9.2 depicts a generalized approach for detecting lung cancer.

Setio et al. [42] suggested a technique for detecting pulmonary nodule by training a multi-view CNN. Three techniques, huge solid, sub-solid, and solid, were blended to identify only potentially malicious tumors. On the LIDC-IDRI database, which is freely available to the public, the implemented model was trained and evaluated. The research work attained a sensitivity level of 85.4% at one false-positive and 90.1% at four false-positives per test. An added assessment was carried out using independent databases from the ANODE09 challenge and the Danish Lung Cancer Screening Trial (DLCST).

Dou et al. [43] implemented a novel approach for lowering false positives in automatic pulmonary nodules' diagnosis from volumetric CT scan results using 3D CNNs. They

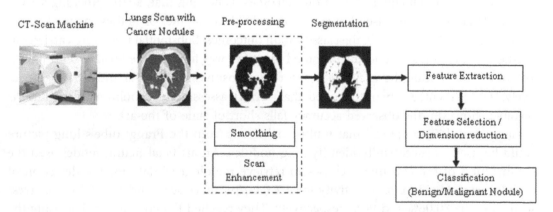

FIGURE 9.2 A generalized approach for lung cancer detection using machine learning.

also proposed a simple yet efficient technique for encoding multi-level contextual information to overcome the difficulties posed by pulmonary nodule variations and hard imitates. The conceptual methodology was extensively validated within the LUNA16 issue, which was carried out in tandem with International Symposium on Biomedical Imaging (ISBI) 2016, in which the maximum competition performance metric (CPM) rank in the false positive reduction track was accomplished.

Shen et al. [44] introduced a multi-crop CNN (MC-CNN) for extracting valuable knowledge from nodule through the use of an innovative multi-crop pooling technique. The results obtained showed that the developed method produced promising outcomes of recognition rate (87.14%) and area under the ROC curve (AUC) outcome (0.93). Furthermore, semantic forecasting and size prediction confirmed the proposed approach's ability in describing nodule-related details.

Van-Griethuysen et al. [45] proposed PyRadiomics for the identification of tumors in order to distinguish between cancerous and non-cancerous nodules. To provide front end code for the 3D slicer, they utilized publicly accessible LIDC dataset and a Python-implemented algorithm.

Tahoces et al. [46] suggested a technique for measuring 3D arterial lumen geometry via an initial contour inside it using a simple incremental approach. The proposed algorithm in 380 of 385 CT cases, the algorithm correctly monitored the aorta geometric features. For aorta cross-section chosen at random from the entire database, the mean dice similarity index was 0.951. For sixteen specific cases, the average distance to a manual process demarcated differentiation of the aortic lumen was 0.9 mm. The suggested solution is remarkable in terms of effectiveness, as well as a high-quality result might be obtained in both common and rare circumstances. The experimental set-up, however, had not been described in detail, and the outcomes also weren't correlated with the state-of-the-art.

To enhance the CT reading process, Xie et al. [47] introduced an automated 2D neural CNN lung nodule identifier. For identifying nodule representatives, they first modified the framework of faster region-based CNN (R-CNN) with two region fully convolution systems and a de-convolution layer, and afterwards three frameworks were designed for three types of slices for subsequent fusion off outcomes. Following that, a strengthening system was created to minimize false positives. Ultimately, the outcomes of all these networks were combined in order to identify the classification outcomes. Substantial tests were carried out on the LUNA16 dataset, and the proposed identifier was found to be 86.42% sensitive. At 1/8 and 1/4 FPs/scan, the accuracy rate for false positives was 73.4% and 74.4%, respectively. The presented scheme revealed that correct assessment of pulmonary nodules is possible. However, the observed accuracy falls short of state-of-the-art.

Jiang et al. [48] proposed that multi-patches cut from the Frangi tube's lung picture could be used to successfully identify lung nodules. An artificial neural model used the combination of the two image classes to retrieve radiologists' data for the detection of nodules from four layers. Sensitivity for 4.7 false-positives/scan and 15.1 false-positives/scan could be 80.06% and 94%, respectively. They reached the conclusion that using the patch-based supervised learning technique in various groups significantly improves performance and reduces false-positives in large amounts of digital images.

Naqi et al. [49] presented a four-step architecture for identifying and diagnosing nodules. First and foremost, the lung area was abstracted using the optimal gray-threshold ascertained through Darwinian particle optimization. Then, in a parametric system, a new technique for identifying candidates was presented, concentrating on the nodules' spatial well-being. Following that, a blended geometrical texture summary was created to best reflect the candidate nodule. Lastly, a deep thinking concept was developed to all those false-positive effects, focusing mostly on piled auto encoder and softmax. The largest publicly available registries, the Lung Image Database Co-operation and the Image Database Network Project, demonstrated that the given solution provided 2.8 false-positives/scan, with an encouraging 95.6% sensitivity. The results emphasize the method's significance through automatic nodule tracking and identification. Furthermore, radiologists would be able to detect nodules with greater precision as a result of this. Subsequently, Naqi et al. [50] proposed an adaptive nodule recognition and grouping technique. First, the lung region was retrieved using the best gray-level criterion. Following that, a hybrid approach was addressed, which relied on the Active Contour Model (ACM), 3D nearby interconnection, and geometry. A fusion feature vector was formed for each nodule candidate by incorporating spatial texture and HOG lowered by PCA (HOGPCA) characteristics. Following extracting features, four different classifiers were used to classify data: Naive Bayesian, k-NN, SVM, and AdaBoost. The LIDC database was used to evaluate the developed classifiers. In terms of performance measures, AdaBoost clearly outperformed all the other classification models. The proposed methodology produced superior results, especially when compared to previously described methodologies in the literature. Although, the approach taken by Naqi et al. [50] is computationally intensive and necessitates the use of multiple resources, its accuracy is not superior to others identified as state-of-the-art.

Asuntha and Srinivasan [51] developed a novel methodology for detecting cancerous lung nodules in a specific lung image and classifying lung cancer and its seriousness. They employed the best feature extraction methods, including HoG, wavelet transform-based characteristics, LBP, Scale Invariant Feature Transform (SIFT), and Zernike Moment. Furthermore, the fuzzy particle swarm optimization (FPSO) approach was utilized to identify the optimal characteristics. In addition, the real-time dataset from Arthi Scan Hospital was examined. The authors found that the novel FPSO-based CNN (FPSOCNN) outperformed other methodologies.

Saba [12] described an automated strategy for detecting and classifying lung nodules that included lesion enhancement, segmentation, and feature extraction of each candidate's tumor. Furthermore, k-fold cross-validation, logistic regression, multilayer perceptron, and voted perceptron classifiers were evaluated in order to categorize lung nodules. The proposed method was tested using the LIDC benchmark dataset, which is freely available to the public. According to the performance assessment, the developed approach outperformed the state-of-the-art method and attained a 100% accuracy rate.

On the LIDC-IDRI dataset, Table 9.2 compares current lung cancer detection methods.

TABLE 9.2

Comparison of Existing Lung Cancer Diagnosis Methodologies on the LIDC-IDRI Dataset

Reference	Method	Dataset	Outcome
Setio et al. [42]	ConvNets	LIDC-IDRI	– Sensitivity 85.4% at 1FP/scan – Sensitivity 90.1% at 4 FPs/scan
Shen et al. [44]	Multi-crop convolutional neural network (MC-CNN)	LIDC-IDRI	– Accuracy 87.14% – Sensitivity 77% – Specificity 93% – AUC 0.93
Xie et al. [47]	2D neural CNN, faster R-CNN	LIDC-IDRI	– Accuracy 86.42% – Sensitivity 73.4% and 74.4% at 1/8 and 1/4 FPs/scan
Jiang et al. [48]	Frangi filter with 4-channel CNN	LIDC-IDRI	– At 4.7 and 15.5 FPs/scan, sensitivity is 80.06% and 94% respectively.
Naqi et al. [49]	For dimension reduction and categorization, a deep learning approach based on stacked autoencoders and softmax was utilized	LIDC-IDRI	– Accuracy 96.9% – Sensitivity 95.6% – Specificity 97% – FPs/scan (2.8)
Naqi et al. [50]	SVM, K-NN, AdaBoost, and Naïve Bayes	LIDC	AdaBoost results: Accuracy 99.2% – Sensitivity 98.3% – Specificity 98% – FPs/scan (3.3)
Asuntha and Srinivasan [51]	HoG, LBP, SIFT, WT, and Zernike moment feature descriptor	LIDC	– Accuracy 95.62% – Sensitivity 97.93% – Specificity 96.32%
Saba [12]	Multiple classifiers voting	LIDC	– Accuracy 100%

9.5 SKIN CANCER

Machine-assisted approaches using dermoscopic image data have indeed been developed in recent years to assist dermatologists in clinical decision making and to identify extremely suspicious instances. These approaches might be utilized as an additional tool by inexperienced healthcare professionals for performing an evaluation and enhancing treatment follow-up [52,53]. In terms of constructive feature extraction from dermoscopic images, these systems are roughly categorized into two classes. One category utilized surgical procedure to diagnose and immediately obtain the same clinical attributes such as uniformity, multiple colors, and unusual differential structures. The other class discovered the patterns in the dataset utilizing machine learning and implemented them with the image's texture and color characteristics [54]. The majority of the work entails the creation of novel machine learning methods for feature extraction, including the Asymmetric information, Border abnormality, Color variation, and Diameter (ABCD) rule, a three-point check-list. As a result, deep convolutional neural networks

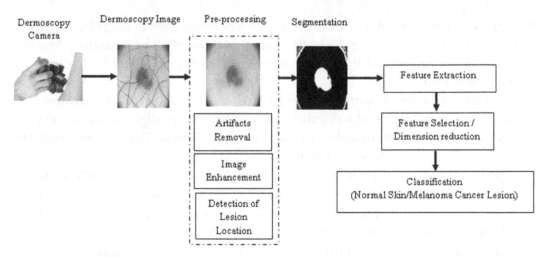

FIGURE 9.3   A general system for skin cancer detection utilizing machine learning.

(DCNNs) achieved significant success in the area of image analysis, where characteristics are primarily generated from digital images.

Figure 9.3 shows a general system for detecting skin cancer.

In an approach identified by Ramya et al. [55], the authors used dynamic histogram equalization methodology as well as a wiener filter for the pre-processing step. They had an active contour segmentation method in their research. The system's features were derived utilizing GLCM, however, for classifying the skin lesion as cancerous or non-cancerous, the researchers used an SVM classification model that had a sensitivity, accuracy, and specificity of 90%, 95%, and 85%, respectively. However, they carried out experiments on a small sample size.

Premaladha and Ravichandran [56] recommended a smart framework for accurate melanoma prediction and classification. Contrast enhancement methodologies include the median filter and contrast-limited adaptive histogram equalization. The innovative segmentation methodology was utilized for separating the nodule from the skin, thus also reducing the issue of differential luminance. From the image segmentation, 15 features were derived and supplied into the trained framework. The prototype was evaluated and validated using nearly 992 images of cancerous and non-cancerous tumors, and it attained an accuracy rate of 93%.

Bareiro Paniagua et al. [13] used dermoscopic images for determining the tumor's malignancy. Following the removal of unwanted hair, the ABCD rule had been used to extract the features from previously segmented affected areas. Finally, utilizing SVM, lesions were categorized as cancerous or non-cancerous. On a database of 104 dermoscopy images, the proposed framework had accuracy, sensitivity, and specificity of 90.63%, 95%, and 83.33%, respectively. These findings are encouraging in terms of diagnosis performance based on traditional advancement in the dermatology domain.

Khan et al. [57] used an approach with various stages, including image enhancement, segmentation, as well as extraction of features, preceded by the use of such features for training and validation of a chosen classifier. They empirically evaluated the proposed technique's effectiveness using the widely known LIDC-IDRI. The outcomes (sensitivity rate of 97.45%) showed that the methodology is remarkably successful for lowering false positive rates (FPRs).

Likewise, Aima and Sharma [58] used CNN to detect initial stage melanoma skin cancer. The proposed method was tested on a 514 dermoscopy digital image dataset from the ISIC repository, which included 138 melanoma skin lesions. The proposed model had 74.76% accuracy and 57.56% validation loss.

Dai et al. [59] used a dataset of 10,015 skin cancer images to train a CNN model. The model was then dispatched on a smart phone, in which the phenomenon of inference occurred, i.e., when introduced to a test dataset, only some simulations were conducted locally whereas the test data managed to remain. With 75.2% model accuracy, this method reduced latency, saved bandwidth, and enhanced confidentiality.

Saba et al. [60] developed a new automated technique for detecting and recognizing skin lesions that makes use of a DCNN. The implemented series structure included three main stages: a) contrast improvement via fast local Laplacian filtering (FlLpF) along hue saturation value (HSV) color transition; b) lesion boundary retrieval via color CNN strategy through the use of exclusive OR process; and c) in-depth feature extraction learning through the use of Inception V3 framework before the fusion of features via hamming distance (HD). For the selection of its most discriminant attributes, an entropy-regulated feature selection technique was incorporated. The authors reported that their technique outperformed existing techniques on some of the benchmark datasets, with accuracy of 98.4%, 95.1%, and 94.8%, respectively.

Readers can refer to Arthur and Hossein [61], and Barata et al. [52] for in-depth reviews of skin cancer. Table 9.3 compares the aforementioned methods for detecting skin cancer.

9.6 ACUTE LYMPHOBLASTIC LEUKEMIA (ALL)

ALL is a kind of bone marrow and blood cancer. In the literature, various computer-assisted ALL categorization methods in healthcare systems are recorded [62,63]. Differentiation of white blood cells (WBC) entails distinguishing the cell from its surroundings, frequently by identifying the cytoplasm as well as nucleus of the cell [64]. This seems to be simple to achieve with image processing operations found in medical technological advances. Figure 9.4 illustrates a general methodology to ALL detection. A few of the stages reported in the literature [65,66] include transferring an image to a distinct color space, contrast flexing, thresholding, cauterization, water-shedding, as well as anatomical filtration. These stages may result in source images of white WBC components that can be used to mask the actual color image. WBC segmentation has been used in several papers to take advantage of morphological findings from grayish image data. Contrast stretching was used to highlight the nuclei of WBCs because they stain darker than most of the other blood components. The WBC diameters were then averaged to create a morphological filter. Using this morphological filter improved WBC

TABLE 9.3
Existing Methods, Datasets, and Outcomes For Detecting Skin Lesions

Reference	Method	Dataset	Outcome
Ramya et al. [55]	SVM	ISIC	– Accuracy 95% – Sensitivity 90% – Specificity of 85%
Premaladha and Ravichandran [56]	Neural networks, hybrid AdaBoost SVM	Skin cancer and benign tumor image Atlas – contents	– Accuracy 91.7% – Sensitivity 94.1% – Specificity 88.7% – Kappa 0.83%
Bareiro Paniagua et al. [13]	SVM	PH2	– Accuracy 90.63% – Sensitivity 95% – Specificity 83.33%
Khan et al. [57]	SVM	Lungs image consortium database	– Sensitivity 97.45%
Aima and Sharma [58]	CNN	ISIC	– Accuracy 74.76% – Validation loss 57.56%
Dai et al. [59]	CNN	Dermatoscopic image dataset	– Accuracy 75.2% – Validation loss 0.71
Saba et al. [60]	DCNN	PH2, ISBI 2016 and ISBI 2017	– Accuracy 98.4%, 95.1%, and 94.8% on PH2, ISBI 2016, and ISBI 2017 dataset, respectively.

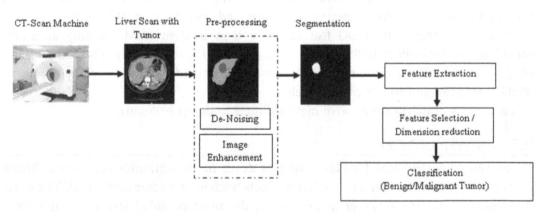

FIGURE 9.4   A generalized methodology for detecting ALL utilizing machine learning.

nuclei whilst also decreasing narrower blood components. Such stages resulted in high-accuracy fixed-dimension sub-images that included centrally located WBCs. Putzu et al. [67] enhanced on just this approach by adding color-space conversion and thresholding stages. Watershed segmentation was also used to separate grouped WBCs, with 92% accuracy.

Normally, health professionals manually check microscopic images to identify ALL, which is a time-consuming and inaccurate process. Patel and Mishra [68] developed an automated method for detecting leukemia early on. They suggested several filtration techniques (k-state categorizing, histogram coordination, and zack) as well as performed classification utilizing. The suggested method was simulated in MATLAB, with a 93.57% accuracy.

In order to identify malignant instances, Khalilabad and Hassanpour [69] created an automated framework for data analysis from microarray image datasets. The proposed system was composed of three stages: image acquisition, analysis, and detection of diseases. Image processing operations included refining image movement, gridding (surveying genes), and retrieving unprocessed information from images. Normalizing the extracted features extracted and choosing the most efficient genes were part of data mining process. Finally, a malignant cell was identified using the collected features. To assess the effectiveness of the developed scheme, a benchmark microarray dataset was used. The findings showed that the suggested scheme had an accuracy of 95.45%, 94.11%, and 100% in identifying the form of cancer based on the data provided.

Sharma and Kumar [70] devised a method for diagnosing leukemia that makes use of an artificial bee colony (ABC) to train a back propagation neural network (BPNN). PCA was initially utilized to extract features from the leukemia dataset. In categorization tests, the ABC-BPNN scheme obtained an accuracy of 98.72%. The results revealed that the ABC-BPNN structure based on PCA is more efficient than that of the GA-based BPNN (GA-BPNN) structure based on PCA.

Zhang et al. [71] utilized three strategies to evaluate the influence of leukocyte type on 5000 images. First, CNN apps were used as SVM input for leukocyte classification, and they performed well, with accuracy, sensitivity, and specificity of 94.23%, 95.10%, and 94.41%, respectively. The HOG features were then used in SVM, yielding accuracy, sensitivity, and specificity of 85.00%, 87.50%, and 83.50%, respectively. The combination of CNN and HOG features resulted in accuracy, sensitivity, and specificity values of 95.93%, 96.11%, and 94.57%, respectively.

Table 9.4 summarizes the above methods used to detect leukemia.

9.7 BREAST CANCER

Breast cancer is the second leading cause of death in women, after melanoma. Breast cancer can affect males and females, but it affects women more frequently [72]. The latest developments in breast cancer diagnosis i.e., the machine-aided structures, improves

TABLE 9.4
A Summary of the Current Methods and Their Results for Diagnosing Leukemia

Reference	Method	Outcome
Patel and Mishra [68]	SVM	– Accuracy 93.57%
Khalilabad and Hassanpour [69]	J48 Tree	– Accuracy 95.45%
Sharma and Kumar [70]	PCA based ABC-BPNN	– Accuracy 98.72% – FAR 0.478% – FRR 0.398%
Zhang et al. [71]	SVM	For combination of CNN and HOG features: Accuracy 95.93% – Sensitivity 96.11% – Specificity 94.57%

radiologists' clinical expertise. Mammography, tomography, breast ultrasound (BUS), MRI, CT scans, and more in-depth PET scans are frequently used for diagnosis of breast cancer [73]. Since the breast is considered the most sensitive organ in the human body, only a subset of these procedures is recommended based on the patient's clinical history. Mammography is considered a reasonable and safe method in the initial stages of cancer, despite the fact that it is inefficient in young women with dense breast tissue. The BUS method is thought to be more beneficial than mammograms [74] in order to avoid unnecessary biopsy. Several breast imaging datasets are publicly accessible, including DDSM, MIAS, Wisconsin Breast Cancer Dataset (WBCD), Breast Cancer Digital Repository (BCDR), and National Biomedical Imaging Archive (NBIA) [75]. Before segmentation, various pre-processing functions, like pectoral muscle deletion and artifact removal, are conducted in addition to image acquisition. The segmentation process is an essential step in the computer-assisted framework for improving accuracy and reducing false positives of the presence of disorder [76]. Figure 9.5 depicts a general framework for detecting breast cancer. Several studies [77–79] suggested the GLCM method for analyzing texture-based features. Likewise, LBP is a remarkable method used in texture extraction to distinguish benign and malignant masses [80].

To classify tumors as malignant or benign, numerous machine learning techniques, including neural networks, k-NN, decision trees, ensemble classifiers, and SVM, are used for the feature classification process [72,81]. Etemadi et al. [82] proposed a hybrid selection model for identifying biased genes. A decision tree classifier was used to address the issue with several groups, and the forecasting of breast cancer sub-types using the same or fewer genes was observed to be completely accurate.

The use of machine learning methodologies, particularly deep learning models, is advancing life sciences and yielding promising results. CNN is currently attracting

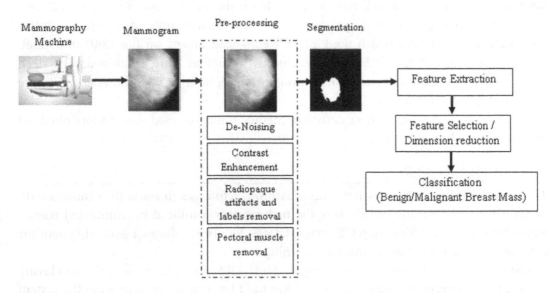

FIGURE 9.5   A general framework for detecting breast cancer using machine learning.

scientists for breast tumor classification and detection. AlexNet, CiFarNet [83], GoogLeNet [84], VGG16, and VGG 19 [39,85] are examples of CNN structural designs.

Using CNN-based techniques, Abdel-Zaher and Eldeib [86] proposed an unsupervised mechanism of profound faith beliefs with a regressive propagation path to detect breast carcinoma. In the experiments, the WBCD was used, and the accuracy was stated to be 99.68%.

Sun et al. [87] created a CNN classifier that utilizes large amounts of data points for variable training and fine-tuning, and the suggested arrangements are only anticipated to use a small fraction of the clearly labeled provided dataset. Data measuring, work compilation, data segregation, training, and CNN were the four major components of the diagnostic tool. Their investigation contained 3158 Regions of Interest (ROI) with 1874 mammographic combinations each. One hundred ROIs were deemed to be recognized data, while the remaining were considered unidentified. The sample's AUC was 0.8818, and the precision of CNN was 0.8243 for combined marking and unlabeled findings.

Zhou et al. [88] introduced the Inception V3 and Inception-ResNet V2 structures, and 90% of Tongji Hospital datasets were eligible as well as verified. Five radiologists' success was associated with the methods. The accuracy, flexibility, and specificity of the models' performance were evaluated. The highest performing CNN, iteration V3, acquired an AUC of 0.89 in the forecasting of the ultimate prognosis therapeutic of auxiliary node metastasis in the autonomous testing methodology. In this model, 85% responsiveness and 73% characteristics were determined.

Based on five datasets, in the classification, Acharya et al. [89] used thorough knowledge, k-means, auto encoder, and enhanced loss feature (ELF) to manage misdiagnosis by improving picture quality and processing time. Histopathological pictures were captured and pre-processed with linear transformation filtration system and stain regularization. These images were size corrected and analyzed in such a way that relevant information on tissue and cell rates was visible on the image data. ResNet 50-128 and ResNet512 were used to train the patches. Auto-encoders were utilized to improve cluster outcomes with k-means, which used a latent enhanced image, on the 128/128 dataset. The loss function of the SVM and the objective function were combined. The deep learning model enhanced breast cancer prognosis precision to 97%; however, the time taken was 40 seconds longer.

Aforementioned breast cancer detection methods, dataset used, and results obtained are summarized in Table 9.5.

9.8 LIVER CANCER

The majority of researchers used machine learning techniques to assess liver tumors [90]. Form, shape, and kinetic curves were the major features utilized by automated frameworks that used a multiple-step CT image dataset. Figure 9.6 shows a general system for diagnosing liver cancer using machine learning.

Hamm et al. [91] used deep learning system (DLS) evolved from CNN to classify hepatic tumors on multi-phase MRI. CNN was built by recursively improving the system

TABLE 9.5
Existing Methodologies, Datasets, and Outcomes for Detecting Breast Cancer

Reference	Method	Dataset	Outcome
Abdel-Zaher and Eldeib [86]	Backward propagation	WBCD	– Accuracy 99.68% – Sensitivity 100% – Specificity 99.47%
Sun et al. [87]	CNN	FFDM	– Accuracy 82.43% – Sensitivity 81% – Specificity 72.26%
Zhou et al [88]	Three different CNNs of Inception V3, Inception-ResNet V2, and ResNet-101	MIASTongi Hospital	– Accuracy 94% – Sensitivity 85% – Specificity 73% – AUC 0.89
Acharya et al. [89]	Enhanced loss function (ELF)	BI-RADS	– Accuracy 97%

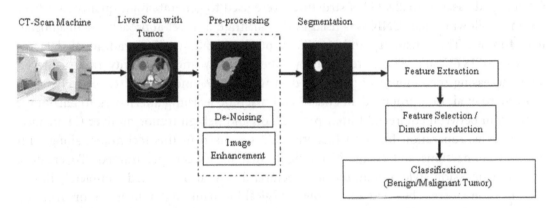

FIGURE 9.6   A general system for liver cancer detection utilizing machine learning.

topology and training instances. A total of 494 liver lesions with specific features from six different groups were used in the study. The DLS achieved accuracy, sensitivity, and specificity of 92%, 92%, and 98%, respectively. Test set effectiveness averaged 90% sensitivity and 98% specificity in a single run of random unknown instances. The mean sensitivity/specificity for radiologists on such types of cases was 82.5%/96.5%. The findings demonstrate that radiologists had a sensitivity of 60%/70% for categorizing hepatocellular carcinoma (HCC). The true positive and false positive rates for HCC categorization were 93.5% and 1.6%, respectively, with AUC of 0.992.

Wen et al. [92] used CNNs to develop an automated methodology in order to segment lesions from CT images. The researchers compared CNN models to popular machine learning algorithms. The average, variability, and contextual characteristics were all considered when developing these classification models. Utilizing leave-one-out cross validation, 30 portal phase-improved CT images were evaluated experimentally. The average dice similarity coefficient (DSC), precision, and recall were 80.06%, 1.63%; 82.67%, 1.43%; and 84.34%, 1.61%, respectively.

Xu et al. [93] described a texture-specific Bag of Visual Words (BoVW) technique for representing focal liver lesions (FLLs). The rotation-invariant consistent local binary technique was used to divide pixel values in the field of interest into nine texture subgroups. For each texture group, the BoVW-based features were computed. In addition, for describing the geolocation data of the visual words within ROI, a recognition method based on spatial cone matching (SCM) was suggested. The designed system outperformed the other BoVW methodologies in differentiating distinct lesions, according to the results. Because it added spatial data to the BoVW model, the SCM technique had an effect on retrieval performance. Using the retrieval system, clinicians' diagnostic accuracy increased from 66 to 80% in the prospective study.

To improve CNN's accuracy in medical image categorization, Frid-Adar et al. [94] recommended generative adversarial networks (GANs) for synthesized medical image creation. The proposed system was evaluated utilizing a sample of 182 liver lesions using CT image dataset. Initially, GAN structures were used to generate high-quality ROI liver lesions. Following that, CNN was used to demonstrate a novel approach for diagnosing liver tumors. The sensitivity and specificity of classification using traditional data increased to 78.6% and 88.4%, respectively. The accuracy and sensitivity rates achieved after increasing the amount of synthetic data were 85.7% and 92.4%, respectively.

Romero et al. [95] proposed an end-to-end machine learning alternative to encourage distinction between colorectal tumor progression and benign tumor on liver CT images. The effective separation function Inception V3 was used in this technique, along with residual connections and Image Net weights that have been pre-trained. To create a probabilistic lesion style output, the architectural design also included completely linked classification layers. They had an in-house surgical bio bank of 230 liver tumors from 63 subjects. Without defining the experimental setup or using a standard database, the generated values of accuracy and F1-score were 0.96 and 0.92, respectively.

Parsai et al. [96] compared retrospectively conjoined fluorodeoxyglucose (FDG) PET/CT and MRI (PET/MRI) to FDG PET/CT and MRI for determining cancerous or noncancerous indeterminate focal liver tumors in subjects with pre-existing basic malignancy. The HERMES® software was utilized to combine PET/CT and MRI scans that were then evaluated by two viewers that use the Likert scale to categorize lesions as noncancerous or cancerous. Histopathology or follow-up image analysis determined the confirmed diagnosis. The results of fused PET/MRI were evaluated by comparing to those of PET/CT and MRI on its own. MRI and fused PET/MRI identified all tumors, whereas PET/CT identified 89.4%. The sensitivity, specificity, accuracy, PPV, and NPV of fused PET/MRI for identifying malignant tumors remained higher than those of PET/CT and MRI.

Jansen et al. [97] proposed a classifier for distinguishing five common forms of tumors from clinical DCE-MR, T2-weighted image datasets, and risk variables. The image dataset was used to compute texture features such as the contrast graph, grayscale histogram, and

TABLE 9.6
A Comparison of Existing Methodologies, Datasets, and Outcomes for Detecting Liver Cancer

Reference	Method	Modality	Outcome
Hamm et al. [91]	CNN	MRI	– Accuracy 92% – Sensitivity 92% – Specificity 98% – True positive rate 93.5% – False positive rate 1.6%
Wen et al. [92]	CNN	CT	– Average Dice Similarity Coefficient (DSC) 80.06% ± 1.63% – Precision, 82.67% ± 1.43% – Recall 84.34% ± 1.61%
Xu et al. [93]	BoVW model	CT	– Accuracy 80%
Frid-Adar et al. [94]	CNN	CT	– Sensitivity 85.7% – Specificity 92.4%
Romero et al. [95]	End-to-end discriminative deep network	CT	– Accuracy 96% – F1-score 0.92 – AUC 0.97 – Precision 1.00 – Recall 0.94 – Specificity 0.85
Parsai et al. [96]	Restrospective fusion of PET with MRI	CT/ PET/MRI	– Accuracy 94.7% – Sensitivity 91.9% – Specificity 97.4% – PPV 97.1 – NPV 92.5
Jansen et al. [97]	Random Tree	MRI	– Accuracy 77% – Average sensitivity 79% – Average specificity 77%

grayscale co-occurrence matrices in the first step. Furthermore, risk variables such as fatty liver, chronic liver damage, and a tumor were utilized as attributes. Fifty of the attributes with the best ANOVA F-scores were chosen and given to Random Tree classifier. Overall, the classification accuracy was 0.77. The sensitivity/specificity ratios for adenoma, cyst, hemangioma, HCC, and metastasis were 0.8/0.7, 0.9/0.9, 0.8/0.8, 0.7/0.5, and 0.6/0.7, respectively.

The foregoing liver cancer detection methods are compared in Table 9.6.

9.9 CONCLUSION

Over the last few decades, there has been a revolution in cancer diagnosis and therapy with the aid of machine learning. As a result, this chapter has conducted a comprehensive summary of existing methods in the diagnosis and treatment of several cancers that have a negative impact on humans. The aim of this review is to assess the machine learning techniques used to diagnose various types of cancer. However, the accuracy of classification for each type of cancer is indeed a long way away from level headed. The vast majority of researchers still do not use benchmark datasets or have only tested their methods on small datasets. The significant issues in the cancer diagnostic and therapeutic procedures are redesigning the research workflow, understanding cancer growth concepts, developing pre-clinical designs, precisely handling complex cancers, early therapy, efficient strategies for creating and implementing clinical studies, and improving accuracy that will be beneficial for health professionals as just a second viewpoint.

REFERENCES

[1] Sung H., Ferlay J., Soerjomataram I., Siegel R.L., Laversanne M., Soerjomataram, Jemal A., Bray F. Global cancer statistics 2020: GLOBOCAN estimates of incidence and mortality worldwide for 36 cancers in 185 countries. *CA Cancer J Clin* 2021; 0: 1–41.

[2] Kurihara Y., Matsuoka S., Yamashiro T., Fujikawa A., Matsushita S., Yagihashi K., et al. MRI of pulmonary nodules. *Am J Roentgenol* 2014; 202: W210–W216.

[3] White C. *New techniques in thoracic imaging*. Boca Raton: CRC Press; 2001.

[4] Breast Cancer Surveillance Consortium. https://www.bcsc-research.org/data/mammography dataset.

[5] Iftikhar S., Fatima K., Rehman A., Almazyad A.S., Saba T. An evolution based hybrid approach for heart diseases classification and based hybrid approach for heart diseases classification and associated risk factors identification. *Biomed Res* 2017; 28(8): 3451–3455.

[6] Ejaz K., Rahim M.S.M., Rehman A., Chaudhry H., Saba T., Ejaz A., et al. segmentation method for pathological brain tumor and accurate detection using MRI. *Int J Adv Comput Sci Appl* 2018; 9(8): 394–401.

[7] Tahir B., Iqbal S., Khan M.U.G., Saba T., Mehmood Z., Anjum A., et al. Feature enhancement framework for brain tumor segmentation and classification. *Microsc Res Tech* 2019; 82(6): 803–811.

[8] Husham A., Alkawaz M.H., Saba T., Rehman A., Alghamdi J.S. Automated nuclei segmentation of malignant using level sets. *Microsc Res Tech* 2016; 79(10): 93–97.

[9] Saba T., Sameh A., Khan F., Shad S.A., Sharif M. Lung nodule detection based on ensemble of hand crafted and deep features. *J Med Syst* 2019; 43(12): 332.

[10] Mittal A., Kumar D., Mittal M., Saba T., Abunadi I., Rehman A., et al. Detecting pneumonia using convolutions and dynamic capsule routing for chest X-ray images. *Sensors* 2020; 20(4): 1068.

[11] Mario J., Venkataraman, S., Dialani V., Slanetz P.J. Benign breast lesions that mimic cancer: Determining radiologic-pathologic concordance. *Appl Radiol* 2015; 44(9):24–32.

[12] Khan M.A., Akram T., Sharif M., Saba T., Javed K., Lali I.U., et al. Construction of saliency map and hybrid set of features for efficient segmentation and classification of skin lesion. *Microsc Res Tech* 2019; 82(6): 741–763.

[13] Khan M.Q., Hussain A., Rehman S.U., Khan U., Maqsood M., Mehmood K., et al. Classification of melanoma and nevus in digital images for diagnosis of skin Cancer. *IEEE Access* 2019; 7: 90132–90144.

[14] Jones O.T., Ranmuthu C.K.I., Hall P.N., Funston G., Walter F.M. Recognising skin cancer in primary care. *Adv Ther* 2020; 37: 603–616.

[15] Abbas N., Mohamad D., Abdullah A.H., Saba T., Al-Rodhaan M., Al-Dhelaan A. Nuclei segmentation of leukocytes in blood smear digital images. *Pak J PharmSci* 2015; 28(5): 1801–1806.

[16] Norouzi A., Rahim M.S.M., Altameem A., Saba T., Rada A.E., Rehman A., et al. Medicalimage segmentation methods, algorithms, and applications. *IETE Tech Rev* 2014; 31(3): 199–213.

[17] Stewart B., Wild C.P. *World cancer report*; 2014. p. 2014.

[18] Ben-Cohen A., Greenspan H. Liver lesion detection in CT using deep learning techniques. *Handbook of medical image computing and computer assisted intervention*. London: Academic Press is an imprint of Elsevier; 2020.

[19] Ben-Cohen A., Diamant I., Klang E., Amitai M., Greenspan H. Fully convolutional network for liver segmentation and lesions detection. *Deep learning and data labeling for medical applications*. New York: Springer; 2016.

[20] Schmauch B., Herent P., Jehanno P., Dehaene O., Saillard C., Aubé C., et al. Diagnosis of focal liver lesions from ultrasound using deep learning. *Diagn Interv Imaging* 2019; 100: 227–233.

[21] Menze B.H., et al. The multimodal brain tumor image segmentation benchmark (BRATS). *IEEE Trans Med Imaging* 2015; 34(10): 1993–2024.

[22] Saba T. Automated lung nodule detection and classification based on multiple classifiers voting. *Microsc Res Tech* 2019; 2019: 1–9.

[23] Bareiro Paniagua L.R., Leguizamón Correa D.N., Pinto-Roa D.P., Vázquez Noguera J.L., Toledo S., Lizza A. Computerized medical diagnosis of melanocytic lesions based on the ABCD approach. *Clei Electron J* 2016; 19: 6-6.

[24] Naqi S.M., Sharif M., Jaffar A. Lung nodule detection and classification based on geometric fit in parametric form and deep learning. *Neural Comput App l* 2018: 1–19.

[25] Khan M.W., Sharif M., Yasmin M., Saba T. CDR based glaucoma detection using fundus images: a review. *Int J Appl Pattern Recogn* 2019; 4(3): 261–306.

[26] Ramzan F., Khan M.U.G., Rehmat A., Iqbal S., Saba T., Rehman A., et al. A deep learning approach for automated diagnosis and multi-class classification of alzheimer's disease stages using resting-state fMRI and residual neural net-works. *J Med Syst* 2020; 44(2): 37.

[27] Lu Z., Bai Y., Chen Y., Su C., Lu S., Zhan T., et al. The classification of gliomas based on a pyramid dilated convolution ResNet model. *Pattern Recognit Lett* 2020; 133(5): 173–179.

[28] Nayak D.R., Dash R., Majhi B. Automated diagnosis of multi-class brain abnormalities using MRI images: a deep convolutional neural network based method. *Pattern Recognit Lett* 2020; 138: 385–391.

[29] Qureshi I., Khan M.A., Sharif M., Saba T., Ma J. Detection of glaucoma base don cup-to-disc ratio using fundus images. *Int J Intell Syst Technol Appl* 2020; 19(1): 1–16.

[30] Nazir M., Khan M.A., Saba T., Rehman A. Brain tumor detection from MRI images using multi-level wavelets. 2019, IEEE International Conference on Computer and Information Sciences (ICCIS) 2019: 1–5.

[31] Khan M.A., Sharif M., Akram T., Raza M., Saba T., Rehman A. Hand-crafted and deep convolutional neural network features fusion and selection strategy: an application to intelligent human action recognition. *Appl Soft Comput* 2020; 87: 105986.

[32] Vaishnavee K., Amshakala K. An automated MRI brain image segmentation and tumor detection using SOM-clustering and proximal support vector machine classifier. In: 2015 IEEE International Conference on Engineering and Technology (ICETECH). 2015. pp. 1–6.

[33] Nie D., Zhang H., Adeli E., Liu L., Shen D. 3D deep learning for multi-modal imaging-guided survival time prediction of brain tumor patients. In: International Conference on Medical Image Computing and Computer-Assisted Intervention. 2016. pp. 212–220.

[34] Ellwaa A., Hussein A., Alnaggar E., Zidan M., Zaki M., Ismail M.A., et al. Brain tumor segmantation using random forest trained on iteratively selected patients. *International Workshop on Brainlesion: Glioma, Multiple Sclerosis, Strokeand Traumatic Brain Injuries* 2016: 129–137.

[35] Abbasi S., Tajeripour F. Detection of brain tumor in 3D MRI images using local binary patterns and histogram orientation gradient. *Neurocomputing* 2017; 219: 526–535.

[36] Mehmood I., Sajjad M., Muhammad K., Shah S.I.A., Sangaiah A.K., Shoaib M., et al. An efficient computerized decision support system for the analysis and 3D visualization of brain tumor. *Multimed Tools Appl* 2019; 78(10): 12723–12748.

[37] Das D., Mahanta L.B., Ahmed S., Baishya B.K., Haque I. Automated classification of childhood brain tumours based on texture feature. *Songklanakarin Journal of Science & Technology* 2019;41(5):1014–1020.

[38] Iqbal S., Ghani Khan M.U., Saba T., Mehmood Z., Javaid N., Rehman A., et al. Deep learning model integrating features and novel classifiers fusion for brain tumor segmentation. *Microsc Res Tech* 2019; 82: 1302–1315.

[39] Saba T., Mohamed A.S., El-Affendi M., Amin J., Sharif M. Brain tumor detection using fusion of hand crafted and deep learning features. *Cogn Syst Res* 2020; 59: 221–230.

[40] Ramzan F., Khan M.U.G., Iqbal S., Saba T., Rehman A. Volumetric segmentation of brain regions from MRI scans using 3D convolutional neural networks. *IEEE Access* 2020; 8: 103697–103709.

[41] Shen W., Zhou M., Yang F., Yang C., Tian J. Multi-scale convolutional neural networks for lung nodule classification. In: International Conference on Information Processing in Medical Imaging. 2015. pp. 588–599.

[42] Setio A.A.A., Ciompi F., Litjens G., Gerke P., Jacobs C., Van Riel S.J., et al. Pulmonary nodule detection in CT images: false positive reduction using multi-view convolutional networks. *IEEE Trans Med Imaging* 2016; 35: 1160–1169.

[43] Dou Q., Chen H., Yu L., Qin J., Heng P.A. Multilevel contextual 3-D CNNs for false positive reduction in pulmonary nodule detection. *IEEE Trans Biomed Eng* 2016; 64: 1558–1567.

[44] Shen W., Zhou M., Yang F., Yu D., Dong D., Yang C., et al. Multi-crop convolutional neural networks for lung nodule malignancy suspiciousness classification. *Pattern Recognit* 2017; 61: 663–673.

[45] Van-Griethuysen J.J., Fedorov A., Parmar C., Hosny A., Aucoin N., Narayan V., et al. Computational radiomics system to decode the radiographic phenotype. *Cancer Res* 2017; 77(21): e104–e107.

[46] Tahoces P.G., Alvarez L., González E., Cuenca C., Trujillo A., Santana-Cedrés D., et al. Automatic estimation of the aortic lumen geometry by ellipse tracking. *Int J Comput Assist Radiol Surg* 2019; 14: 345–355.

[47] Xie H., Yang D., Sun N., Chen Z., Zhang Y. Automated pulmonary nodule detection in CT images using deep convolutional neural networks. *Pattern Recogn* 2019; 85: 109–119.

[48] Jiang H., Ma H., Qian W., Gao M., Li Y., Hongyang J., et al. An automatic detection system of lung nodule based on multi group patch-based deep learning network. *IEEE J Biomed Health Inform* 2018; 22(4): 1227–1237.

[49] Naqi S.M., Sharif M., Jaffar A. Lung nodule detection and classification based on geometric fit in parametric form and deep learning. *Neural Comput Appl* 2018: 32; 4629–4647.

[50] Naqi S.M., Sharif M., Lali I.U. A 3D nodule candidate detection method supported by hybrid features to reduce false positives in lung nodule detection. *Multimed Tools Appl* 2019; 78: 26287–26311.

[51] Asuntha A., Srinivasan A. Deep learning for lung cancer detection and classification. *Multimed Tools Appl* 2020; 79: 7731–7762.

[52] Barata C., Celebi M.E., Marques J.S. A survey of feature extraction in dermoscopy image analysis of skin cancer. *IEEE J Biomed Health Inform* 2018; 23(3): 1096–1109.

[53] Rehman A., Khan M.A., Mehmood Z., Saba T., Sardaraz M., Rashid M. Microscopic melanoma detection and classification: a framework of pixel-based fusion and multilevel features reduction. *Microsc Res Tech* 2020; 83(4): 410–423.

[54] Saba T., Al-Zahrani S., Rehman A. Expert system for offline clinical guidelines and treatment. *Life Sci Journal* 2012; 9(4): 2639–2658.

[55] Ramya V.J., Navarajan J., Prathipa R., Kumar L.A. Detection of melanoma skin cancer using digital camera images. *ARPN Journal of Engineering and Applied Sciences* 2015; 10: 3082–3085.

[56] Premaladha J., Ravichandran K. Novel approaches for diagnosing melanoma skin lesions through supervised and deep learning algorithms. *J Med Syst* 2016; 40(4): 1–12.

[57] Khan S.A., Nazir M., Khan M.A., Saba T., Javed K., Rehman A., et al. Lungs nodule detection framework from computed tomography images using support vector machine. *Microsc Res Tech* 2019; 82(8): 1256–1266.

[58] Aima A., Sharma A.K. Predictive approach for melanoma skin Cancer detection using CNN. *Ssrn Electron J* 2019. Available at SSRN 3352407.

[59] Dai X., Spasi'c I., Meyer B., Chapman S., Andres F. Machine learning on mobile: an on-device inference app for skin cancer detection. In: 2019 Fourth International Conference on Fog and Mobile Edge Computing (FMEC). 2019. pp. 301–305.

[60] Saba T., Khan M.A., Rehman A., Marie-Sainte S.L. Region extraction and classification of skin cancer: a heterogeneous framework of deep CNN features fusion and reduction. *J Med Syst* 2019; 43(9): 289.

[61] Arthur F., Hossein K.R. Deep learning in medical image analysis: a third eye for doctors. *J Stomatol Oral Maxillofac Surg* 2019; 120(4): 279–288.

[62] Abbas N., Saba T., Mehmood Z., Rehman A., Islam N., Ahmed K.T. An automated nuclei segmentation of leukocytes from microscopic digital images. *Pak J Pharm Sci* 2019; 32(5): 2123–2138.

[63] Abbas N., Saba T., Rehman A., Mehmood Z., Javaid N., Tahir M., et al. Plasmodium species aware based quantification of malaria, parasitemia in light microscopy thin blood smear. *Microsc Res Tech* 2019; 82(7): 1198–1214.

[64] Rawat J., Bhadauria H., Singh A., Virmani J. Review of leukocyte classification techniques for microscopic blood images. *Computing for sustainable global development (INDIACom)*. In: 2015 2nd International Conference on. 2015. pp. 1948–1954.

[65] Ramoser H., Laurain V., Bischof H., Ecker R. Leukocyte segmentation and classification in blood-smear images. Engineering in medicine and biology society, 2005. In: *IEEE-EMBS 2005. 27th Annual International Conference of the*. 2006. pp. 3371–3374.

[66] Su M.C., Cheng C.Y., Wang P.C. A neural-network-based approach to white blood cell classification. *Sci World J* 2014; 4: 796371.

[67] Putzu L., Di Ruberto C. White blood cells identification and counting from microscopic blood image. In: *Proceedings of World Academy of Science, Engineering and Technology*. 2013. p. 363.

[68] Patel N., Mishra A. Automated leukaemia detection using microscopic images. *Procedia Comput Sci* 2015; 58: 635–642.

[69] Khalilabad N.D., Hassanpour H. Employing image processing techniques for cancer detection using microarray images. *Comput Biol Med* 2017; 81: 139–147.

[70] Sharma R., Kumar R. A novel approach for the classification of leukemia using artificial Bee Colony optimization technique and back-propagation neural networks. *Proceedings of 2nd International Conference on Communication, Computing and Networking* 2019: 685–694.

[71] Zhang C., Wu S., Lu Z., Shen Y., Wang J., Huang P., et al. Hybrid adversarial-discriminative network for leukocyte classification in leukemia. *Med Phys* 2020; 47(8):3732–3744.

[72] Sadad T., Munir A., Saba T., Hussain A. Fuzzy C-means and region growing based classification of tumor from mammograms using hybrid texture feature. *J Comput Sci* 2018; 29:34–45.

[73] Kumar A., Singh S.K., Saxena S., Lakshmanan K., Sangaiah A.K., Chauhan H., et al. Deep feature learning for histopathological image classification of canine mammary tumors and human breast cancer. *Inf Sci (Ny)* 2020; 508: 405–421.

[74] Kelly K.M., Dean J., Comulada W.S., Lee S.J. Breast cancer detection using auto-mated whole breast ultrasound and mammography in radiographically dense breasts. *Eur Radiol* 2010; 20(3): 734–742.

[75] Dora L., Agrawal S., Panda R., Abraham A. Optimal breast cancer classification using Gauss–Newton representation based algorithm. *Expert Syst Appl* 2017; 85: 134–145.

[76] Mughal B., Sharif M., Muhammad N., Saba T. A novel classification scheme to decline the mortality rate among women due to breast tumor. *Microsc Res Tech* 2018; 81: 171–180.

[77] Saba T., Khan S.U., Islam N., Abbas N., Rehman A., Javaid N., et al. Cloud based decision support system for the detection and classification of malignant cells in breast cancer using breast cytology images. *Microsc Res Tech* 2019; 82(6): 775–785.

[78] Yousaf K., Mehmood Z., Saba T., Rehman A., Munshi A.M., Alharbey R., et al. Mobile-health applications for the efficient delivery of health care facility to people with dementia (PwD) and support to their carers: a survey. *Biomed Res Int* 2019; 2019: 1–26.

[79] Khan S., Islam N., Jan Z., Din I.U., Rodrigues J.J.C. A novel deep learning based framework for the detection and classification of breast cancer using transfer learning. *Pattern Recognit Lett* 2019; 125: 1–6.

[80] Rabidas R., Midya A., Chakraborty J., Arif W.A. Study of different texture features based on local operator for benign-malignant mass classification. *6th International Conference On Advances In Computing & Communications, Procedia Computer Science* 2016: 389–395.

[81] Vijayarajeswari R., Parthasarathy P., Vivekanandan S., Basha A.A. Classification of mammogram for early detection of breast cancer using SVM classifier and Hough transform. *Measurement* 2019; 146: 800–805.

[82] Etemadi R., Alkhateeb A., Rezaeian I., Rueda L. Identification of discriminative genes for predicting breast cancer subtypes. *IEEE International Conference on Bioinformatics and Biomedicine (BIBM)* 2016: 1184–1188.

[83] Roth H., Lu L., Liu J., Yao J., Seff A., Cherry K., et al. Improving computer-aided detection using convolutional neural networks and random view aggregation. *IEEE Trans Med Imaging* 2016; 35(5): 1170–1181.

[84] Szegedy C., Liu W., Jia Y., Sermanet P., Reed S., Anguelov D., et al. Going deeper with convolutions. *Proceedings of the IEEE Conference on Computer Vision and Pattern Recognition* 2015: 1–9.

[85] Ejaz K., Rahim M.S.M., Bajwa U.I., Rana N., Rehman A. An unsupervised learning with feature approach for brain tumor segmentation using magnetic resonance imaging. *Proceedings of the 2019 9th International Conference on Bioscience, Biochemistry and Bioinformatics* 2019: 1–7.

[86] Abdel-Zaher A.M., Eldeib A.M. Breast cancer classification using deep belief networks. *Expert Syst Appl* 2016; 46: 139–144.

[87] Sun W., Tseng T.L.B., Zhang J., Qian W. Enhancing deep convolutional neural network scheme for breast cancer diagnosis with unlabeled data. *Comput Med Imaging Graph* 2017; 57: 4–9.

[88] Zhou L.Q., Wu X.L., Huang S.Y., Wu G.G., Ye H.R., Wei Q., et al. Lymph node metastasis prediction from primary breast cancer US images using deep learning. *Radiology* 2020; 294: 19–28.

[89] Acharya S., Alsadoon A., Prasad P., Abdullah S., Deva A. Deep convolutional network for breast cancer classification: enhanced loss function (ELF). *J Super-comput* 2020: 1–18.

[90] Chang C.C., Chen H.H., Chang Y.C., Yang M.Y., Lo C.M., Ko W.C., et al. Computer-aided diagnosis of liver tumors on computed tomography images. *Comput Methods Programs Biomed* 2017; 145: 45–51.

[91] Hamm C.A., Wang C.J., Savic L.J., Ferrante M., Schobert I., Schlachter T., et al. Deep learning for liver tumor diagnosis part I: development of a convolutional neural network classifier for multi-phasic MRI. *Eur Radiol* 2019; 29(7): 3338–3347.

[92] Li W., Jia F., Hu Q. Automatic segmentation of liver tumor in CT images with deep convolutional neural networks. *J Comput Commun* 2015; 3: 146–151.

[93] Xu Y., Lin L., Hu H., Wang D., Zhu W., Wang J., et al. Texture-specific bag of visual words model and spatial cone matching-based method for the retrieval of focal liver lesions using multiphase contrast-enhanced CT images. *Int J Comput Assisted Radiol Surg* 2018; 13(1): 151–164.

[94] Frid-Adar M., Diamant I., Klang E., Amitai M., Goldberger J., Greenspan H. GAN-based synthetic medical image augmentation for increased CNN performance in liver lesion classification. *Neurocomputing* 2018; 321: 321–331.

[95] Romero F.P., Diler A., Bisson-Gregoire G., Turcotte S., Lapointe R., Vandenbroucke-Menu F., et al. End-to-End discriminative deep network for liver lesion classification. In: *2019 IEEE 16th International Symposium on Biomedical Imaging (ISBI 2019)*. 2019. pp. 1243–1246.

[96] Parsai A., Miquel M.E., Jan H., Kastler A., Szyszko T., Zerizer I. Improving liver lesion characterisation using retrospective fusion of FDG PET/CT and MRI. *Clin Imaging* 2019; 55: 23–28.

[97] Jansen M.J., Kuijf H.J., Veldhuis W.B., Wessels F.J., Viergever M.A., Pluim J.P. Automatic classification of focal liver lesions based on MRI and risk factors. *PLoSOne* 2019; 14(5): e0217053.

CHAPTER 10

Human Papillomavirus and Cervical Cancer

Surekha Manhas, Zaved Ahmed Khan, and Shakeel Ahmed

CONTENTS

10.1   INTRODUCTION

Cervical cancer is a major mortality cause in females globally and is mainly initiated with infection with a high-risk, severe HPV strain. According to WHO statistics, common cancer has become a prevalent mortality cause all over the world, accounting for approximately 10 million deaths in the year 2020. In a 2018 report, around 9.6 million

DOI: 10.1201/9781003185604-10

people were estimated to die because of cancer [1]. Human papillomavirus (HPV) represents the DNA virus class that acts as a causative agent of viral infection, specifically in sexually transmitted infections in humans throughout the world. Due to the ubiquitous nature of HPV, infection has been observed in broad spectrum from animals to humans. Viral infection is also the leading cause of cancer formation in which it contributes up to 15–20% from various other types of cancers in humans. Infection caused by the oncogenic virus could be more able to promote various other associated stages of oncogenesis. Two hundred different HPV strains have been recorded by analyzing their different DNA sequencing pattern studies showing genomic variations. In addition, 85 genotypes of HPV have been carefully characterized [2]. Of the numerous varied types of HPV, around 30 different strains of HPV play a role in genital tract infection. The correlation between HPV and its role in cancer formation has been established.

Moreover, HPV plays a role in the cellular-based transformation process in the epithelial cells of the cervix. Still, alone it's not enough to cause disease, whereas various other molecular-based events and cofactors act as an inducer to boost cancer development mechanisms. The severe risk of cervical cancer can be prevented by means of early detection by treating it through medication, which is directly helpful to halt cancer progression [2]. There are various HPV types, from which around 15 strains are directly linked to causing cancer. Despite effective strategies with varied approaches, it's still a major health concern. The one recognized cancerous virus is HPV, causing infection through sexual transmission, and its highly causative risk DNA presence is found in around 99.9% of cervical cancer patients [3]; 90% infection of HPV is usually inactive due to continuous exposure of 12–24 months. In addition, conditions worsen in high-risk HPV viruses, which enhance the progression rate of cervical cancer [4].

10.2 HPV

HPV belongs to the papovaviridae family containing the double-stranded structure of DNA. Almost 200 varied forms of HPV have been identified, of which 40 strains colonize the tract of the genital organs. All infectious strains of HPV are classified into two well-established groups. Strains with a high risk of infection and associated with carginogenic properties are 58, 51, 16, 39, 18, 52, 31, 59, 33, 56, 45, and 35, whereas 52, 82, 53, 73, 66, and 70 are classified based on having greater potential high risk [5]. HPV18/16 is designated as the leading cause of invasive cancer of the cervix. These two virulent strains have a genotype with high risk; 70% of cervical cancer is mostly caused by these two virulent strains of HPV [5]. The HPV genome consists of highly conserved dsDNA with the size of about 8,000 bp. This 8,000 bp DNA molecule has greater complexity. Among 8,000 bp of DNA, 4,000 bp DNA consists of three oncoproteins, including E7/E5/E6. Six early complex proteins and three proteins play a role in regulatory processes, including E4, E1, and E2. All of these participate in the cellular transformation and replication process of cells. The rest of the 3,000 bp portion of viral DNA encodes the other two structure-based proteins, including L2/1, which display its role in virus capsid formation. Transcriptional-dependent regulatory elements and the replication process of viral DNA are functionally controlled by the long control region of about 1,000 bp [6].

10.3 HPV-16 CAUSES

As far as HPV 16/18 causes, sexual behavior represents itself as a strong point for increasing cervical malignancy. Despite sexual behavior, there are several other factors responsible for disease development. It is worthy to note that not all HPV strains are able to cause malignancy, although two HPV strains (16/18) mostly contribute to cervical malignancy. Additional factors include contraceptive pills, smoking, tobacco use, and sexual activities [7]. The role of oncogenes, ras and fos, in which mutations have been identified in cervical cancer by detecting infected cells in in vivo studies and proliferation, is unpredicted [7]. Other HPV-associated factors enhance disease development, including impaired immunity, virus persistence, steroid administration, smoking, etc. [7]. Anti-tumor genes lead to oncogenes inactivation. Despite that, female steroid hormones, including estrogen, progesterone, etc., display a tremendous role in disease progression. Already, it has been reported that females who used to take estradiol develop lesions of HSIL, which ultimately result from converting itself into a progressive one [8,9]. In addition, estrogen also affects the defense system [10,11]. Haptoglobin, referred to as glycoprotein, found in body fluids, is reported to correlate with tumors that modulate Th/2 response [12–15]. It is also considered to be responsible for the defense tolerance mechanism associated with human fertility [12,13,16]. HP polymorphism also enhances women's susceptibility for viral infection [12,13]. Prominent evidence in cervical cancer, which is greatly reported in 80% of studies, is sexual behavior. This marked factor suffers due to a lack of authenticated data. Available data only show that increased CIN incidence ratio among females under 25–31 years might be because of disastrous changes, population immigration, population migration, population mixing, economic migration, etc. [17].

10.4 PATHOGENESIS

The cervical oncogenesis mechanism involves the uncontrollable division of cells by means of HPV-dependent gene integration that infects the host cellular machinery through which cells undergo various cellular changes. Alone, HPV is not that potent to induce cancer development. Other epigenetic factors also are needed to carry out the process. When the host is exposed to viral infection, several other DNA-dependent changes occur in which host DNA process machinery gets mutated. The presence of various cellular and environmental factors plays a leading role in viral genomic integration and simultaneously operating host cellular machinery to synthesize their products to increase cellular division by halting the apoptotic mechanism.

Oncogenic dependent the viral strain, HPV-16 potential is based on regulatory actions of transcriptional factors of the virus. During the initial stage of infection, the genome of HPV-16 may be represented as an unintegrated minute DNA-based molecule designated as an episome, which results in the appearance of lesions of pre-cancerous cervix infection. However, HPV 16 might have the potential to start its integration mechanism leading to the formation of cervical carcinoma [18]. Genomic integration of viral genomic content is involved in the E2 protein dysregulation, oncoproteins repression, and promotion of carcinogenesis. E2 dysregulation causes an increase in E7/6 protein expression by causing drastic changes in apoptotic mechanisms [6]. Alone, E6 protein along with E7 protein is not that efficient to develop cancer despite various other epigenetic factors that need to be well established. A variety of different HPV strains that mostly show highly close relation with cancer development include 68, 58, 73, 18, 39, 51, 56, 33, 18, 45, 51, and 35 [5]. Almost 50% of various other forms of cervical cancer are directly related to HPV-16 [19].

In HPV-16 infected cells, viral genes, including E7/E6, are mostly and highly retained, integrated, and expressed in the host genome. In addition, in some other viral genome-integrated host cells, overexpression of these two genes might be absent. However, the overexpressive nature of E6/E7 is recognized in different types of HPV-infected cells [17,20]. These two viral proteins are designated as small proteins, consisting of about 150 and 100 monomers of proteins without any recognized specific activity of enzymes. Despite that, they are potent to induce host cell activity, forming a close association with various cellular proteins. For illustration, E6 shows binding with E6AP, which is a ubiquitin ligase that directly causes changes in the structure of E6. All these changes allow this protein to bind with p53, cell cycle-dependent tumor inhibitor, and form a complex called trimeric complex consisting of E6/E6AP/p53, as shown in Figure 10.1. Binding causes p53 degradation and thus increases the cell proliferation rate. On the other hand, E7 protein binds with pRb, causing it to switch off pRb activity and degrade it [21].

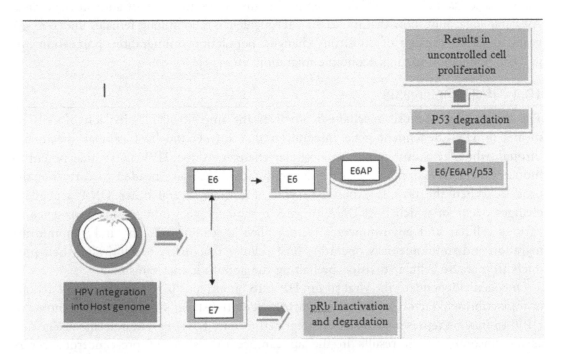

FIGURE 10.1　Pathogenesis of HPV leads to p53 and PRb degradation.

10.5   EPIDEMIOLOGY

Cervical cancer is designated as genital cancer, which is the leading cancerous disease among females throughout the world, with almost 50 hundred thousand new cases arising per year [22]. In a report from 2015, around 526,000 females developed genital cancer worldwide, causing 239,000 mortalities [23]. Squamous cell cancer is commonly found in cervical cancer. The mortality rate of cervical cancer varies according to different geographically dependent regions. The incidence rate based on age-standardization is reduced in developed countries, around 8 per 100,000 [23]. The mortality rate based on age-standardization for cervical cancer is greatly reduced in developed nations, around 2.2 per 100,000 rather than developing countries, around 4.3 per 100,000. For illustration, in Africa, 34.8 new cases were found with 22.5 deaths per 100,000 females, whereas in Asia, around 4.4 new cases were found with 1.9 deaths per 100,000 females in 2012 [24]. In addition, Northern America is recognized as a region marked at the third position throughout the world for increasing incidence of cervical cancer [23].

10.6   IMPORTANCE OF HPV VIRUS IN ONCOGENESIS

Many HPV strains are clearly distinguished by observing the clinically identified symptoms and the effect assigned during cancer development among males and females [25]. It is well documented that HPV plays a role as a precursor for induction of carcinogenesis in the genital tract. In approximately 70% of cases, including all cancers, HPV16/18 are severe strains in which 99.7% of cancer cases already are detected [26]. Despite that, HPV onco-genic drastic effect was already confirmed on squamous epithelial layers of cells correctly in the penis, vagina, and vulva, as shown in Figure 10.1. In addition, it also shows its oncogenic activity in the oral cavity, throat, palatine tonsils, larynx, conjunctivitis, lungs, and paranasal sinuses [27]. It is notable to mention that in organs with cancer, hrHPV detection estimates range from 0 to 78% [28]. Malignant disease development is also induced by physical factors, including place of residence and improper health conditions such as drinking al-cohol, smoking etc., but also cancer is being analyzed. Similarly, other results were observed by examining head/neck cancer cases. Simultaneously, it has already been proved that malignancy in those body parts contributed by HPV responds better to treatment compared to those that had a negligible effect from the virus [29] (Figure 10.2).

10.7   HPV'S ROLE IN CERVICAL CANCER DEVELOPMENT

Cervical cancer is fourth among all the cancers in females across the world, causing approx 275,000 deaths each year [30,31]. Numerous factors are responsible for this cancer development, including sexual intercourse status, socio-economic position, ex-cessive alcohol consumption, genetic load, birth control drug use especially in young females, etc. [32]. The most impactful factor that displays a decisive role in cervical cancer formation is the continuous exposure of two HPV severe strains hrHPV (16/18) that cause infection at an uncontrollable level. Transmission of HPV commonly occurs through sexual intercourse, infecting around 6.2 million people annually, which makes it

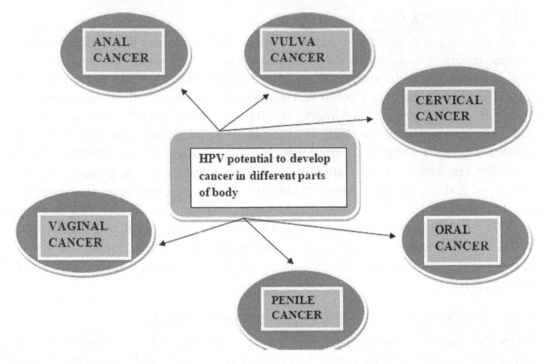

FIGURE 10.2   HPV potential to promote various cancer formation in different body parts.

the most infected virus across the globe. Regardless of male or female gender, and depending on degree of sex-related activities, HPV infection risk is about 50% throughout the life cycle in males and females [25]. In general, females often get infected with this virus between the age of 15 and 25. In immunocompetent females, infection usually is transmitted asymptomatically after HPV infection of about at least 24 months. HPV-dependent malignancy mostly lacks symptoms that are the hallmark associated with HPV viral infection, which undoubtedly contributes to increasing cases due to ignoring continuous tests of patients to analyze the presence/absence of HPV pathogen threat, allowing the pathogen to initiate persistent viral infection [33]. If the virus doesn't subside within 10–30 days, then viral replication can be drastically accompanied through neoplastic changes that will concern the cervix endothelium, called cervical intraepithelial neoplasiab, or CIN. In the findings based on histopathological studies, CIN classified into CIN-1 represents advanced neoplasia, CIN-2 represents average-sized neoplasia, and CIN-3 is the pre-cancerous stage [25,34]. Thoroughly analyzing previous data of cervical cancer studies related to the aetiology of cervix malignancy, it was clearly found that the system associated with cytological examinations and their evaluation doesn't constitute an appropriate diagnostic toolset that infected individuals can use. Recently, it was highly recommended to use an extended molecular-based algorithm to diagnose disease. Using it, it's not just possible to detect HPV virus but also make it easy to identify the specific disease-causing strains. In addition, certain limitations are associated with cytology, including low repeatability and sensitivity, which leads to hindrance in result accuracy.

Furthermore, with repeated cytological examinations, incorrect diagnosis numbers were increased, increasing per unit time. Cytology works to detect squamous cell malignancy in the cervix. Cervical adenocarcinoma is not detected by using this approach, unfortunately [30,31,35]. It is possible to notice the disproportion appropriately characterizing the rate of cervical malignancy incidence across the globe. Abnormally, the number is higher in females living in undeveloped areas, up to 85% of cases, including SE Asia, Central America, and Saharan Africa. The morbidity and mortality rate is lower in those specific countries where efficient, appropriate screening-based strategies with varied approaches are available, resulting in malignancy falling for years [30,31].

10.8 SYMPTOMS OF CERVICAL CANCER

In one of the studies, a list of symptoms was prepared and presented to the participants to ask about symptoms and other associated risk factors. The majority of selected members recognized various risk factors such as more sexual partners and infection in the cervix from sexually transmitted viral particles; 88.3% of participants agreed on increased risk factors due to multiple partner intimacy, whereas 82% agreed on sexually transmitted infection due to virus. A third of the participants agreed on multiparity, tobacco, and cigarette use as high risk factors in cervical cancer cases. The common symptoms are pain in the lower abdomen region, vaginal discharge with offensive odor, postmenopausal bleeding, dyspareunia, vaginal bleeding during the intermenstrual phase, etc. [36].

10.8.1 Perceived Cervical Infection Causes

The observable causes of viral infection include not washing the female's genitals after sexual intimacy, sexual intimacy with polygamous males, prolonged birth control injections/pills, and sexual intercourse in rough ways leading to physical trauma to the female's genitals [36].

10.9 RISK FACTORS

Keeping in mind the correlation between HPV and cervical malignancy, the primary factor that is thought to contribute to HPV infection is early age. Infection probability increases as several sex mates increase at any point of time in a specific individual's life. Data from epidemiological studies show that sex hormones also are responsible for making females highly prone to the viral infection and development of this severe cervical disease [37]. Further data analysis on cervical cancer, indicated by means of having multiple sex mates and age at full-term pregnancy, referred to as FTP, more commonly found that early pregnancies through multiparity displayed alterations in female hormonal levels during pregnancy and high parity related to a higher risk of HPV infection [38]. Although immune suppression directly shows association with pregnancy, with more affinity for HPV infection in pregnancy, defense mechanism cannot eliminate existing conditions that make it more vulnerable towards the risk of continuous progression of neoplastic changes (Figure 10.3).

Oral contraceptive medication use also increases the risk of disease. It was found that females who used contraceptive pills for five years or more had a three-fold increased

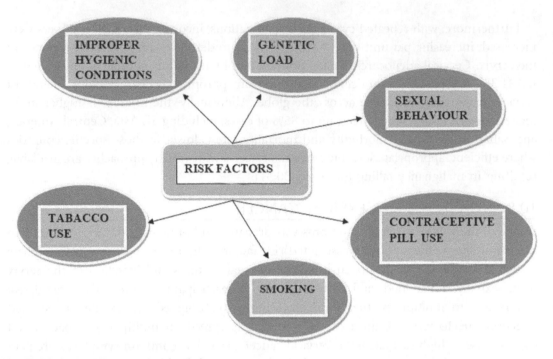

FIGURE 10.3   HPV-associated risk factors.

chance of cancer formation than those who generally did not use it. Available data explain cervical cancer incidence rate and higher risk in multifarious females and ladies using contraceptives for longer duration and confirm the data-based study that women's hormones favor malignancy risk. More commonly, cervical cancer has been found in females who usually ignored pap smears. Similarly, in females who commonly had orthodox-based religious beliefs like churchgoers [39,40]. Human semen is recognized as a biologically marked basis in the case of sex-associated behavior, which enhances viral HPV infection, which leads to cervical cancer. In the cervix, chronic inflammation occurs due to certain changes at the cellular and molecular level, which are already reported to be triggered with continuous exposure to semen [35,41]. In addition, semen also commonly interacts with the epithelial lining and cells of the cervix, which ultimately affects the chemokines/cytokines synthesis that generates the immune response [42]. PGE2, major prostaglandin, is detected in human semen, which displays its role as an inflammatory mediator. PGE2 is detected basically in 10,000-fold extra higher concentration during inflammation at inflammatory sites [35,41,43]. Upregulated level of PGE2 is marked to be an influencer of cervical malignancy. Various other studies demonstrated that the semen of a smoker is highly concentrated with certain tobacco-based carcinogens that might play a role in cancer development [44,45]. In addition, various procedures associated with birth control, like intrauterine devices and tubal ligation, cause 80% of cancer in the cervix, especially in developing nations [46,47].

10.10   SCREENING OF CERVICAL CANCER

It is very well established that cancer screening reduces the risk of increasing cervical cancer and mortality rates [48]. Different nations have adopted various strategies to overcome this problem. Few countries have specific programs based on population whereby susceptible women are identified individually and invited to attend the screening programs. In opportunistic screening, the process of invitation totally depends on the individual's decision and also on encounters with healthcare organizations.

Organized programs of cervical screening might set proper standards for equal participation at decided daily intervals and equal access. In addition, high-quality standards must be set for disease diagnosis. Potentially, it's a more practical approach compared to opportunistic screening [49,50]. Organized screening programs exist in highly developed countries, including Singapore, Canada, UK, and Australia. On the other side, countries in eastern Europe also have a method of screening that is opportunistic screening designated as low coverage screening results in the increasing incidence of cervical cancer and higher mortality rate. In varied countries of central Asia, an opportunistic approach is usually based on cytology testing or by Ramanowsky staining use [51]. At last, cervical cancer screening contributes to reduction in the incidence of cervical cancer and mortality [52].

10.11   DIAGNOSIS

At low-risk strain, diagnosis is clinically carried out by detecting genital warts. Genital warts have the potential to transmit sexually in cauliflower form, referred to as small elevated warts. During disease progression, benign intraepithelial lesions are formed. Differential diagnosis is usually carried out by means of three different procedures associated with molecular assays, including non-amplified based hybridization, signal amplification, and target amplification [53]; in addition, pap smear-based diagnostic procedure mostly used in females. Sampling from the cervix region is done by screening methods and identifying the malignancy signs [53]. However, this diagnostic procedure shows the abnormal condition of cells, and still, it does not have that much potential for accurate diagnosis of disease. The colposcopic biopsy is another way to overcome this issue [54].

10.12   HPV VACCINATION

Currently, the vaccine is available on the market, commercialized in developed and developing nations, indicating an effective preventive measure against hrHPV. Data from various sources confirmed that 60% of cases contributed to HPV-16 infection, 18% by HPV-18 infection, 8% by means of HPV-45 infection, and only 5% contributed by HPV-31. The developed vaccine consists of purified virus-like particle designated as VLP [25,33].

The basis of statistical data collected from the last few years suggests that HPV vaccine utilization is much more effective for disease prevention and infection associated with specific genotypes of the viral genome [52]. Various approachable vaccination programs have been implemented successfully in several countries throughout the world [52,55]. Commercially, three prophylactic vaccines are available in the health sector, including Cervarix: bivalent vaccines show action against HPV16/18 strains; Gardasil. tetravalent vaccine plays a role against HPV 6/11/16/18 strains; and Gardasil 9:9 valent vaccines show protective action against HPV 6, 16, 18, 31, 33, 45, 52, and 58. These subunit vaccines are non-infectious, consisting of viral-like particles derived from the L1 protein of the capsid part of HPV in the case of yeast that is Gardasil. In other cases, it is derived from insect cells called Cervarix. Vaccine administration is done by means of intramuscular injection with repeated three doses for six months. Data shows that even with a single dose, chances of the infection get reduced [56]. A long-lasting response of antibody is generated that is documented [57] (Figure 10.4).

The primary approved vaccine formulation was Gardasil, referred to as quadrivalent formulation. Recently, it has replaced by the newest generation-based vaccine that is Gardasil 9, referred to ninevalent vaccine show anti-carcinogenic actions against varied strains of HPV, including 45, 16, 11, 18, 31, 52, 11, and 58. Its efficacy against infection prevention is almost comparable with second Cervarix vaccine available in the market referred to a bivalent vaccine for HPV16/18 infections. It is highly recommended to everyone to vaccinate girls in the stage of adolescence under the age of 9–15 yrs. Before active in sexual life, vaccinate them with two doses, preferably each dose after six months. WHO guidelines recommend that the administration of the vaccine should be in three doses. It is well mentioned that 80% of cases of malignancy caused through hrHPV persistent infection leads to introduce various changes in cervical regions in females, so it is worth noting that vaccination of young boy is also needed at the age of 11–12 yrs. Twelve years have been completed to introduce the vaccine in the market by the recommendations of WHO, prophylaxis programs associated with vaccine functions in 74 recognized countries, and no side-effects have been confirmed to date [58]. In Poland, HPV vaccinations are highly recommended but not financed by the health ministry budget.

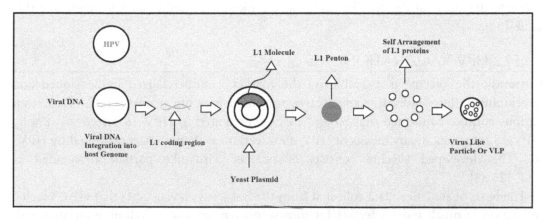

FIGURE 10.4   Preparation of vaccine by using yeast as vector.

10.13   CONCLUSION

HPV increases the risk of infection, has a drastic role in females' associated sex life problems, and marks major hazardous effects in women in the dreadful form of malignancy, especially cervical cancer, which is referred to as a major well-illustrated cause of death among all cancers in developing nations. Ignorance of screening procedures and cultural taboos promote infection transmission. In a developing country, women mostly do not know about it and are illiterate about regular screening. To prevent cervix carcinogenesis, early change detection is a way of prevention and takes care of other factors responsible for forming etiopathogenetic relationships with organ malignancy. Ignorance of cervical screening promotes HPV infection. Disease abundance indicates the higher mortality rate of cancer with a lack of screening approaches and poor awareness among females. Actual incidences in malignancy make it very important. More awareness must be spread to women of the deadly disease. Enhancing awareness among females related to causative factors is a marked priority emphasized for the introduction of preventive measures. HPV testing incorporation into disease screening strategies makes the task easier to reduce the mortality risk associated with cervical cancer. Knowledge about HPV prevalence and pathogenesis contributes to vaccine development. The major projects related to educational health should be introduced in societies for continuous disease exposure. Governments should be the part of implementation and HPV vaccination programs.

REFERENCES

[1] Chan K.C., Aimagambetova G., Ukybassova T. et al. (2019) Human papilomavirus infection and cervical cancer: Epidemiology, screening, and Vaccination-Review of current perspectives. *Journal of oncology*, 2019: 3257939.

[2] Burd M.E. (2003) Human Papillomavirus and cervical cancer. Clinical microbiology reviews, 1–17.

[3] Walboomers M.M.J., Jacobs M.V., Manos M.M. et al. (1999) Human paillomavirus is a necessary cause of invasive cervical cancer worldwide. *The journal of pathology*, 18(19): 12–19.

[4] Asiaf A., Ahmad S.T., Mohammad S.O. and Zargar M.A. (2014) Reviews of the current knowledge on the epidemiology, pathogenesis and prevention of Human papilomavirus infection. *European journal of cancer prevention*, 23(3): 203–224.

[5] Reid R., Stanhope C.R., Herschman B.R. et al. (1982) Genital warts and cervical cancer. I. Evidence of an association between subclinical papilomavirus infection and cervical malignancy. *Cancer*, 50(2): 377–387.

[6] Jing Y., Wang T., Chenz et al. (2018) Phylogeny and polymorphism in the long control regions E6, E7 and L1 of HPV type 56 in women from southwest china. *Molecular medicine reports*, 17(5): 7131–7141.

[7] Stanely M. (2006) Immuneresponses to human papillomavirus. *Vaccine*, 24: S10–S16.

[8] de Villiers E.M. (2003) Relation ship between steroid hormone contraceptives and HPV, cervical intraepithelial neoplasia and cervical carcinoma. *Int J Cancer*, 103(6): 705–708.

[9] Elson D.A., Riley R.R., Lacey A., Thordarson G., Talamantes F.J., Arbeit J.M. (2000) Sensitivity of the cervical transformation zone to estrogen induced squamous carcinogenesis. *Cancer Research*, 60: 1267–1275.

[10] Paavonen T., Andersson L.C., Adlercreutz H. (1981) Estradiol enhances human B cell maturation via inhibition of suppressor T cells in pokeweed mitogen stimulated cultures. *JEM*, 154: 1935–1945.

[11] Hughes G.C., Clark E.A. (2007) Regulation of Dendritic cells by female sex steroids: relevance to immunity and auto immunity. *Auto immunity*, 40: 470–481.

[12] Langlois M.R., Delanghe J.R. (1996) Biological and clinical significance of haptoglobin in human. *Eur J Clin Chem*, 42: 1589–1600.

[13] Quaye I.K. (2008) Haptoglobin inflammation and disease. *Trans R soc trop medi hyg*, 102(8): 735–742.

[14] Vilerberghe H.V., Langlois M., Delanghe J. (2004) Haptoglobin polymorphisms and iron homeostasis in health and in disease. *Clin chimica acta*, 345: 35–42.

[15] Guetta J., Strauss M., Levy N.S., Fahoum L., Levy A.P. (2007) Haptoglobim genotype modulates the balance of Th1/Th2 cytokines produced by macrophages exposed to freehaemoglobin. *Artherosclerosis*, 191: 48–53.

[16] Bottini N., Gimelfarb A., Gloria-Bottini F., La Torre M., Lucarelli P., Lucarini N. (1999) Haptoglobin genotype and natural fertility in humans. *Fertility and a Sterility*, 72: 293–296.

[17] Argyri E., Tsimplaki E., Daskaloporlou D. et al. (2013) E6/E7 mRNA expression of high risk HPV type in 849 Greek women. *Anticancer Research*, 33(9): 4007–4011.

[18] Lehoux M., Abramo C.M.D., Archambaut J. (2009) Molecular mechanism of Human papilomavirus- induced carcinogenesis. *Public health genomics*, 12(5-6): 268–280.

[19] Mirabello L., Clarke M.A., Nelson C.W. et al. (2018) The intersection of HPV epidemiology genomics and mechanistic studies of HPV-mediated carcinogenesis. *Viruses*, 10(2).

[20] Cattani P., Zannoni G.F., Riccic et al. Clinical performance of Human papilomavirus E6 and E7 mRNA testing for high grade lesions of cervix. *Journal of clinical microbiology*, 47(12): 3895–3901.

[21] Zhang B., Chew W. and Roman A. (2006) The E7 protein of low and high risk Human papilomavirus share the ability to target the pRb family members' p130 for degradation. *Proceedings of the national academy of science*, 103(2): 437–442.

[22] Ferlay J., Soerjomataram I., Dikshit R. et al. (2015) Cancer incidence and mortality worldwide: sources, methods and major pattern in GLOBOCAN 2012. *International Journal of Cancer*, 136(5): E359–E386.

[23] Altobelli E., Rapacchietta L., Profeta F.V., Fagnano R. (2019) HPV –vaccination and cancer cervical screening in 53 WHO European Countries: an update on prevention programs according to income level. *Cancer Medicine*, 8(5): 2524–2534.

[24] Bruni L., Rosan B.L., Albero G. et al (2014) Human papilomavirus and related disease in Kazakhstan, "Tech. Rep. ICO Information center on HPV and Cancer, Barcelona Spain, 2014, summary report.

[25] Inrle L. (2009) Zakażenia wirusem HPV-problem medyczny i społeczny. *Ginekol Prakt* 17: 8–12.

[26] Broniarczyk J., Koczorowska M.M., Durzyńska J., Warowicka A., Goździcka-Józefiak A. (2010) Struktura i właściwości wirusa brodawczaka ludzkiego. *Biotechnologia* 3: 126–145.

[27] Morshed K. (2004) Udział wirusa brodawczaka ludzkiego (HPV) w etiopatogenezie nowotworów głowy i szyi. *Otorynolaryngologia* 3: 91–96.

[28] Zhai K., Ding J., Shi H.Z. (2015) HPV and lung cancer risk: A meta-analysis. *J Clin Virol* 63: 84–90.

[29] Doorbar J., Quint W., Banks L., Bravo I.G., Stoler M., et al. (2012) The biology and Life-Cycle of Human Papiillomaviruses. *Vaccine* 30: F55–F70.

[30] Dijkstra M.G., Snijders J.F., Arbyn M., Rijkaart D.C., Berghof J., et al. (2014) Cervical cancer screening: n the way to a shift from cytology to full molecular screening. *Annals of Oncology* 25: 927–935.

[31] Reels J., Jones D., Chen H., Macleod U. (2018) Interferations to improve the uptake of cervical cancer screening among lower socio-economic groups: a systematic review. *PrevMed* 111: 323–335.

[32] Stefanek A., Durka P. (2014) Poziom świadomości kobiet na temat profilaktyki raka szyjki macicy. *Polski Przegląd Nauk o Zdrowiu* 1.

[33] Molijn A., Berhard K., Quint W., van Doorn L.J. (2005) Molecular diagnosis of human papillomavirus (HPV) infections. *J Clin Virol* 32: S43–S51.

[34] Ronoco G., Dillner J., Elfstrom K.M., Tunesi S., Snijders P.J.F., et al. (2014) Efficacy of HPV-based screening for prevention of invasive cervical cancer: follow-up of four European randomised controlled trials. *Lancet* 383: 524–532.

[35] Sharkey D.J., Macpherson A.M., Tremellen K.P., Robertson S.A. (2007) Seminal plasma differentially regulates inflammatory cytokine gene expression in human cervical and vaginal epithelial cells. *Mol hum rep*, 13(7): 491–501.

[36] Mwaka D.A., Orach G.C., Were M.E. et al. (2015) Awareness of cervical cancer risk factors and symptoms: cross-sectional community survey in post –conflict Northern Uganda. *Health expectations*, 19: 854–867.

[37] Chung S.H., Franceschi S., Lambert P.F.: Estrogen and ER-α:Culprits in cervical cancer. *The Cell* 2010, 21: 504–511.

[38] International Collaboration of Epidemiological studies of cervical cancer cervical carcinoma and reproductive factors: collaborative reanalysis of individual data on 16,563 women with cervical carcinoma and 33,542 women without cervical carcinoma from 25 epidemiological studies. *Int J Cancer* 2006, 119: 1108–1112.

[39] International Collaboration of Epidemiological Studies of Cervical Cancer, Appleby P., Beral V., Berrington de González A., Colin D., Franceschi S., Goodhill A., Green J., Peto J., Plummer M., Sweetland S. (2007) Cervical cancer and hormonal contraceptives: collaborative reanalysis of individual data for 16,573 women with cervical cancer and 35,509 women without cervical cancer from 24 epidemiological studies. *Lancet*, 370: 1609–1621.

[40] Curado M.P., Edward B.K., Shin H.R., Storm H. (2007) Cancer incidence in five continents. *29th Meeting of the International Association of Cancer Registries.*

[41] Baniyash M. (2006) Chronic inflammation, immuno-supression in cancer: new insights and outlook. *Seminar cancer biology*, 16(1): 80–88.

[42] Kelly R.W. (1995) Immunosuppressive mechanism in semen: Implications for contraceptions. *Human reproduction*, 10(7): 1686–1693.

[43] Sales K.J., Katz A.A., Millar R.P., Jabbour H.N. (2002) Seminal plasma activates cyclooxygenase-2 and prostaglandin E2 receptor expression and signalling in cervical adenocarcinoma cells. *Molecular human reproduction journal*, 8(12): 1065–1070.

[44] Herfs M., Herman L., Hubert P., Minner F., Arafa M., Roncarati P., Henrotin Y., Boniver J., Delvenne P. (2009) High expression of PGE2 enzymatic pathways in cervical (Pre) neoplastic lesions and functional consequences for antigen-presenting cells. *Cancer immunology journal*, 58(4): 603–614.

[45] Hung P.H., Froenicke L., Lin C.Y., Lyons L.A., Miller M.G., Pinkerton K.E., VandeVoort C.A. (2009) Effects of environmental tobacco smoke in vivo on rhesus monkey semen quality, sperm function, sperm metabolism. *Reproductive toxicology*, 27(2): 140–148.

[46] Schiffman M., Castle E.P., Jeronimo J., Rodriguez A.C., Wacholder S. (2007) Human papillomavirus and cervical cancer. *Lancet*, 370(9590): 890–907.

[47] Wellings K., Collumbien M., Slaymaker E., Singh S., Hodges Z., Patel D., Bajo N. (2006) Sexual behaviour in context: a global perspective. *Lancet*, 368(9548): 1706–1728.

[48] International Agency for Research on Cancer, Cervix cancer screening. *International agency for research on cancer, in IARC handbooks of cancer prevention*, 10: 1–302, IARC press, Lyon, France, 2005.

[49] Zucchetto A., Ronco G., Rossi G.P. et al. Screening patterns within organized programs and survival of Italian women with invasive cervical cancer. *Preventive medicine*, 57(3): 220–226.

[50] Bucchi L., Baldacchini F., Msncini S. et al. Estimating the impact of an organized screening programme on cervical cancer incidence: a 26 year study from northern Italy. *International journal of cancer*, 144(5): 1017–1026.

[51] Rogovskaya S.I., Shabalova I.P., Mikheeva I.V. et al. (2013) Human papillomavirus prevalence and type –distribution, cervical cancer screening practices and current status of vaccination implementation in Russian Federation, the western countries of the former Soviet Union, Caucasus region and central Asia. *Vaccine*, 31(7): H46–H58.

[52] Peirson L., Lewis F.D., Ciliska D. and Warren R. (2013) Screening for cervical cancer: a systematic review and meta-analysis. *Systematic reviews*, 2(1): 35.

[53] Baay M.F., Quint W.G., Koudstaal J., Hollema H., Duk J.M., Burger M.P., Stolz E., Herbrink P. (1996) Comprehensive study of several general and type specific primer pairs for detection of human papillomavirus DNA by PCR in paraffin embedded cervical carcinomas. *Journal of clinical microbiology*, 34: 745–747.

[54] Van Doorn L.J., Molijn A., Kleter B., Quint W., Colau B. (2006) Highly effective detection of human papillomavirus 16 and 18 DNA by a testing algorithm combining broad spectrum and type specific PCR. *Journal of clinical microbiology*, 44: 3292–3298.

[55] Brotherton J.M.L. (2019) Impact of HPV vaccination: achievements and future challenges *Papillomavirus research*, 7: 138–140.

[56] Tanaka H., Shirasawa H., Shimizu D. et al. (2017) Preventive effect of human paillomavirus vaccination on the development of uterine cervical lesions in young Japenese women. *Journal of obstetrics and gynaecology research*, 43(10): 1597–1601.

[57] Schiller J. and Lowy D. (2018) Explanations for the high potency of HPV prophylactic vaccines. *Vaccine*, 36(32): 4768–4773.

[58] Sabeena S., Bhat P.V., Kamath V., Arunkumar G. (2018) Global Human virus vaccine implementation: an update. *The journal of obstetrics and gynaecology research*, 44(6): 989–997.

CHAPTER 11

Case Studies/Success Stories on Machine Learning and Data Mining for Cancer Prediction

Chander Prabha and Geetika Sharma

CONTENTS

DOI: 10.1201/9781003185604-11

11.1   INTRODUCTION

Cancer is one of those diseases in which multiple unusual cell(s) grows in an uncontrolled manner any place in the human body. These unusual cells are named as tumor cells, harmful cells, or cancer cells. These cells can penetrate through any body tissues. Many unusual cells and the cancer cells that make the cancer tissue are additionally recognized by the name of the tissue that the unusual cells started from (like brain cancer, skin cancer, oral cancer, lung cancer). Cancer is not bound to human beings only, but it can affect other living organisms as well. In all existing cancer types, several body tissues start dividing and spreading around the cells without stopping. The human body is composed of millions of cells, so the cancer can begin at any place in the body. As per the requirement of the human body, tissues grow and also divide in order to form new tissues. With time, cells may damage or die, so they get replaced by new cells. But this process breaks down after the development of cancer. With cancer, cells become increasingly unusual. As they get older or destroyed, then they are supposed to die, but they survive, and new cells are develop that are not required in the body [1]. This may result in tumor formation as extra cells divide into more cells without stopping. Figure 11.1 shows various types of cancer.

Machine learning (ML) techniques are well suited to medical applications, especially in complex problems like cancer detection and diagnosis. This artificial intelligence (AI) approach is a growing trend towards personalized predictive treatment. Due to the increasing significance of cancer detection and the growing reliance on ML techniques, we assumed that it would be of immense concern to carry out a review on recently published research papers using ML techniques in detecting cancer and its diagnosis [2].

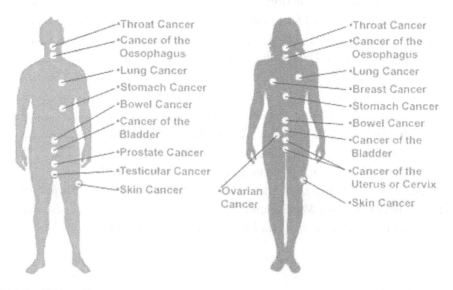

FIGURE 11.1   Types of cancer.

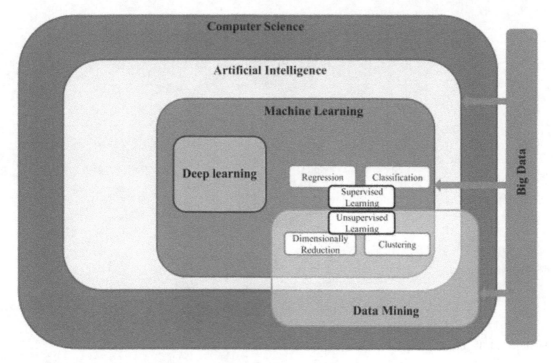

FIGURE 11.2   Machine learning and data mining [9].

Figure 11.2 shows correlation between ML and data mining. Unlike statistics, ML techniques can work with an absolutely conditional (if-then-else), unconventional optimization strategy to classify patterns; these ML techniques actually resemble the human approach to learn and classify. ML techniques have advanced the domain of computer vision, leading to a powerful tool for various applications such as detection, segmentation, and classification. Some of the main uses of ML are predictive analysis and classification [3–8].

Data mining in short involves finding patterns in data, basically extracting all knowledge possible from the data. It can be done in an automatic or semi-automatic way. It aids in understanding the data in an easier manner, whereas ML involves arguments that improve automatically through experience based on data [10]. Both ML and data mining are dependent on data, but in data mining we explicitly program for specific trends, whereas in ML we create a model and that model learns without explicitly programming for specific parts. Figure 11.3 shows various data mining techniques.

11.2 LITERATURE SURVEY

This literature survey is divided into various sections in which papers are discussed for the detection of different types of cancer using ML and data mining. The first section contains research done on detection of oral cancer. The second section gives a review on approaches used for detection of skin cancer, which is followed by brain cancer detection in the next section. The fourth section contains the work done by various researchers on ovarian

FIGURE 11.3   Data mining techniques [11].

cancer using ML approaches. The fifth section contains a review on lung cancer detection. The last section contains a review on breast cancer detection.

11.2.1   Oral Cancer Detection

Oral cancer affects the pharynx as well as the mouth and is quite dreadful because of its late detection. At a later stage, the only treatment left is surgery and chemoradiation, which does not give good results and leads to death of patients. As far as detecting oral cancer, Suhas Vittal et al. [12] used the Medusa algorithm in parallel with binary classification. For predicting oral cavity squamous cell carcinoma (OCSCC), Andres M. Bur et al. (2019) used an ML algorithm and ROC, or receiver operating characteristic, curve for measuring performance, which is then compared with a DOI model [13]. Also, varied data mining algorithms used for detecting oral cancer were used by ArushiTetarbe et al. (2017). The main endeavor is to categorize dataset, collect valuable material from the data, and select an opposite algorithm for a precise prognostic model [14]. Then, various algorithms like RFN and support vector machine (SVM) are trained by Saunak Chatterjee et al. (2018) using various features like morphological, histogram features, texture and intensity, and color extracted from patients who are suffering from oral leukoplakia (LKP), oral squamous cell carcinoma (OSCC), and oral sub-mucous fibrosis (OSF) [15].

11.2.2   Skin Cancer Detection

For the detection of skin cancer, an earlier biopsy method was used, which is very painful and also time-consuming. So, the researchers worked to develop a new system which did not require any kind of skin sample. For this, NaserAlfed et al. (2015) proposed an efficient system comprised mainly four stages, i.e., pre-processing, pigment network extraction, feature extraction, and classification. The system will use dermoscopic images in detecting skin cancer [16]. An illustrative segmentation scheme based on SVM was used by Prachya Bumrungkun et al. (2018) for skin cancer detection [17]. Soniya Mane et al. (2018) also used SVM for the categorization of skin images as melanoma skin cancer or normal skin [18]. Firstly, Gaussian Filter was used for pre-processing. After that, image segmentation and feature extraction was done.

11.2.3 Brain Cancer Detection

Various researchers have worked to augment speed and precision of detection as there is a large database available because the tumor may occur in any part or any place or may be of any size and shape. So, for these reasons, S. Pereira et al. (2016) used a convolutional neural network (CNN) algorithm for brain tumor detection. For brain tumor segmentation, data augmentation is used on different MRI images [18]. A deep neural network (DNN) model founded on the fully automatic brain tumor segmentation method was used by Mohammad Havaei et al. (2017) for the detection of cancer [19]. Xiaomei Zhao et al. (2018) used 2D image slices and image patches in order to guide a segmentation model founded on deep learning. For the said purpose, they first trained the fully convolutional neural networks (FCNNs) using image patches, and then secondly, FCNNs parameters and image slice were used to train conditional random fields (CRFs) as recurrent neural networks (CRF-RNNs) [20]. Then, thirdly, an image slice was used for fine-tuning of CRF-RNNs and FCNNs. For brain cancer detection, all the above researchers used the databases named BRATS2013 and BRATS2015 to get better results.

11.2.4 Ovarian Cancer Detection

For detecting ovarian cancer, a number of researchers have done tremendous research in this field. For example, Hemita Pathak et al. (2015) devised a method founded on ML that can accurately classify between malignant and benign tumors that cause ovarian cancer [21]. For this wavelet, transform was used for pre-processing, and then grey level co-occurrence algorithm was employed for feature extraction and then SVM for categorization. Also, with the detection of ovarian cancer, the stage of the cancer was also detected by Beant Kaur et al. (2017) [22]. Two classifiers were used, namely SVM and CNN, and their performances were also compared.

11.2.5 Lung Cancer Detection

In order to replace the ancient trial of chest X-ray screening by doctors, various research scholars carried out extensive research in the said field. For example, Moffy Vas et al. (2017) developed an automated model for segmenting lung regions by using various mathematical morphological operations that help in detecting lung cancer [23]. Artificial neural network (ANN) classifier was used on positron emission tomography/computed tomography (PET/CT) images to get improved accuracy. K. Punithavathy et al. (2015) have used fuzzy C-mean (FCM) clustering, whose aim is to develop a methodology for PET/CT images for automatically detecting lung cancer. First, Wiener filtering and CLAHE were used to remove noise. Receiver operating characteristics (ROC) curve was used for evaluating performance of the projected methodology. Janee Alam et al. (2018) used a multiclass SVM classifier for detecting lung cancer. The probability of lung cancer can also be predicted using this system by applying segmentation and image enhancement at every stage of classification [24]. Also, the proposed algorithm that is based on Watershed transform, GLCM, and SVM classifier was compared with other algorithms like region growing, morphological smoothing, FCM clustering, region growing, and neural network.

11.2.6 Breast Cancer Detection

For detecting breast cancer, Chadaporn Keatmanee et al. (2017) discovered a novel method designed specifically for US-based imaging modalities for an automatic initialization of active contour model. The automatic initialization methods like Poisson inverse gradient (PIG), center of divergence (COD), and fast field segmentation (FFS) are compared with the proposed method [25]. For detecting breast cancer in mammographic images, Pavel Kral et al. (2016) developed a novel method based on local binary patterns (LBP). The proposed method was composed of four steps: image preprocessing, local binary patterns computation, image representation creation, and cancer detection. A PNN classifier was used by Anu Appukuttan et al. (2016) for detecting breast cancer and for the classification of micro calcifications and circumscribed masses as normal, benign, and malignant [26]. For this Curvelet Transform was used for features extraction, and for texture analysis, gray level co-occurrence (GLCM) matrix was used. For early stage breast cancer detection, Qinwei Li et al. (2015) proposed a direct extraction method by using ultra-wide band (UWB) microwave images based on ensemble empirical mode decomposition (EEMD) [27,28]. The projected approach was able to detect a 4 mm tumor that was situated inside the glandular area in one breast model, and furthermore by the model that was situated between the interface of the organ and the fat, respectively. Tom Botterill et al. (2014) described a computerized system for measuring 3D surface motion accurately. The proposed system was able to detect a 10 mm tumor in a silicon phantom breast. Modern optical flow implementation was used to measure surface motion, and then optical flow was fused with reconstructed surfaces by trajectories of points on the 3D surfaces [29]. On tracking skin surface motion, the validation of proposed work on humans showed that it gave better performance compared with other earlier marker-based systems (Table 11.1).

11.3 CASE STUDY

Cancers are classified according to the location in the body where they first developed. There are various cancers, like oral, skin, lung, ovarian, breast, and many more. ML has done a lot in the field of cancer prediction, and this approach takes less time and is cost effective also. Many researchers to this date have done extensive research in the domain of breast cancer prediction, skin cancer prediction, lung cancer prediction, brain tumor prediction, oral cancer prediction, and many more. Now, we will see some case studies on different cancer prediction by using ML:

TABLE 11.1
Comparative Analysis of Work Done by Various Researchers on Different Cancers

Authors	Type of Cancer	Approach Used	Outcomes
SuhasVittal et al. (2018) [12]	Oral cancer	Graph-based and supervised algorithm provides a Medusa algorithm in parallel with binary classification.	Confusion matrix, % error, root mean square error measures of prediction accuracy were calculated for the binary classification.
Andres M. Bur et al. (2019) [13]	Oral cancer	ML algorithm (decision forest algorithm)	AUC, sensitivity, specificity was measured and Delong test was used to compare the performance of DOI.
ArushiTetarbe et al. (2017) [14]	Oral cancer	Different algorithms like Naive Baye, J48, SMO, REP tree and random tree of data mining.	Accuracy, mean absolute error, and ROC area were measured for accurate prognostic algorithm among different algorithms.
Saunak Chatterjee et al. (2018) [15]	Oral cancer	SVM, K-nearest neighbor, Naive Bayes, Random Forest, decision tree	Comparison of various algorithms on the basis of precision and recall value. 90% accuracy was achieved using Random Forest classifier.
NaserAlfed et al. (2015) [30]	Skin cancer	Pigment-network based efficient system	A high detection accuracy in the form of false positive rate and the false negative rate was calculated for the proposed system.
PrachyaBumrungkun et al. (2018) [16]	Skin cancer	SVM and snake active contour algorithm	Snake algorithm and SVM algorithm were used to analyze in terms of accuracy.
Soniya Mane et al. (2018) [17]	Skin cancer	SVM	SVM was compared with other algorithms like radial basis function and Bayes net classifier on the basis of performance parameters like accuracy, F-measure, and recall, and SVM classifier proved to be best.
Sergio Pereira et al. (2016) [18]	Brain cancer	CNN	Dice similarity coefficient metric like complete, core, and enhancing region were calculated.
Mohammad Havaei et al. (2017) [19]	Brain tumor	DNN	The proposed architecture was compared with other

(Continued)

TABLE 11.1 (*continued*)

Authors	Type of Cancer	Approach Used	Outcomes
			currently published state-of-the-art in terms of complete, core, and enhancing region.
XiaomeiZhao et al. (2018) [20]	Brain tumor	FCNN is integrated with CRFs	The proposed method was compared with other methods on the basis of dice, sensitivity, and positive predictive value.
Hemita Pathak et al. (2015) [21]	Ovarian cancer	SVM	The proposed system was used to classify ovarian cancer as malignant or benign tumors, and an accuracy of 86% and 92% by relief-F was achieved.
Beant Kaur et al. (2017) [22]	Ovarian cancer	CNN and SVM	By using CNN classifier, the proposed system realized an exactness of 98.8%, and by using SVM classifier, an accuracy of 85.01% was achieved.
Moffy Vas et al. (2017) [23]	Lung cancer	Mathematical morphological operations and ANNs	An accuracy of 96% was achieved in the training phase, and an accuracy of 92% was achieved in the testing phase, sensitivity of 88.7% and specificity of 97.1% were achieved.
K. Punithavathy et al. (2015) [31]	Lung cancer	CLAHE (contrast limited adaptive histogram equalization) and Wiener filtering, FCM, and ROC curve.	ROC curves were used for evaluating the performance of the proposed system in terms of exactness, specificity, and sensitivity. Total accuracy achieved was 92.67%.
JaneeAlam, et al., (2018) [24]	Lung cancer	SVM	The proposed algorithm achieved a precision of 87% for prediction of cancer and 97% for identification of cancer.
ChadapornKeatmanee, et al., (2017) [25]	Breast cancer	ACM (active contour model) and FCM	The results of the proposed algorithm accomplished high accuracy of 69% in

(*Continued*)

TABLE 11.1 (*continued*)

Authors	Type of Cancer	Approach Used	Outcomes
			comparison with other algorithms.
Pavel Kral et al. (2016) [26]	Breast cancer	LBP	The proposed method achieved an accuracy of 84%.
AnuAppukuttan et al. (2016) [27]	Breast cancer	PNN classifier	Various parameters like accuracy, precision, recall, and F-measure were evaluated, and images were categorized as normal, benign, or malignant.
Qinwei Li et al. (2015) [28]	Breast cancer	EEMD	A tumor of size 4 mm was detected that was situated inside the glandular area in one breast model.
Tom Botterill et al. (2014) [29]	Breast cancer	Computer vision system and DIET (digital IMAGE-based elasto tomography)	In a silicon phantom breast, a 10 millimeter tumor was detected by using the computer vision based proposed system.

11.3.1 Prediction of Breast Cancer Using ML: A Case Study

Breast cancer is the biggest health problem faced by women all over the world. One of the major causes of breast cancer is being overweight [32]. In order to diagnose these problems and make predictions, many classifications using ML have been employed. In breast cancer detection, basically women are divided on the basis of their BMI and also on whether they are affected by breast cancer or not i.e. (1) No cancer with BMI less than 25 kg/m^2. (2) No cancer with BMI greater than 25 kg/m^2. (3) Breast cancer with BMI less than 25 kg/m^2. (4) Breast cancer with BMI greater than 25 kg/m^2. Besides BMI, two other factors are also used, i.e, glucose metabolism and insulin resistance [33]. The detection process is done by using any ML algorithm in which we first collect data on age, BMI, glucose, lepton, insulin, Resistin, Adiponectin, etc., and then pre-process this data. For implementing the ML algorithm, two libraries were used. One was ML lib, which provides many ML algorithms for cluster reduction, regression, dimensionality reduction, classification, and also for model evaluation, and the other library was ML package for ML routines, which provides an API to perform cross validation [34]. Mainly, K-nearest neighbor, decision tree, classification and regression tree (CART), Naive Bayes, and SVM were used for breast cancer detection at an early stage.

11.3.2 Prediction of Lung Cancer Using ML: A Case Study

Every year, around 25,000 people are diagnosed with one cancer in a country. The key to improve the survival rate is detection. If the system of detection can be made more efficient and effective for radiologists, then this will be a key step to achieving the goal of early detection. For lung cancer, we are specifically looking for tumors by the use of CT scans and biopsy, but this process is often wasted and time-consuming [35]. So, various researchers have used ML, in which they have worked on different scenarios in lung cancer detection. A few have worked on finding the life expectancy of lung cancer patients using various data mining algorithms. Also, in some research, various algorithms such as decision tree, Naive Bayes, and ANN were compared for lung cancer detection. In a few papers, the accuracy rate for different classifiers like KNN, SVM, and logistic regression was obtained for a lung cancer dataset. Out of them, SVM got the accuracy of 99.3%. Various segmentation algorithms like Naive Bayes, Hidden Markov model, and many others are discussed for lung cancer detection. So, in short, ML and data mining techniques have reduced the time consumed by multiple tests done by doctors for the detection of lung cancer. Also, they have minimized the unnecessary checkups that sometimes patients have to undergo in order to diagnose lung cancer.

11.3.3 Prediction of Skin Cancer Using ML: A Case Study

The increase in the development rate of skin cancer and also in the cost of its cure and in the fatality rate of persons affected by skin cancer is the major cause for detecting skin cancer at an early stage. In previous times, a manual process was used for the diagnosis of skin cancer, which was very expensive and time-consuming [36]. But nowadays, due to advancements in the world of science, we can diagnose it through ML, which has also made the detection process very easy. Most researchers are working on skin cancer detection along with malignant or benign diagnosis. Until now, many researchers have done tremendous work in this detection field. For example, one of the researchers in the preprocessing phase used a Wiener filter and a histogram equalization technique. For segmentation, they used an active contour. GLCM was utilized for an extracting feature, and lastly SVM was utilized as a classifier with an achieved accuracy of 95%, and sensitivity and specificity of 90% and 85%, respectively [2]. This classifier was used basically to categorize whether the skin lesion was malignant or benign. In the next research, the author used an image enhancement technique named median filter (MF) and an adaptive histogram equalization (AHE) method. For image segmentation, an original technique known as normalized Otsu's method was used, and due to this technique, the variable illumination problem became easier than earlier. A neural network and hybrid AdaBoost SVM were used as classifiers, which used the 15 features extracted from a segmented image. In this, 9.92 images (both malignant and benign) were used as a dataset, and 93% accuracy was achieved in the end [37]. In another research, the author used the ABCD rule for extracting features after removing unwanted details, and SVM was used as a classifier, which achieved sensitivity of 95%, accuracy of 90%, and specificity of 83%.

11.3.4 Prediction of Brain Tumors Using ML: A Case Study

Brain tumors have four degrees. If the tumor spreads slowly, then this type is known as Grade 1 and Grade 2. If it spreads quickly and treatment is a bit harder, then it is known as Grade 3 and Grade 4. The uncontrollable growth of cells leads to the origin of the tumor within the body. Sometimes, a malformed mass of tissue is formed within the brain, where the cells start increasing abruptly and ceaselessly [38]. Also, many times a brain tumor can be related to various issues with the heart. Magnetic resonance imaging (MRI) is used to identify the region affected by the tumor. For treatment, the radiologist needs to measure the size of the tumor. There are a lot of risks to life because of this brain tumor. Many ML techniques and many data mining techniques were developed for the prediction and detection of brain tumors at an early stage. First, the pre-processing phase is done for noise removal, and non-brain tissues are removed from the input image in order to improve accuracy [39]. Also, for noise removal and for contrast enhancement, a Wiener filter, fast non-local mean, and partial differential diffusion filter are used. Next, for brain tumor segmentation, K-mean clustering, FCM, and Otsu threshold methods are used. For feature extraction, local binary patterns (LBP), histogram orientation gradient (HOG), and Gabor Wavelet transform (GWT) are used. For feature selection, principal component analysis (PCA) and genetic algo (GA) are used. Now, for classification many authors have used different approaches and achieved different results. In one research work, SVM classifier was used along with an anisotropic diffusion filter for eliminating noise, and 81% dice similarity was achieved [40]. In another work, 3D-CNN brain tumor segmentation was used, which achieved 89.9% accuracy, 92.19% sensitivity, and 88.22% specificity. In the next research work, Random Forest classifier was applied on the BRATS 2013 dataset, and in another, the author used 3D-CNN for segmenting multiple brain regions, and an accuracy of 80.11% was achieved.

11.3.5 Prediction of Oral Cancer Using ML: A Case Study

In the past decades, oral cancer was considered to be an incurable disease, but nowadays, with advancements in the medical field, it has become a curable disease. Due to various factors like alcohol, smoking, human papillomavirus (HPV), or any cancer family history, there is a tremendous increase in the number of cells that further affect their neighboring tissues located in various parts of the body, like the mouth, cheeks, lips, tongue, throat, etc. [41]. For oral cancer detection, many data mining algorithms were used. One of the proposed approaches used WEKA, which consisted of many data mining algorithms with 10-cross validation in order to compute and collate productivity [42]. In the other proposed work, a decision support system was used for detecting cancer with the help of an AI classifier and data mining algorithms. The result of this work was calculated on the basis of precision and the duration to develop the same. In another research, different algorithms like SVM, Naive Bayes, DF, and boosted DT were compared on the basis of precision, recall, F1 score, specificity, sensitivity, and accuracy. Also, the performance of these algorithms was compared for depth of invasion in which boosted decision tree algorithm achieved the highest accuracy. In another research work, the authors compared the performance of SVM, linear regression, and decision tree in predicting oral cancer [43]. The accuracy calculated by these algorithms was linear regression 88%, SVM 87%, and decision tree 70%.

11.4 IMPORTANCE OF MACHINE LEARNING AND DATA MINING IN CANCER PREDICTION

Every year, there are around 14 million cancer patients around the world. This problem of cancer has been diagnosed and prognosed for decades. The success rate in diagnosing cancer is around 97% by pathologists, which is pretty good, but the problem is in the accuracy of prognosis by pathologists, which is only 60% according to the Oslo University Hospital.

Here, prognosis means prediction of the development or spreading of disease after it has been diagnosed. This is the reason why we require a better approach for the diagnosis and prognosis of cancer with a high accuracy rate. For this purpose, ML and data mining techniques take a main role. First, we will see the ML, which is part of AI. It is a technique in which we take data as input then find patterns in it. Then, the machine trains itself using this data and provides an outcome. Now, we will see how we can say that ML is better than a trained pathologist.

The major advantage is that machines can work much faster than humans. Take, for example, a pathologist who wants to conduct a biopsy. This process will take 10 complete days, whereas a computer can perform simultaneously 1,000 biopsies in a few seconds [44].

Another advantage can be if at any point in time we want to repeat any step again and again for better results; we can do it using machines. On the other hand, this will become a little bit hectic in the case of pathologists.

The most important usage is accuracy. Nowadays, with the vast Internet of Things technology, the huge quantity of data present in the world cannot be gained by humans in one sitting, but this is possible with machines because of their faster speed and tendency to provide more accurate results.

Since we have already seen the advantages of a machine over humans, we can also say that data mining techniques will provide far better results than any pathologist for cancer prediction. Data mining from the name itself means extracting important information from a raw bulk amount of data. With high classification ability and high diagnostic capability, data mining's reputation is on the rise in the medical field. In a large dataset relationship, unknown and valid patterns will be first discovered by any data analysis tool that includes an ML algorithm and statistical models. For the diagnosis of cancer in a particular patient, first it is necessary to assemble, integrate, and clean up. Now, this developed system will be used by many physicians and patients in order to identify the patient's cancer status and its seriousness. It is also used to save large amounts of important information about any disease and its treatment.

11.5 RELATION BETWEEN DATA MINING AND MACHINE LEARNING

Data mining is basically a part of business analytics that is used to explore different unidentified patterns, relationships, and anomalies from an existing large dataset. Also, it helps in finding new insights that we are not expecting. In short, different data mining algorithms are used to identify patterns and trends in retail.

ML is a part of AI that is used to analyze and then find patterns in large datasets, which will further help in making predictions. With the assistance of ML, a lot of information is gathered from data without the help of humans. In simple language, ML basically means learning from our successes and failures like human do and also tracking the computer to learn by interpreting information. There are a lot of similarities between ML and data mining, like both of them are used for analytical processing and also for pattern recognition. We can use them for improving decision making by learning from data, and both can work on large datasets. Sometimes ML can use data mining methods in order to identify patterns and also design models and vice versa, i.e., sometimes data mining can use ML algorithms for generating more accurate analysis. Besides these similarities, there are a lot of differences between ML and data mining, like data mining only finds the patterns that exist in the data, but ML learns from the past in order to predict future outcomes. For this, it uses pre-existing data. Another dissimilarity is rules or patterns are not known in the beginning of the process in the case of data mining, whereas these rules and patterns are fed to the machine in ML for better understanding. Also, data mining is dependent on an existing dataset in order to identify patterns, whereas ML depends on a trained dataset. In order to make predictions about a new dataset, this trained dataset will teach the computer how to make sense of the data. We can also say that data mining is a more manual process or is more dependent on human intervention and decision making, whereas with ML, once the rules are fed into the machine, all the processes like information extraction, learning, and refining are automatically done without the support of humans.

11.6 ISSUES AND CHALLENGES WITH DATA MINING AND MACHINE LEARNING

- By using data mining and ML, many cutting-edge applications have been developed. We are using these applications in our everyday life, but in spite of the useful features and applications of data mining and ML, there are certain issues and challenges that are faced by any practitioner who uses data mining and ML for developing any application from scratch to production.

- The most common hurdle is the memory requirement in order to store a large amount of data. In order to get an efficient and effective data mining and ML product, one needs to find a more efficient method to overcome this challenge of memory and to discover facts, store them, and also access them whenever required.

- A lot of expenditure and time has been invested in natural language processing, but there is still a long way to go in order to have a better understanding of languages. This has become a major hurdle, even for deep networks to teach computers how to represent languages and also to replicate reasoning based on it.

- In the human visual system, we generally concentrate on highly robust things and integrate them into a rich set of features, whereas in data mining and ML, it focuses on tiny things one at a time and then integrates them in the end. So, there is a need to develop a neural network that works the same as the human visual system.

- A lot of effort has been done in the field of data mining and ML, but still we don't know how exactly these deep training nets work. We can't make any real progress until we know the actual working of them.

- We are still working with static images; we haven't used any video training data. For better models, we should make machines learn from videos by listening and observing. As in the case of human beings, we have a better understanding by watching videos instead of static images. So, this can be another challenge with machines.

- Data collection is also another issue with data mining and ML. Every data scientist spends almost 60% of their work on data collecting. For just doing an experiment, we can collect data from Kaggle, UCI ML Repository, etc. But when we want to implement real-world scenarios, then we will require more real data, and to gather that it will be a challenge.

- A lot of training data will be required in order to make a simple algorithm because every time we have to train the model, we need a lot of data. For example, if a child needs to distinguish between two animals, then a smaller number of samples will be required in order to train the child. But in the same case, data mining and ML will require a large dataset for learning. Thus, for any complex problems like image classification and speech recognition, data mining and ML will require datasets in the millions.

- Many times, by processing inappropriate data, the system makes false predictions, so it is very important to select a good quality dataset. Then, data processing should be done on it, which includes filtering missing values, extracting, and rearranging as per the requirement of the model.

- Last but not the least, a major challenge with data mining and ML is overfitting and underfitting. If we select fewer features while training our model, then the problem of underfitting will arise, whereas if we select a large number of features in the training phase, then sometimes a problem of overfitting will arise. That will sometimes create a big problem in achieving higher accuracy.

11.7 CONCLUSION AND FUTURE SCOPE

This chapter discusses two techniques for cancer prediction: ML and data mining. Learning is carried out with a plan drawn on various new technologies used in the detection of cancer in different parts of the body. Traditional technology, used by pathologists for a considerable period of time, was very time-consuming and not that efficient. These problems were addressed by data mining and ML. The importance of data mining and ML is discussed in detail for cancer prediction and also how they are related to each other, followed by various issues and challenges that are being faced with the use of these technologies. It has been observed that there is a lot more scope to improve the accuracy while using these technologies. But in the literature survey, state-of-art accuracy has not been reached to achieve the desired result. In such a scenario, advanced deep learning techniques like VGG16, Inception V3, and Inception V4 can be utilized to deal with this issue and get better accuracy. Further, we can also work for a greater number of images with a greater number of features extracted from these images and then apply different classifiers in order to achieve the desired result. Moreover, we can find more parameters on the basis of which to compare our algorithms [45–68].

REFERENCES

[1] Aryan A., Aiman A., Grace B., Marco A., Increase in detection of oral cancer and precursor lesions by dentists, *JADA*, 531–539 (2019).

[2] Roman C., Michael W., Jochen S., Achim H., Carola B., Axel H., Systematic outperformance of 112 dermatologists in multiclass skin cancer image classification by convolutional neural networks. *Elsevier*, 119, 57–65 (2019).

[3] Pandey S., Solanki A., Music instrument recognition using deep convolutional neural networks. *Int. J. Inf. Technol.* 13(3), 129–149 (2019).

[4] Rajput R., Solanki A., Real-time analysis of tweets using machine learning and semantic analysis. In: *International Conference on Communication and Computing Systems (ICCCS2016), Taylor and Francis, at Dronacharya College of Engineering, Gurgaon, 9–11 Sept* 138(25), 687–692 (2016).

[5] Ahuja R., Solanki A., Movie recommender system using K-Means clustering and K-Nearest Neighbor. *Accepted for Publication in Confuence-2019: 9th International Conference on Cloud Computing, Data Science & Engineering, Amity University, Noida.* 1231(21), 25–38 (2019).

[6] Tayal A., Kose, U., Solanki, A., Nayyar, A., Saucedo, J.A.M., Efficiency analysis for stochastic dynamic facility layout problem using meta-heuristic, data envelopment analysis and machine learning. *Comput. Intell.* 36(1), 172–202 (2020).

[7] Singh, T., Nayyar, A., Solanki, A., Multilingual opinion mining movie recommendation system using RNN. In: Singh, P., Pawłowski, W., Tanwar, S., Kumar, N., Rodrigues, J., Obaidat, M. (eds.), *Proceedings of First International Conference on Computing, Communications, and Cyber-Security (IC4S 2019). Lecture Notes in Networks and Systems*, vol. 121. Singapore: Springer (2020). 10.1007/978-981-15-3369-3_44.

[8] Agarwal, A., Solanki, A., An improved data clustering algorithm for outlier detection. *Selforganology* 3(4), 121–139 (2016).

[9] Vougas, K., Machine learning and data mining frameworks for predicting drug response in cancer: An overview and a novel in silico screening process based on association rule mining. *Pharmacology and Therapeutics* 203, 107395 (2019).

[10] Hengameh M., Tim K., Ghassan H., *Skin lesion tracking using structured graphical models.* Elsevier (2015).

[11] https://medium.com/@tanmayct/data-mining-techniques-24d01a8fb71e

[12] Vittal, S., Karthikeyan, G., Modeling association detection in order to discover compounds to inhibit oral cancer. *Journal of Biomedical Informatics*, 159–163 (2018).

[13] Mbur, A., Holcomb, A., Goodwin, S., Woodroof, J., Karadaghy, O., Shnayder, Kiran Kakarala, Y., Brant, J. and Shew, M., "Machine learning to predict occult nodal metastasis in early oral squamous cell carcinoma", *Oral Oncology*, pp. 20–25, 2019.

[14] Tetarbe, A., Choudhury, T., Toe, T. and Rawat, S., "Oral cancer detection using data mining tool", *International Conference on Applied and Theoretical Computing and Communication Technology*, pp. 35–39, 2017.

[15] Chatterjee, S., Nawn, D., Mandal, M., Chatterjee, J., Mitra, S., Pal, M. and Paul, R., "Augmentation of Statistical Features in Cytopathology Towards Computer Aided Diagnosis of Oral Precancer/Cancer", *2018 4th International Conference on Biosignals, Images and Instrumentation (ICBSII)*, pp. 1–4, 2018.

[16] Bumrungkun, P., Chamnongthai, K. and Patchoo, W., "Detection skin cancer using SVM and snake model", *International Workshop on Advanced Image Technology(IWAIT)*, pp. 1–4, 2018.

[17] Mane, S., Shinde, S., "A Method for Melanoma Skin Cancer Detection Using Dermoscopy Images", *2018 Fourth International Conference on Computing Communication Control and Automation (ICCUBEA)*, pp. 1–7, 2018.

[18] Pereira, S., Pinto, A., Alves, V. and Silva, C., "Brain Tumor Segmentation Using Convolutional Neural Networks in MRI Images", *IEEE Transactions on Medical Imaging*, pp. 1240–1251, 2016.

[19] Havaei, M., Davy, A., Warde-Farley, D., Biard, A., Courville, A., Bengio, Y., Pal, C., Jodoin, P. and Larochelle, H., "Brain tumor segmentation with Deep Neural Networks", *Medical Image Analysis*, pp. 18–31, 2017.

[20] Zhao, X., Wu, Y., Song, G., Li, Z., Zhang, Y., Fan, Y., "A deep learning model integrating FCNNs and CRFs for brain tumor segmentation", *Medical Image Analysis*, pp. 98–111, 2018.

[21] Pathak, H., Kulkarni, V., "Identification of Ovarian mass through Ultrasound Images using Machine Learning Techniques", *2015 IEEE International Conference on Research in Computational Intelligence and Communication Networks (ICRCICN)*, pp. 137–140, 2015.

[22] Kaur, B., Mann, K. and Grewal, M., "Ovarian Cancer stage based detection on Convolutional Neural network", *Proceedings of the 2nd International Conference on Communication and Electronics Systems (ICCES 2017)*, pp. 855–859, 2017.

[23] Vas, M., Dessai, A., "Lung cancer detection system using lung CT image processing", *2017 International Conference on Computing, Communication, Control andAutomation (ICCUBEA)*, pp. 1–5, 2017.

[24] Alam, J., Alam, S., and Hossan, A., "Multi-Stage Lung Cancer Detection and Prediction Using Multi-class SVM Classifier", *2018 International Conference on Computer, Communication, Chemical, Material and Electronic Engineering (IC4ME2)*, pp. 1–4, 2018.

[25] Keatmanee, C., Makhanov, S., Kotani, K., Lohitvisate, W. and Thongvigitmanee, S., "Automatic Initialization For Active Contour Model In Breast Cancer Detection Utilizing Conventional Ultrasound And Color Doppler", *39th Annual International Conference of the IEEE Engineering in Medicine and Biology Society (EMBC)*, pp. 3248–3251, 2017.

[26] Kral, P., Lavlenc, L., "LBP Features for Breast", *2016 IEEE International Conference on Image Processing (ICIP)*, pp. 2643–2647, 2016.

[27] Appukuttan, A., Sindhu, L., "Curvelet And PNN Classifier Based Approach For Early Detection And Classification Of Breast Cancer In Digital Mammograms", *2016 International Conference on Inventive Computation Technologies (ICICT)*, pp. 1–5, 2016.

[28] Li, Q., Xiao, X., Wang, L., Song, H., Kono, H., Liu, P., Lu, H., and Kikkawa, T., "Direct Extraction of Tumor Response Based on Ensemble Empirical Mode Decomposition for Image Reconstruction of Early Breast Cancer Detection by UWB", *IEEE Transactions On Biomedical Circuits And Systems*, pp. 710–724, 2015.

[29] Botterill, T., Lotz, T., Kashif, A. and Chase, J., "Reconstructing 3-D Skin Surface Motion for the DIET Breast Cancer Screening System", *IEEE Transactions On Medical Imaging*, pp. 1109–1118, 2014.

[30] Alfed, N., Khelifi, F., Bouridane, A. and Seker, H., "Pigment network-based skin cancer detection", *37th Annual International Conference of the IEEE Engineering in Medicine and Biology Society (EMBC)*, pp. 7214–7217, 2015.

[31] Punithavathy, K., Ramya, M. and Poobal, S., "Analysis of Statistical Texture Features for Automatic Lung Cancer Detection in PET/CT Images", *International Conference on Robotics, Automation, Control and Embedded Systems*, pp. 1–5, 2015.

[32] Fatima, N., Liu, L., Sha, H., Ahmed, H., "Prediction of Breast Cancer, Comparative Review of Machine Learning Techniques and their Analysis", 10.1109/ACCESS.2020.3016715, IEEE Access.

[33] Hung, P., Hanh, T., Diep, V., "Breast Cancer Prediction Using Spark MLlib and ML Packages", ICBRA '18, December 27–29, 2018, Hong Kong, Hong Kong, 2018 Association for Computing Machinery, ACM ISBN 978-1-4503-6611-3/18/12.

[34] Singh, S., Thakral, S., "Using Data Mining Tools for Breast Cancer Prediction and Analysis", *2018 4th International Conference on Computing Communication and Automation (ICCCA)*.

[35] Radhika, P., Rakhi, A., " A Comparative Study of Lung Cancer Detection using Machine Learning Algorithms", 978-1-5386-1507-2/18/2018, IEEE.

[36] Dmitrijs B., Katrina B., Aleksandrs S., Kamran A., *"Towards the Scalable Cloud Platform for Non-Invasive Skin Cancer Diagnostics"*, Elsevier, 2017.

[37] Sertan S., Hasan D., *"Gabor wavelet-based deep learning for skin lesion classification"*, Elsevier, 2019.

[38] Hemanth, G., Janardhan, M., Sujihelen, L., "Design and Implementing Brain Tumor detection using Machine Learning approach", *Third International Conference on Trends in Electronics and Informatics (ICOEI 2019)*, IEEE Xplore Part Number: CFP19J32-ART, ISBN: 978-1-5386-9439-8.

[39] Amin, J., Sharif, M., Raza, M., Saba, T., Anjum, M., *"Brain Tumor Detection using Statistical and Machine Learning Method"*, Elsevier (2019), PII: S0169-2607(18)31378-6.

[40] Ozyurt, F., Sert, E., Avcı, D., *"An expert system for brain tumor detection: Fuzzy C-means with super resolution and convolutional neural network with extreme learning machine"*, Elsevier (2019): 0306–9877.

[41] Morikawa T., Kozakai A., Kosugi A., Bessho H., Shibahara T., *"Image processing analysis of oral cancer, oral potentially malignant disorders, and other oral diseases using optical instruments"*, Elsevier, 2019.

[42] Carlander A.F., Gronhoj Larsen C., Jensen D.H., Garnaes E., Kiss K., Andersen L., "Continuing rise in oropharyngeal cancer in a high HPV prevalence area", *A Danish population-based study from 2011 to 2014*.

[43] Shan J., Si Y., Xiuping M., Chengkun W., *"One step synthesis of red-emitting fluorescence turn-on probe for nitroreductase and its application to bacterial detection and oral cancer cell imaging"*, Elsevier, 2020.

[44] Balaji V.R., Suganthi S.T., Rajadevi R., Krishna Kumar V., Saravana Balaji B., Pandiyan Sanjeevi, *"Skin disease detection and segmentation using dynamic graph cut algorithm and classification through Naive Bayes classifier"*, Elsevier, 2020.

[45] Islam, M., Liu, D., Wang, K., "A Case Study of HealthCare Platform using Big Data Analytics and Machine Learning", HPCCT 2019, June 22–24, 2019, Guangzhou, China, 2019 Association for Computing Machinery, ACM ISBN 978-1-4503-7185-8/19/06.

[46] Ketut Agung Enriko, I., "Comparative Study of Heart Disease Diagnosis Using Top Ten Data Mining Classification Algorithms", ICFET 2019, June 1–3, 2019, Beijing, China, 2019, Association for Computing Machinery. ACM ISBN 978-1-4503-6293-1/19/06.

[47] Hafinaz Hassan, F., Yong Kah Wye, A., Syafiqah Syed Yusof, S., "Predicting Risk of Getting Smoking-Related Cancer: A Comparison of Three Prediction Models", LOPAL '18, May 2–5, 2018, Rabat, Morocco, 2018 Association for Computing Machinery., ACM ISBN 978-1-4503-5304-5/18/05.

[48] Omobolaji Alabi, R., Elmusrati, M., Sawazaki-Calone, I., Paulo Kowalski, L., Haglund, C.D., Coletta, R., Antti, A., "*Comparison of supervised machine learning classification techniques in prediction of locoregional recurrences in early oral tongue cancer*", Elsevier (2019), PII: S1386-5056(19)30614-8.

[49] Omobolaji Alabi, R., Antti, A., Pirinen, M., Elmusrati, M., Leivo, I., Almangush, A., "*Comparison of nomogram with machine learning techniques for prediction of overall survival in patients with oral tongue cancer*", Elsevier (2020), PII: S1386-5056(20)31013-3.

[50] Hameed, N., Shabut, A., Ghosh, M., Hossain, M., " *Multi-class multi-level classification algorithm for skin lesions classification using machine learning techniques*", Elsevier (2019).

[51] Hasan, M., Das Barman, S., "Skin Cancer Detection Using Convolutional Neural Network", ICCAI '19, April 19–22, 2019, Bali, Indonesia, 2019 Association for Computing Machinery, ACM ISBN 978-1-4503-6573-4/19/02.

[52] Saba, T., "*Recent advancement in cancer detection using machine learning:Systematic survey of decades, comparisons and challenges*", Elsevier (2020).

[53] Dona M.G., Spriano G., Pichi B., Rollo F., Laquintana V., Covello R., "Human papillo-mavirus infection and p16 overexpression in oropharyngeal squamous cell Carcinoma": a case series from 2010 to 2014. *Future Microbiol*, pp. 1283–1291, 2015.

[54] Saulle R., Semyonov L., Mannocci A., Careri A., Saburri F., Ottolenghi L., "Human pa-pillomavirus and cancerous diseases of the head and neck": a systematic review and meta-analysis. *Oral Dis*, pp.417–431, 2015.

[55] Agalliu I., Gapstur S., Chen Z., Wang T., Anderson R.L., Teras L., "Associations of oral alpha-, beta-, and gamma-human papillomavirus types with risk of incident head and neck cancer", *JAMA Oncol* 2016.

[56] Chaturvedi A.K., Engels E.A., Pfeiffer R.M., Hernandez B.Y., Xiao W., Kim E., "Human papillomavirus and rising oropharyngeal cancer incidence in the United States. *J Clin Oncol*", pp. 4294–4301, 2011.

[57] Tinhofer I., Johrens K., Keilholz U., Kaufmann A., Lehmann A., Weichert W., "Contribution of human papilloma virus to the incidence of squamous cell carcinoma of the head and neck in a European population with high smoking prevalence", *Eur J Cancer*, pp. 514–521, 2014.

[58] Maria G., Barbara P., Francesca R.,* Maria B., Alessandra L.,Valentina L., Raul P., Manuela C., Mirko F., Massimo G., Antonio C., "*Human papillomavirus detection in matched oral rinses, oropharyngeal and oral brushings of cancer-free high-risk individuals*", Elsevier Ltd., 2019.

[59] Lang-Ming C., Yung-Chin H., Kun-Yi C., Szu-Fan C., Yao-Ning C., "*Assessment of candidate biomarkers in paired saliva and plasma samples from oral cancer patients by targeted mass spectrometry*", Elsevier, 2019.

[60] Sumul A.G., Jeremy K., "*Skin Cancer Epidemiology, Detection, and Management*", Elsevier, 2015.

[61] Heather R., Katherine M., "Assessing Skin Cancer Prevention and Detection Educational Needs: An Andragogical Approach", *The Journal for Nurse Practitioners*, Volume 11, No. 4, April 2015.

[62] DelBoz J., Fernandez T., Padilla-Espana L.,Aguilar M., Rivas-Ruiz F., DeTroya M., *"Skin Cancer Prevention and Detection Campaign at Golf Courses on Spain's Costa del Sol"*, Elsevier, 2014.

[63] Hyejun R., Emilio G., Md J., Bonnie L., Alex L., Irfan Ali K., Lawrence J., Jean Y., Christopher H., "Detection of Non- Melanoma Skin Cancer by in-vivo Fluorescence imaging", *Neoplasia* Vol. 17, No. 2, 2015.

[64] Shivangi J., Vandana J., Nitin P., "Computer aided Melanoma skin cancer detection using Image Processing", *International Conference on Intelligent Computing, Communication & Convergence*, 2015.

[65] Wiem A., Dorra S., *"Automatic Skin Lesions Classification Using Ontology-Based Semantic Analysis of Optical Standard Images"*, Elsevier, 2017.

[66] Teck Y., Li Z., Chee P., *"Intelligent skin cancer diagnosis using improved particle swarm optimization and deep learning models"*, Elsevier, 2019.

[67] Dascalu A., David E.O., *"Skin cancer detection by deep learning and sound analysis algorithms: A prospective clinical study of an elementary dermoscope"*, Elsevier, 2019.

[68] Amira S., Walid B., *"An image-based segmentation recommender using crowdsourcing and transfer learning for skin lesion extraction"*, Elsevier, 2019.

Index

Note: *Italicized* page numbers refer to figures, **bold** page numbers refer to tables